MINING AND THE STATE IN BRAZILIAN DEVELOPMENT

Perspectives in Economic and Social History

Series Editor: Robert E. Wright

Titles in this Series

Forthcoming Titles

Welfare and Old Age in Europe and North America: The Development of
Social Insurance
Bernard Harris (ed.)

Financing India's Imperial Railways, 1875–1914
Stuart Sweeney

MINING AND THE STATE IN BRAZILIAN DEVELOPMENT

BY

Gail D. Triner

Routledge
Taylor & Francis Group

LONDON AND NEW YORK

First published 2011 by Pickering & Chatto (Publishers) Limited

Published 2016 by Routledge
2 Park Square, Milton Park, Abingdon, Oxfordshire OX14 4RN
711 Third Avenue, New York, NY 10017, USA

First issued in paperback 2015

Routledge is an imprint of the Taylor & Francis Group, an informa business

BRITISH LIBRARY CATALOGUING IN PUBLICATION DATA

Triner, Gail D.
Mining and the state in Brazilian development. – (Perspectives in economic and
social history)
1. Mineral industries – Economic aspects – Brazil. 2. Mineral industries –
Government policy – Brazil. 3. Economic development – Brazil – History.
I. Title II. Series
338.2'0981-dc22

ISBN-13: 978-1-138-66438-8 (pbk)
ISBN-13: 978-1-8489-3068-1 (hbk)

Typeset by Pickering & Chatto (Publishers) Limited

CONTENTS

For Carter, as always

ACKNOWLEDGEMENTS

Like many other scholarly publications, this book has taken longer than anticipated to produce and it has benefited hugely from the generosity of others. Mining is an under-researched topic among historians, and this book has taught me why that is – it is a very difficult subject to research. I could not have done so without the support, guidance and help of others.

Many colleagues and friends helped me throughout this project to identify and access the source material. Marshall Eakin and Douglas Cole Libby pointed me to sources in the mining areas of Minas Gerais, the most notable of which is the meticulous archive maintained by the St John d'el Rey Mining Company at Morro Velho, Nova Lima (now a part of the Anglo-Gold-Ashante Corporation). Douglas has provided advice, housing, great ideas and companionable dinners throughout the project. At Morro Velho, the company was incredibly gracious in supporting my work. Roberto de Carvalho (then president of the company) granted access; Mary Gill made living arrangements for me, Victor Rodrigues educated me about their archives, eased my access and offered cheerful companionship; the Real Estate department opened their extensive and rare documentation for me; the geologists who were also lodged in the guest housing taught me about mining and geology, and the IT department saved my computer. Other important sources for mining historians, companies and government agencies, chose an opposite route and firmly maintained their exemptions from federal disclosure requirements. Paulo Roberto de Almeida offered much appreciated support in my search to open organizational and judicial records. The chief municipal judges of Sabará and Itabira allowed me access to the notarial files of land sales. Amilcar Martins opened the library of his family's historical foundation in Belo Horizonte to me, where all of the staff made me welcome and kept me caffeinated; Amilcar also used his keen book-searching interests to acquire for me one of the most useful (and unknown) sources of the project. The library at the State Assembly of Minas Gerais kindly shared their spreadsheets from an on-going project to list all of the state legislation from 1891 forward. Andréa Val Costa at the Judiciary of the state of Minas Gerais assisted in finding other sources from the state and in gaining access to the rare book collection at the Universidade Federal de Ouro Preto. Margareth Moraes, of the Companhia de Pesquisa de Recursos Minerais's Rio de Janeiro library facilitated my work there, and made it more companionable. Diego de Barros, at the library of the Rio de Janeiro museum of the National Department of Mining Production helped me look for information (beyond the point that was in his own better interests). Maria Teresa Ribeiro de Oliveira shared with me her collection of colonial and early nineteenth-century legislative actions and offered valuable opportunities to develop some of the ideas in Chapters 2 and 3.

The ideas of this book have evolved greatly over the life of the project. Conversations with colleagues have been instrumental in that process. Within Brazil, some (but not all) of the people who have shared ideas include Sérgio Birchal, Monica Dantas, Silvia Figueirôa, Eduardo Gomes, Hildebrando Herrmann, Luciana Lopes, Teresa Marques and André Villela. Maria Antonieta Leopoldi has especially helped me to develop the project and has supported my efforts; as a colleague and a friend, she has helped to keep it going. During a semester in 2007 at the graduate programme in political science at the Universidade Federal Fluminense, under the auspices of a Fulbright Fellowship, my graduate students were instrumental in helping me to figure out the 'on the ground' dynamics of Brazilian institutional arrangements. Doing so provided them a great deal of amusement and I learned more from them than they learned from me. Within the US, many colleagues planted important ideas for the book, often without realizing they were doing so. Some of these include Alan Dye, Aurora Gómez-Galvarriato, Anne Hanley, Joe Love, Carlos Marichal, Aldo Musacchio, Richard Sicotte, Bill Summerhill, Catalina Vizcarra, Simone Wegge, the Columbia University Seminar in Economic History, and my colleagues in the departments of history and economics at Rutgers University. Ian Capps, a Brazilophile from outside of academia, first honed my attention onto mineral rights during a casual dinner conversation, as I was shaping my research.

Conferences and seminars served as the fora for the most trenchant commentary on the ideas of this book. These have included presentations at the Business History Conferences (2004 and 2006), Universidade Federal de Minas Gerais (2004) Universidade Estadual de Campinas - Instituto de Geociências (2006) and Instituto de Economia (2008; for which I thank Pedro Paulo Zaluth Bastos), the Middlebury-University of Vermont Economic History Workshop (2006), the Universidade de São Paulo-Ribeirão Preto (2007), the Universidade Federal de Rio Grande de Sul (2007) the Economic History Association (2007), the Associação Brasileira de Pesquisadores de História Econômica (2008), the Washington DC Area Economic History Workshop (2009), the Columbia University Brazil Seminar (2008), Brazilian Studies Association (2008), the XIII Seminário Sobre a Economia Mineira: Economia História, Demografia e Políticas Públicas (2008), the World Economic History Association (2009), the

Harvard-MIT Workshop on the Political Economic of Development in Brazil (2009) and New Frontiers in Latin American Economic History (2010). Portions of Chapters 2 and 3 have appeared in 'Property Rights, Kinship Groups, and Business Partnership in Nineteenth and Twentieth Century Brazil: The Case of the St. John d'el Rey Mining Company' (in *Enterprise and Society*, 8:1 (January 2007), pp. 35–67).

I have been especially fortunate in the research assistance that has contributed to the project. In Minas Gerais, Marcus Neves provided terrific energy in archives and notarial offices, and he tracked source material with admirable stubbornness. In Rio de Janeiro, Soraia Marcelino proved herself a natural archival researcher, a consistently dedicated worker and a delightful companion; Daniel Heller collected data with great accuracy, charm and dedication; Victor Miranda undertook last-minute searches and provided bibliographic assistance at the end of the project. At Rutgers University, Yasu Denda thoroughly researched US archival catalogues and offered interesting insight into some of the questions that I was trying to resolve and AnnaLinden Weller provided final formatting and proofreading assistance. Long ago, Tamara Swedburg manipulated the map which appears as Figure 3.2, and more recently, she saved me from a file organization mishap.

Two individuals deserve special recognition. Herb Klein supported my scholarship before I had produced any; he taught me the skills and showed me the satisfaction of the endeavour. Tamás Szmrecsányi also encouraged my scholarship, and was especially helpful in the early phases of this project with bibliographic suggestions and an invitation to the Instituto Geociências (Unicamp). I can only hope that this book meets the standards that he would have set for it, had he been here to read it.

At Pickering & Chatto, Daire Carr and Stephina Clarke improved the manuscript by honing their editorial eyes on it.

In the face of this support and contribution of good ideas, I remain responsible for any errors of fact or reasoning.

Carter Kaneen has carried much of the burden of this book, in the time and distraction from everyday life that it has required; I hope that he enjoyed much of the adventure as well. The editing and research that he has cheerfully provided are only small portions of his contribution. I can only believe that, if he thinks this project has been worthwhile, then it has.

LIST OF FIGURES AND TABLES

NOTE ON THE TEXT

Currency

For a brief history of the Brazilian unit of currency please see the Global Financial Data information below, available at http://www-globalfinancialdata.com.

Prior to November 1942	*Real*
	1 *mil-réis* = 1,000 *réis*
	1 *conto (de réis)* = 1,000 *mil-réis*
November 1942 – February 1967	*Cruzeiro*: 1 *cruziero* = 1 *mil-réis*
	Beginning of multiple administered exchange rates
February 1967 – February 1986	New *cruzeiro*: 1 new *cruzeiro* = 1 *cruzeiro*
February 1986 – January 1989	*Cruzado*: 1 *cruzado* = 1,000 *cruzeiros*
January 1989 – March 1990	New *cruzado*: 1 new *cruzado* = 1,000 *cruzados*
March 1990 – August 1993	*Cruzeiro*: 1 *cruzeiro* = 1 *cruzado*
August 1993 – July 1994	*Cruzeiro real*: 1 *cruzeiro real* = 1,000 *cruzeiro*
July 1994 –	*Real*: 1 *real* = 2750 *cruzeiro réis*

Note: Global Financial Data calculates that (including changing par value of currency), 1 *real* (1994) = $2750*10^{15}$ old *réis*.

Names

Brazilians typically refer to all individuals, regardless of their public standing, by their first names, and the usage of family names varies. Recognizing its English-language readership, I refer to individuals by their family names in this book. When naming conventions or spelling discrepancies arise, I try to use the most common and recent spelling.

Within Brazil, the Companhia Vale do Rio Doce, one of the most important actors in this book, is commonly referred to as 'Vale'. For purposes of succinctness, I use this nomenclature.

Translations

All translations by the author, unless noted otherwise.

Figures and Tables

Sources and notes accompanying the figures and tables can be found in the end-note indicated after each caption.

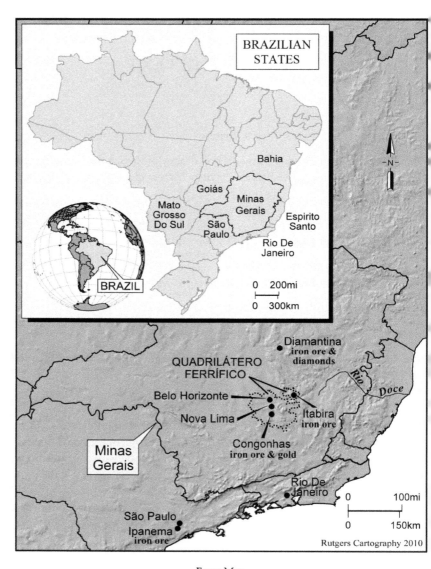

Front Map

INTRODUCTION

This book is about attempts in Brazil to use its endowment of minerals as a tool for creating wealth and the evolution of the economic role of the Brazilian state. These topics are surprisingly intertwined. The focus is on political economy, rather than the extraction of minerals from the ground, because political economy impeded extraction. Substantive change in the political-economic institutions related to mineral extraction initiated Brazil's emergence as an industrial economy and as a global powerhouse in supplying iron ore in the second half of the twentieth century. These outcomes occurred nearly four and a half centuries after the first attempts of Europeans to realize wealth from the land's minerals. As one result of this process, the Brazilian state became the nation's largest industrial producer and commercial agent, as well as one of the world's prime examples of state-capitalism.

The questions framing this study are: How did political-economic institutions shape efforts to exploit mineral resources within Brazil, and reciprocally, how did these efforts shape political-economic institutions? The interactions between the rules and practices governing property, business enterprise, capital markets and the state reveal themselves to be as important to mineral development as the structure of the individual institutions and as important as the presence of minerals. The argument developed here is that creating wealth from the subsoil required the coordination and accommodation of these institutions, and further, that the interaction between institutions and resources was instrumental in shaping the economic governance of Brazil. Understanding the institutional dynamics of the changing economic role of the state in order to extract minerals also sheds important light on two persistent questions of Brazilian economic history (as well as that of other 'late developing' economies): What were the impediments to the evolution of business organization practices that would have promoted large-scale, de-personalized private capital accumulation? And what were the parameters of the shifting divide between public and private spheres in economic activity?

The economic history of mineral rights is not widely studied, and the subject typically focuses on the establishment, rather than change, of property rights.[1]

In Brazil, the Portuguese established the principle that the subsoil was sovereign property early during colonial rule. After a gold 'rush' from 1695 until about 1750, ambitions of garnering mineral wealth continually fell short of miners' goals. From the late eighteenth century, government policy began to search for the means to vitalize mineral production. As miners juggled competing institutional and infrastructure demands with difficulty, their efforts presaged later activity and policy. In 1891, the federal government abruptly privatized mineral rights by attaching the subsoil to land, effectively transferring the subsoil and its contents to landowners. Privatization required significant changes to the definitions of two institutions: public domain and subsoil property. The motivation for these reforms was to promote economic modernity. Mining was only one of many arenas subject to modernizing efforts at the turn of the twentieth century, although historians have subsequently questioned the commitment to fundamental reform.[2] Change to subsoil rights achieved very limited success, and its reversal began in 1930. By 1942, after years of controversy and the shift of attention from precious to industrial minerals, state-owned enterprises emerged to mine and export iron ore and to produce steel in order to meet the superordinate goal of economic development. The new enterprises were the largest in Brazil at the time. They set the precedent for state capitalism in natural resources and mining, and Brazil became one of the world's major providers of iron ore and steel in a relatively short time frame. Although policy makers and legal authorities focused their attention on the property rights attached to the subsoil, competing institutional demands with respect to capital and various categories of property proved to be the binding constraints on mineral development. To meet goals for industrialization, without threatening long-standing arrangements that governed economic relationships extending far beyond minerals, the public sector entered into the business of industrial production and commerce.

Although minerals have always lurked in the background (and sometimes in the foreground too) of Brazilian political economy, they have received surprisingly little historical attention. The neglect of the topic parallels the inability to develop a base of economic activity sustained by minerals. Non-renewable natural resources generate unique issues with respect to political economy and governance for a variety of reasons. The resources are natural and non-renewable, rather than produced and reproducible by identifiable actors. Because these resources are natural, this study belongs to the corpus of environmental history, as well as economic, business and political history. It is concerned with human interaction with the natural world in the effort to convert a raw material into a marketable commodity. However, in keeping with the norms of the time periods under examination here, the effects of exploiting the natural environment were not objects of consideration to decision makers or to miners.

The analysis in this book draws heavily on the 'new institutional economic history'. Loosely defined, institutions are the 'rules of the game'.[3] While the term has an impersonal and abstract tone to it, institutions represent the understandings that individuals have reached through innumerable interactions, often over long periods of time and subject to evolution. They reflect the accumulated agreements about norms and practices of social interaction. With all of their ambiguities, institutions identify the parameters of interactions among actors, and they regulate those interactions. Institutions take many forms, including specific organizations, social custom, or laws and government. They shape and govern behaviour and reflect the interests of the participating actors. Institutions are negotiated outcomes that represent an accumulation of myriad transactions. Negotiations may be formal or informal; they may also be among parties of relatively equal influence or among unequal parties (coercion). The outcomes fall on a continuum of possibilities, strongly influenced by interest group activity and political strength.

Neo-institutional scholarship concentrates on interactions among private sector actors. This literature postulates the state as an important tool for shaping and enforcing institutional arrangements and also as a tool of interest groups. States provide the forum for negotiating many institutional constraints (legislatures specifying laws); they also provide the infrastructure to regulate interactions and enforce agreements among private parties as well as between private parties and public authorities. Latin America has provided a prominent setting for these studies, even if most of their authors have their intellectual homes in the US.[4]

Property rights are a fundamental theme of the new institutional economic history; they are taken as a crucial element in determining the trajectory of economic growth and business development. The underlying tenet of current research is that well-specified property rights are a prerequisite for sustained economic growth and market formation.[5] The literature assumes that effective property rights delineate the limits to owner autonomy with respect to asset use, transformation and transfer. Effective rights do not easily give rise to counter-claims on property that render autonomy uncertain, and clear procedures exist when counterclaims arise. Law (common or statutory) specifies and protects property ownership and use.[6] While paying lip service to the diversity possible in specifying property rights, there is an impressive dearth of research observing specific features of property rights that prove to be ineffective.

Contracts operationalize property rights in transactions between economic actors. Whether formal or informal, contracts serve to specify the terms of exchange transactions and to anticipate problems of contingent claims that may arise in the process of exchange. The evolution towards more sophisticated forms of property rights and larger, more complex organizations requires more complex contracting. However, asset specificity (the ability to reallocate or transform assets/property) and asymmetric information impose constraints on the ability to specify complete contracts. 'Complex contracts are invariably incomplete, and many are maladaptive. The reasons are two: Many contingencies are unforeseen (and unforeseeable), and the adaptations to those contingencies that have been recognized for which adjustments have been agreed to are often mistaken.'[7] The judicial system may offer one avenue for settling disputes about contingencies that disrupt contracts. Judicial remedy is limited by the confidence the parties put in the courts, the ability of courts to deal with complex problems expeditiously and by their costs. Therefore, as contracts become more complex, the parties develop incentives to build in credible commitments that bind them to the terms and intent of their contract and to peaceful extra-judicial settlement.[8]

The physical characteristics of different types of assets shape feasible structures for their rights. Land and financial assets are the types of property whose rights have been most thoroughly studied. These assets have an important characteristic that eases their understanding. They are nearly infinitely divisible, yielding large samples of transactions that demonstrate their dynamics. Therefore, analysts can observe institutional development in the daily practices of multiple small and large economic actors. The few recent studies of Brazilian institutional economic history share this characteristic.[9] In contrast, the case of minerals in the formation of a large-scale industrial base presents significant difficulties.

In sub-surface mining, asset specificity and asymmetric information are particularly vexing problems. Mines seldom can be converted to other uses of equal economic value, and mine owners closely hold information about the likelihood of finding minerals or other resources. The number of actors was small in Brazil. Relatively few cases had large impact and they did not occur along a smooth time path. In short, mineral-related transactions were lumpy. As a result, establishing rights to minerals had particular conceptual and practical difficulties, with respect to uncertainty and asymmetry of geological knowledge, high fixed costs and time dimensions. Causality was bi-directional; the specific nature of the iron ore deposits in the Minas Gerais region of Brazil (the central locus of early mining) both constrained institutional responses, and the ability to extract those deposits was constrained by institutions. These characteristics challenge both methodology of the new institutionalism and the understanding of historical experience.

Despite its usefulness, the new institutionalism also brings theoretical and methodological limitations. One divergence from mainstream neo-institutional scholarship in this study is the inclusion of non-human actors: iron ore deposits and the state. This book posits that the state is simultaneously an actor, a tool for interest groups and an enforcement agent.[10] The effort to develop iron ore production of industrial scale resulted in a fundamental transition of the economic role of the state. This outcome resulted from the decision to develop through the medium of a state-owned enterprise, one of the strongest forms of economic intervention. Doing so initiated the state in the role of an important actor in production and commerce, at the same time that the state's more usual activities of regulation and mediation grew stronger. Development economists have studied the economic role of the state in detail. In addition to the nature and scope of regulation, state-owned enterprise (SOE) has been an important, if controversial, tool for managing development. However, business and economic historians of the developing world have generally neglected these firms and their origins.

In addition, rather than limiting this analysis to a single institution, interaction among different institutions provides a key to understanding how complex institutions change over time in this project. Different categories of property – familial, business, subsoil – carry distinct considerations, and these categories are not mutually exclusive. The preponderance of the property rights literature has assumed a dichotomy between individual and corporate ownership structures. This assumption is at odds with Brazilian history.[11] The literature ignores *familial* property, a form that has been mandated through Brazilian history.[12] Further, protection of existing accumulations of property could prevent the division of fixed real assets (such as mineral veins). The effects of these constraints for Brazilian business practices are crucial for understanding this history. The consideration of multiple institutions also complicates our understanding of the process of institutional change. If institutions represent the cumulative result of the actions and interests of actors, then changing institutions needs to accommodate both existing and new interest groups.

Researching institutional change, incorporating the implications of multiple institutions, non-human actors and the multiple roles of the state has methodological implications for this study. The theoretical and econometric models used by the new institutionalism have difficulty incorporating the multidimensionality of institutional interaction, and have given rise to its most effective criticism.[13] As a result, methodological constraints are powerful determinants of the application of neo-institutional analysis. A strange dichotomy divides the literature between large, generalized questions and topics that are very narrowly defined.[14] They take advantage of nearly infinite divisibility appropriate to the standard tools of econometric analysis: model specification and accumulating large data samples for empirical testing. These studies gain much of their strength from applying either very generalized or narrowly defined institutional arrangements to a small range of often-repeated actions in a manner that can accommodate divisibility. However, their usefulness is limited by not explaining clear avenues of causality (in the overly generalized studies) or by explaining very narrowly defined and not readily replicable circumstances of narrowly defined institutions. These studies have not addressed the large-scale industrial transformation that occurred in the middle of the twentieth century in many economies.[15] To do so requires a more multidimensional approach than recent methods support.

In the case of mineral extraction, in which scale matters and economic importance is high, the repeated actions of economic actors are not available for analysis.[16] The economists' tools of precisely parameterized models reflecting narrowly defined questions do not allow for an understanding of the messy realities of institutional interaction and path dependence (historical specificity). Further, data availability hinders the possibility of empirical analysis of the optimum rate of resource extraction (to test the desirability of policy options at different times).[17] Here, economic concepts combined with historians' tools allow a broader insight on the political-economic question of the development of the role of the Brazilian state within the productive economy. The quantitative data appropriate to the questions of each chapter (analyses of laws, land sales, concession-granting and equity-market data) present sufficient constraints that econometric testing would obscure, rather than clarify, their implications. These data present pictures of circumstances that can be understood most clearly through narrative analysis in conjunction with documents from archival sources, government and company records and the very active business press of the period. The historical approach allows for the nuanced and widely considered study of a case that is important both to the theories of institutions and to the history of Brazil.

Theories of public choice provide the prism for understanding the evolution of the economic role of the state by considering the interaction between collective and individual interests.[18] When economic activity generates externalities (benefits that extend beyond those accruing to the provider) the incentive of any private sector economic actor (person or enterprise) to engage in that activity diminishes, because of the benefit that actor cannot capture. If the externality, or collective good, is sufficient, then the state, as the public authority, may step in to provide it. Conflict over the public provision of a good or service is often fraught with political competition. Strong interest groups identify externalities that they have no incentive to provide, or cannot capture, and they attempt to influence the state to provide for their collective creation. Once decided upon, the state can provide goods and services through a variety of arrangements. State-owned corporate enterprise, operating in the economic marketplace, is only one of many possible arrangements.[19] The implementation of Brazil's first large-scale iron ore projects relied on state-owned enterprise in order to accommodate a range of competing economic and political goals.

This book's focus on the political economy and institutional accommodation to initiate industrial-scale iron ore mining defines its scope. A general history of mining or of the iron and steel industry in the twentieth century are (potentially rich) projects left to other scholars.

The argument of the book impinges upon many topics that are crucial to understanding Brazil's history and its current reality. It also raises issues that continue to impact resource use in Brazil and throughout Latin America. At the beginning of the twenty-first century, Brazil is one of the world's largest providers of iron ore, one of the most sophisticated producers of steel and is energy self-sufficient. Efforts to achieve these goals began as early as the seventeenth century. Difficulties in bringing together the resources, technology and capital were frustrated repeatedly by the desire to not challenge the accepted underpinnings of society and economy. The resolution of these issues required Brazilians to face questions regarding the boundaries between public and private property, forms of governance and economic participation. The pendulum of political and economic support for public enterprise oscillates with circumstance. This book offers a detailed and long-term case study of one of the largest and (perhaps) most successful public enterprises of the developing world. The global economic crisis of the first decade of the twenty-first century brings the issues considered here back to prominence.

The book's organization reflects both chronology and thematic issues. After a chapter to establish the historical context, Chapter 2 delineates the legal history of mining. Readers uninterested in the topic or in gaining insight on the interaction between law and economic concerns may wish to go directly to Part II, which analyses the historical trajectory of the subsoil and its development in three chapters. The first two efforts that the state brought to the topic, an early attempt to develop local industry within Brazil as the colonial era ended at the beginning of the nineteenth century and the subsequent benign neglect in the hope of attracting foreign capital and technology through the remainder of the nineteenth century, are explored in Chapter 3. Chapter 4 analyses the first major change in subsoil rights, privatization in 1891. The chapter considers the effects of the privatization and the impediments to fuller mining development, as interest shifted from precious to industrial metals. The successful organization of iron ore mining into a large-scale industrial endeavour is the topic of Chapter 5. The concerns of the chapter are the historical path by which this outcome arose and the effects for the Brazilian economy with respect to the introduction of state capitalism, capital markets and the structure of business organization. The chronological story beyond the launching of industrial iron ore receives only sketchy attention here because the early transformation set the broad parameters of subsequent development. Inserting the history of developing iron ore production into the broader perspectives of Brazilian history is the task of Part III with chapters on two especially pertinent themes. Chapter 6 asserts the tight and pragmatic relationship between mining development and economic ideology. Chapter 7 articulates the precedent that iron ore development set for the subsequent history of petroleum and for economic governance, and it offers a brief consideration of the retrenchment from state capitalism during the second half of the twentieth century. These chapters build the argument that the practices governing many different categories of property, capital markets, business structure and economic governance evolved together in order to turn Brazil into one of the major global providers of a basic industrial commodity, iron ore, at the same time that they structured the Brazilian economy.

PART I: THE SUBSOIL IN BRAZILIAN HISTORY

1 HISTORICAL SETTING

Efforts to extract wealth from the subsoil began with the earliest colonization of Brazil by Portugal, but they achieved success only in the middle of the twentieth century, with the massive exploitation of iron ore. As entrepreneurs experimented with a range of approaches, they faced shifting definitions of 'success'. Finally emerging as a mineral producer required significant transformation in Brazilian economic governance. Leveraging extremely rich iron ore deposits into wider economic benefit had unexpected and fundamentally important impact on the Brazilian economy. Mineral extraction is a relatively neglected area of historiography, despite its centrality in production and in the institutions of political economy. Scholarship by Gavin Wright demonstrates the very tight connection between industrialization and mineral endowment in the US.[1] This book, using different methods, a longer time frame and a focus on political economic institutions, examines this connection as it unfolded in Brazil. The book places iron ore mining at the centre of the story, because iron ore is the mineral that brought success.[2] This chapter offers the relevant historical background. In focusing on the general features of Brazilian political and economic structures that have been relevant to the institutional developments necessary for iron ore mining and metallurgy, the chapter gives short shrift to the broader range of individuals, conflict, contention, nuance and non-linearity of Brazilian history.

Political and Economic Structure

The Colony

Initial Portuguese exploration of Brazil, after first finding themselves in the 'New World' in 1500, did not seem to promise much that would motivate settlement and exploitation. The large settled populations and precious minerals that

Spanish expeditions found were not present in the region where the Portuguese landed. Although explorers remained hopeful of gold or silver discoveries, it was timber, the dyes from Brazilwood and then the commoditization of sugar based on plantation and slave agriculture that slowly motivated European settlement. Settlers found abundant iron ore in the region that is currently São Paulo in 1554; but this mundane mineral was not their goal. The discovery of rich gold veins and precious stones by settlers pushing inland, almost 200 years later, at the end of the seventeenth century, is variously mythologized as the consequence of heroic actions by brave and noble settlers or analysed as the accidental results of *bandeirantes* on expeditions to clear land and to hunt for indigenous slaves.[3]

The Portuguese organized their colonies in Brazil to reflect their interests and their background. The result was that a very broad base of Indians, Africans (introduced by the largest and longest-lasting importation of slaves in the Americas) and their descendents supported a much smaller, well-defined, highly nuanced and stratified social hierarchy of Europeans and their descendents. While seemingly a rigid hierarchy, movement among its strata was quite fluid. Property and the exploitation of natural resources defined the hierarchy. These principles set the course of future social, political and economic organization.

Laws and practices evolved to protect the interests of existing property owners. The imperial state had two goals in this regard: to benefit as much as possible from the extraction of natural resources and to protect the interests of its constituency: European-descended property owners. Sometimes these goals conflicted; but usually the interested parties could find resolutions that reconciled or circumvented conflicts. The hope of finding precious minerals motivated the earliest property laws and the discovery of gold instigated a significant extension of administrative regulatory authority (Chapter 2). Given available technology, the first gold discoveries were substantially depleted within fifty years.

Imperial interests turned to local conditions within the Brazilian colonies during the thirteen-year interregnum, 1808–21, when the Portuguese imperial court sat in exile in Rio de Janeiro. The unique circumstance of an imperial government abandoning its capital during siege and transplanting itself to its most important colony introduced fundamental changes in many aspects of Brazilian life.[4] For the purposes of this book, the most important change was the developmentalist perspective that need and proximity induced in imperial leaders. Imperial participation within the colonial economy took new forms in order to construct the infrastructural underpinnings required for further extraction of resources at the turn of the nineteenth century. The need for physical infrastructure to support local industry, whether for domestic or export-market production, had received sparse attention in the policies of the previous three centuries, which had focused narrowly on extraction and mercantilism.

Iron ore mining and forging (which producers and policy makers considered jointly) was an integral component of the changed perspective. Persistent shortages in machinery and tools, contributing to production bottlenecks for export goods, were prominent among local problems. The Crown sponsored efforts to expand iron ore mining and forging without inhibiting the pursuit of more lucrative endeavours by private producers of sugar and precious minerals (Chapter 3). As with many of the policy innovations of the period, support for iron mining and forging ended with the return of the Portuguese Crown to Lisbon, and the subsequent march towards independence.

Incomplete Independence: Brazilian Empire

Brazilian independence came in 1822, sharing many of the dynamics that motivated political independence in the former colonies of other European powers. Two features, however, distinguished the process in Brazil: the relative lack of violence surrounding the independence movement and the construction of a Brazilian 'empire' to govern instead of the Portuguese Crown. Members of the Portuguese royal family ruled the Brazilian political entity until 1889.

The developmental policies of the immediately preceding years did not continue while the Brazilian state presented itself as an independent empire. The conflation of fiscal and trade policies by the imperial government rendered both ineffective.[5] Inability to establish sources of revenues other than exports inhibited fiscal policy. As a result, public resources did not exist to support aggressive intervention in the economy. Perhaps the most important governmental intervention in the economy supported commodity producers by subsidizing railroad mainlines and offering concessions to build connecting trunk-lines.[6] Despite prudent practices,[7] money and finance developed slowly and in manners that did not give incentive to large-scale, de-personalized capital accumulation.[8] Traditional land-extensive plantation agriculture rested on a broad base of slave labour and free-labour subsistence-producers who could not support dynamic local commerce. For all of these reasons, domestic economic development lagged behind efforts in the export sectors.

Agricultural exports dominated the prevailing political and economic constituency. Gold and precious-stone mining continued within the mineral-rich region of Minas Gerais, as well as in pockets of the provinces of Bahia and Goiás; but participants in this sector were not heavily invested in the political process (Chapters 2 and 3). Iron ore mining and forging lost its position on the political economic agenda during the nineteenth century.[9] Even so, isolated activity did occur; the national government funded and opened the *Escola de Minas* (Mining School) with foreign geologists in 1876. The school became the domestic training ground for engineers and geologists.[10]

From the middle of the nineteenth century, policy makers and property owners began to recognize that the existing economic structure did not offer a viable future. The effective abolition of the trans-Atlantic slave trade in 1850 was both a cause and an effect of social change; it marks a convenient point of departure for considering deep economic change. Property owners understood that, given demographic realities of Brazilian slavery, the abolition of the trans-Atlantic trade would result in the eventual end of the slave system.[11] Therefore, some began to turn their attention to preserving their ability to survive the loss of one of their important categories of property – slaves – by instituting reforms that would modernize the Brazilian economy. A Commercial Code to encourage more open business structures, efforts to attract European migrants for labour, and the creation of systematic methods for claiming land ownership with the Land Code were some of the responses that took shape.[12] Applying modern organizational methods and scientific practices to large-scale commercial agriculture, both for export commodities and increasingly for domestic sustenance, gained attention as a way to modernize the country-side. Would-be entrepreneurs worked to introduce a base of industrial manufacturing into the economic system. Reacting to a widespread belief that slaves were unsuitable labour for manufacturing, industrial ambitions also served as a motivation to end slavery.[13] None of these projects progressed quickly, smoothly, or as planned; but with time, they gathered momentum.

Republican Brazil

The abolition of slavery and overthrow of the Empire to introduce republican government, in 1888 and 1889, respectively, signalled continuing political-economic and social transition. Governing Brazil must have become more difficult during the First Republic (1889–1930) than it had been during the Empire. New and traditional interest groups competed in the marketplaces of ideas and political representation. The military emerged as an active force in domestic politics and government. Recently freed slaves and other poor rural folk began moving to cities in large numbers, and they simultaneously constituted a pool of consumers for industrially manufactured goods, a source of labour and uncivilized hordes. Foreign immigrants and freed slaves also flocked to newly opened areas of plantation agriculture. These demographic movements opened opportunities for industrial entrepreneurs and would-be entrepreneurs. Under the guise of republicanism, much governance passed from the national level to the newly designated states. Questions about economic structure moved to the centre of most political agendas. Much historiography has focused on the political and economic transitions of the period.[14]

Some social historians contend that conciliation between different groups, rather than resolution of conflict, created many of the contradictions and inconsistencies in Brazilian life. In accordance with this interpretation and notwithstanding new interest groups and rearranged social organization, rigid social order remained an organizing principal. Social, economic and political hierarchies were mutually reinforcing. Reconciling new material and economic needs with traditional ones required skill, and often they created new sources of conflict. Economic policy debates that juxtaposed export agriculture against support for industrialization began to gain ground in this environment.

Tensions between the interests of commercial agricultural producers and emerging industrialists have received attention. Nevertheless, historians have shown that these sectors tended to advance in tandem, and these were the commercial sectors that accumulated strong political power.[15] The rapid expansion of both sectors required physical infrastructure beyond the existing capacity in Brazil at the end of the nineteenth century. As a result, in areas of dynamic growth the demand for transportation, finance, ports, electrical networks, and basic machine- and tool-manufacture remained ahead of their supply. Iron mining and forging (and by the twentieth century, steel manufacturing) re-emerged as potential solutions to some of the bottlenecks of supplying machinery and tools necessary for industrial manufacturing and for expanded commercial agriculture. At the same time, a new Constitution in 1891 mandated the first change in subsoil property rights since Portuguese colonization, which evolved into a concern with the natural resource and institutional requirements to bring about iron and steel development (Chapter 4).

Post-Republican Brazil

A coup, in the face of election disputes, ended the First Republic in October 1930, and initiated the governmental regimes of Getúlio Vargas (1930–45, 1951–4). The experiment with state-level governance ended and political power was re-concentrated in the national executive branch. Re-centralizing political power was a clear instance of invoking traditional principles in order to serve new goals. A strong and personalized executive branch directed its powers to build a state that incorporated a broad mass of individuals. Its objective was to create and oil the machine of a powerful and economically independent nation. A wide historiography documents the expansion of constituencies with a stake in the national political system and the balance between authoritarianism, patronage and social welfare programmes that the Vargas regime employed to consolidate a strong government at the national level.[16]

Focusing on the economic ambitions that were central to the Vargas regime policies, the mining and metallurgy sector was both an inescapable necessity to these ambitions and a crucial factor shaping the future structure of the Brazilian economy (see Chapter 5). Building this sector propelled Brazil into the top ranks of global iron ore production within two decades and turned the state into the nation's largest commercial entrepreneur. It also ushered in an era of development projects of enormous scale and sweeping ambition that were intended to turn Brazil into the 'country of the future'. The tools for this transition would be exploitation of the nation's vast natural resource endowment, construction of a massive modern industrial sector and transformation of its 'backward' population into a skilled and compliant labour force.[17] The intended results were wealth and independence from the vagaries of the global economy.[18]

Although the post-Vargas regimes are largely outside of the analytic scope of this book, the issues important in the political economy of developing iron ore retained their presence in the institutional aspects of policy debates. National-level governance did not face serious challenge in the second half of the twentieth century. However, the specific forms and locales of governmental and political power have not remained static. Active intervention in the economy, with strong inflationary biases, was an important legacy of the Vargas regime. By 1964, a military coup took control of the state for the purpose of reigning in these influences. Military governments expanded centralized executive governance to new levels in Brazil. With the transition back to republican democracy at the end of military government in 1984, national-level political dynamics continue to predominate relative to local ones, even as governance has slowly broadened with stronger powers for the legislative branch.[19] Among the issues that continued to command attention were the forms of state intervention in the economy, desirability of state capitalism, shifting dynamics between the public and private sectors, property (including the rights to natural resources), economic ideology and development of both capital markets and industrial infrastructure.

Minerals in Brazil

Although Brazil has the richest mineral endowment in Latin America, knowledge about the sector remains elusive. Even such seemingly straightforward information as the current size of the sector relative to the Brazilian economy is vague. By all accounts, the sector was large at the end of the twentieth century. Estimates range from 1) an imprecise comparison of approximating the size of electrical industry and agribusiness in 2002 to 2) accounting for 1.6 per cent of GDP plus 5.3 per cent for the industries transforming mineral ores to primary materials (pig iron, steel, and other processed metals) in 2000 and 3) a very high estimate of 4.6 per cent of GDP plus 25.1 per cent for the transformation industries in 1984.[20] Exploration for minerals has become extensive and technologically sophisticated as the sector has grown. At the beginning of the twenty-first century, Brazilian territory contains an estimated 6.5 per cent of global reserves of iron ore, significant amounts of bauxite and manganese, and dominant proportions of important trace minerals (as of 2002, 90 per cent of known reserves of niobium and 45 per cent of tantalum – trace metals used, respectively, to create super-conducting properties in alloys and in the construction of gas pipelines).[21] Of further interest, the Brazilian Institute of Geography and Statistics estimates that each job in mining creates 8.7 positions in the transformation industries.[22]

While mining is currently important to the Brazilian economy, until recently, the absence of mining was more important. Despite the inability to sustain the early discoveries of precious metals, interest in industrial metals intensified by the end of the nineteenth century. Geologists recognized the iron deposits in the interior state of Minas Gerais as the richest in the world by 1881.[23] An international survey in 1910 estimated that these deposits constituted nearly one-quarter of then-known global reserves.[24] These deposits and the concentrated mining area of central Minas Gerais (the *Quadrilátero Ferrífico*, or Iron Quadrilateral, see front map) provide the focus of this book. The largest deposits became a point of catalysing national controversy, as they promised the ability to support the development of a lucrative new source of commodity exports simultaneously with industrial growth. As in the sixteenth, seventeenth and eighteenth centuries, efforts to benefit from these deposits were stymied by scarcity of transportation and capital in the first half of the twentieth century. Overcoming these scarcities required changes to fundamental institutions that governed the structure of economy and politics (Chapters 4 and 5).

Although the macroeconomic history of Brazilian industrialization is well examined,[25] many of the specific experiences and much of the microeconomic history remain mysterious. In a similarly unexplored vein, the actual benefits from mining, with the exception of iron ore, have fallen short of expectations in Brazil. For iron ore, the strategy that the Brazilian economy invoked was not one that modern neoclassical economists would recommend; but it was consistent with policy trends of its time.

From the early 1940s, Brazilian industrialists and the government developed a massive industrial policy to construct a large and modern capital goods sector in order to provide modern industry with a wide range of intermediate and consumer manufactured goods. This project initiated some of the largest and most enduring industrial concerns in Brazil. The national government was a central participant in this programme, and one of the outcomes was to establish Brazil as a strong exemplar of economic interventionism in the twentieth century.[26] By the mid-1940s, the national government of Brazil was the majority owner of the two largest companies on the Rio de Janeiro stock exchange, Companhia Vale do Rio Doce (Vale, iron ore mining) and Companhia Siderúrgica Nacional (CSN, the National Steel Company). State-owned enterprise (SOE) operating with significant policy preferences was instrumental in building the Companhia Vale de Rio Doce, with the sole initial purpose of exporting iron ore. In the crucial case of iron ore, the state stepped in, as majority shareholder and offering a wide range of financial and policy advantages, to ensure the development of large-scale iron mining and steel manufacturing. These enterprises were among the largest industrial concerns in the Third World. Their formation was the culmination of a long period of enormous effort to bring together natural resources, capital, technology, managerial skill, and policies governing trade, foreign exchange and industrialization. Global geopolitical circumstances of World War II also played a crucial role in shaping the path of these firms. Both companies remain prominent (though reconfigured) at the beginning of the twenty-first century, and they were among the most important of the firms privatized in the 1990s.

Vale was one of three enterprises, along with the national steel and petroleum firms (CSN and Petrobras, respectively) that became iconic representatives of the state's role in the productive sectors of the Brazilian economy. That these companies would be state-owned was not a foregone conclusion, but rather the confluence of ideology and an entrepreneurial history that spanned almost forty years. To understand how this came about, and hence to understand the trajectory of the state becoming the largest entrepreneur in the Brazilian economy, requires an exploration of constraints imposed by fundamental institutions and economic ideologies.

The intersection of mining, industrialization and institutional change offers a fruitful venue for research in Brazil. Establishing these SOEs required extraordinary organizational and political effort and it motivated some of the most contentious public policy debates of the period.[27] To establish the companies, the Vargas regime invoked two parallel strategies that redefined the basic property rights attached to natural resources and to private business. These strategies were to reclaim sovereignty over mineral resources and to expand the perceived range of externalities resulting from commercial endeavour that justified public sector intervention. The legitimacy of both strategies extended beyond their efficacy and rested on their origins in colonial law and practice that prevailed for almost three centuries, from 1603 to 1891.

The effort to understand the rise of iron ore mining in Brazil highlights the importance of identifying institutional change within the contexts of exogenous constraints and interactions with other institutions. In this case, liberalized institutions directly addressed one asset of concern, but did not meet the ambitions of transforming a dormant mining sector into a dynamic industrial activity. Important features of other institutions that constrained the effectiveness of a seemingly crucial property right were the indivisibility of real property and the capacity of capital markets. Indivisibility provisions imposed difficulties on business organization, and by extension limited the support that capital markets could give to mineral extraction and the related infrastructure requirements.

Finally, the interaction of all of these forces had important consequences for shaping the possibilities for private Brazilian enterprise (see Chapters 5 and 7).

Exploring the development of iron ore mining in the context of theories about institutions, public choice and state economic intervention highlights the political economy of allocating to the public domain the property rights to natural resources in order to build an SOE. The Brazilian state reverted to earlier property definitions that protected its sovereignty over the subsoil and mineral resources, and it used the global strategic circumstances of World War II to great advantage. As a result, the state redefined its role in the economy while promoting large-scale industry in the twentieth century. In the middle of the twentieth century, new political and business interest groups invoked long-entrenched traditional practices in order to pursue a fundamentally new trajectory of development.

2 MINERALS, THE SUBSOIL AND PROPERTY LAW

Outlining the pertinent trajectory, characteristics and debates of subsoil property law throughout Brazilian history since European colonization is the purpose of this chapter. It considers intersections of the subsoil with other forms of property, with legal regulation and with political-economic ideology. Brazilian policymakers have continually faced the challenge of balancing ideological commitments to legal theory with the more pragmatic concerns of economic development. In the middle of the twentieth century, the state reintroduced principles of mineral law that originated from early colonial rule, but vastly transformed their scope and intent in order to accommodate the exigencies of modern economic and political reality. By doing so, the format of legal theory had proven sufficiently flexible to allow the predominance of economic goals over ideological commitments.

From the beginning of Portuguese rule, Roman law has formed the basis of the Brazilian legal system. Codification is one of the underpinnings of Roman law, rather than the accumulated and evolutionary fluidity of common law. The efficacy of Roman (or Napoleonic) legal systems for economic development is subject to debate.[1] However, a codified legal system has the advantage for analysis of strictly delineating law, rather than relying on interpretations of 'custom'. Codified law is important for three reasons. First, the legal system is an important institution that provides for the regulation of other institutions. Secondly, the legal system reflects the underlying organizing principles of society; i.e., deeply embedded non-economic institutions such as customary practice, beliefs and culture. Finally, and anticipating one of the important conclusions of this book, the laws that governed property rights to minerals were crucially important for debating and shaping the economic institutions that underpinned Brazilian industrialization and the role of the Brazilian state in the productive economy.

At the time of colonization, the imperial power considered the colony to be within the sovereign's domain.[2] The earliest colonial manifestation of property law was the land allocation from 1532 to 1548, monarchical *doações* of *capitanias hereditárias* (allocations of hereditary captaincies). The *doações* did not serve their intended purpose of promoting land settlement. The Crown withdrew the *doações* and replaced them after only sixteen years with a system of *sesmarias*, granting full property rights over very large holdings.[3] Although the practice of granting *sesmarias* ended with independence from Portugal in 1822, no alternative land law was legislated until the Land Code of 1850.[4] Under both of these systems, land and mining law remained distinct from each other.[5]

The evolution of Brazilian subsoil rights reflects important junctures of economic and political change (Appendix Table A.1A identifies major mining legislation). Precious minerals and stones were the target of regulation from the beginning of Portuguese rule until the end of the nineteenth century. From then, increasing private and public urgency attached to the goal of establishing a modern industrial sector. As a result, attention turned to industrial minerals. This transition directly paralleled the development of mining law.

Pre-Industrial Subsoil Rights

Brazilian law and common practice clearly conceptualized property, and they provided both rights and regulations. The sovereign's claim to the subsoil was not controversial. A logical implication of the claim was the separation of land ownership from rights to subsoil resources.[6] The legal structures and the practices governing property remained remarkably constant over time. Portuguese colonial administration established the principles that would continue to govern property through the nineteenth century. As an agricultural and precious-minerals colony, regulating and monitoring access to natural resources was always at the centre of ideas about property.

Portuguese authorities introduced law to regulate mining in their American colonies even before discovering large mineral deposits.[7] The major gold mines of Minas Gerais were discovered, and widely publicized, at the end of the seventeenth century. Many scholars have identified taxation and regulation of mining as the origin of stronger colonial rule in Portuguese America.[8] Devising incentives to increase mining was in continual tension with the efforts to use regulation to promote order and generate imperial revenues. Pre-industrial practices firmly established the Crown/state's claim to non-renewable subsoil resources. This was the source of the (in)famous *quinto* (one-fifth) that the Portuguese Crown claimed from precious mineral production in 1601, through the collection of rents on concessions granted to individuals.[9]

The second royal *alvará* to govern mining, in 1603, after the imposition of the *quinto*, emphasized the indivisibility of fixed assets. This *alvará* established that mineral veins were indivisible at the same time that it protected miners against imprisonment for debt default.[10] Europeans first found large gold deposits during the 1690s. By 1702, the *Regimento dos Superintendentes, Guardas-mores e*

Oficiais Deputados (an official superintendency) appeared in the mining area of Minas Gerais to distribute and regulate mining claims. Officials paired the initial practice of granting mining concessions with establishing refining and minting houses near rich lodes in 1713 in order to capture fees and tax revenues.[11] In 1721, with the first attempts at deep-shaft mining, the *Guarda-mor* took on the task of regulating the subsurface claims. Further reinforcing the protection of fixed assets, in 1752, the *Lei da Trintena* prohibited the ability of creditors to force the bankruptcy of concessionaires who also had at least thirty slaves working the mines. With the decline of mining in the second half of the century, the benefits of the *Lei da Trintena* extended to all mine operators in 1813.[12] Beyond widening bankruptcy protection, attempts to provide incentive to moribund mining at the beginning of the nineteenth century resulted in early (perhaps the earliest) corporate partnership provisions. A *carta régia* (royal pronouncement) of 12 August 1817 authorized the formation of joint-stock partnerships for gold exploration, long before the Commercial Code of 1850 generally recognized joint-stock organizations.[13]

In addition to the fundamental legislation that controlled mining, ancillary regulation established the bureaucratic infrastructure to enforce control. Some of these actions included: in 1703, opening a *Casa de Registro do Ouro* (registration office for gold), prohibiting clergy from mining areas in 1713; the first attempt to regulate water rights in 1720, controlling the construction of new roads in 1733; forbidding the circulation of precious metal coins in 1808; and creating a fiscal office for the arsenals, factories and foundries in 1811.[14]

Rights to the subsoil intersected with other practices that regulated property. Other unifying principles applied to all forms of property. The overriding principle of business property law in Brazil was to preserve the integrity of fixed assets (mines and sugar plantations, for all practical purposes). Once accumulated, property could not be redivided, if doing so reduced its productive capacity.[15] Deviations from this practice required a cumbersome judicial process. At the same time, one of the most persistent features of personal property law has been to preserve the inheritance of personal estates among all legally recognized heirs, limiting the ability of an individual to determine the distribution of assets within his/her estate.[16] Though much socio-economic historiography emphasizes the difficulty of maintaining estates through inter-generational transfers,[17] problems of dividing property seldom receive consideration. To reconcile the principles of indivisibility and partible distribution of estates, heirs commonly received proportionate shares of estates, without transferring specific assets to individuals. Estates frequently became family partnership enterprises, managed by one or a small number of senior family members. Alternatively, some members purchased the shares of others.[18] Propertied families implemented a wide variety of sophisticated and complex practices to sustain unified holdings for as long as they retained their profitable life.

Without general laws on the composition, functioning and transferability of business partnerships, their success relied on good will and personal relations. The absence of norms providing for freely transferable limited-liability joint-venture organizations meant that personal partnerships were the most efficacious form for dealing with ambiguities about claims. Family inheritance laws, with the opportunity for the future appearance of unknown heirs, left open the possibility of requiring partnerships with unintended and undesirable partners. The complicated requirements of dissolving partnerships, because of either a partner's death or a business disagreement could paralyse a mine's operations until the legal arrangements were finalized.[19] The complexities of these indivisibility provisions compounded the risks inherent in mining and impeded incentives for investment by limiting the ease of accumulating capital among a wide range of investors.

The second application of indivisibility provisions, the physical integrity of mineral veins, was equally troubling as miners slowly began to practice deep-shaft mining. Since the extent and trajectory of veins were unpredictable, exclusive claims to the minerals in any location were uncertain. No specific guidelines governed the limits of concessions as veins merged or split. In principle, all contiguous ore belonged to a single vein. This interpretation of indivisibility remained in effect throughout the middle of the twentieth century.[20] Indivisibility of subsoil assets and their separation from the soil presented significant administrative difficulty. For example, authorities typically demarcated concessions by the surface area, using land measures. By 1702, concessions required that miners had one slave for each two-and-a-half square *braças*[21] allocated in order to assure adequate labour for extracting minerals.

As much as the law tried to keep them distinct, surface and subsoil rights often intersected in complicated manners. Procedures to allocate mining concessions tried to reconcile two principles: the first claim to extraction rights belonged to the discoverer of deposits and the owner of the surface above the deposits (if the surface was privately owned) had a right to a portion of the minerals discovered below his/her soil.[22] The basis for protecting the landowner was that mining the subsoil inevitably disrupted the utility of the surface. Both the discoverer of new deposits and the surface owner were entitled to claim rights to exploit mineral deposits, with the discoverer's share twice that of the land owner. The provisions against division ensured that deposits on privately owned land, explored by an outside party, would be mined in partnership. Constraints on transferring concessions left few avenues for resolving differences that may have arisen in these enterprises.

The concept of *terras devolutas* (literally translated as 'returned lands') defined the treatment of land in the public domain and operationalized beneficial-use regulations. The concept survived the colonial regime and became incorporated within laws governing all resources in independent Brazil.[23] By determining that natural resources[24] previously allocated to private parties were not actively exploited (or in 'beneficial use'), the asset returned to the public domain. Standards of beneficial use applied to all natural resources: agricultural land, water sources, forests, scrublands; mineral veins were only one particular category. With the subsoil and the surface separated, mineral veins could return to public control separately from the land. Private citizens could invoke beneficial-use provisions to have resources returned to the public domain, for the purpose of reallocating the asset to their control.[25] Legal challenges based on beneficial-use requirements generated significant judicial struggle, while they also provided an effective means for resource expropriation.

Independence in 1822 did not bring substantive changes to mining law or to its practical applications. The post-independence Constitution of 1824 was silent on the subsoil and, by default, left it with the same legal status as under imperial rule. Control of subsoil resources passed from the person of the Portuguese monarch to the institution of the Brazilian state.[26] This transfer did not result in changes to practices or business opportunities for miners. Retrospectively, these arrangements were subject to debate and reinterpretation; however, they were not controversial at the time.[27] Although the share of output claimed by the state in exchange for conceding access changed through the nineteenth century,[28] mining and the development of mineral-based industries were not a priority for the Brazilian Empire. Efforts to regulate, control or create incentives for miners resulted in sparse and relatively minor legislation for most of the nineteenth century. During the first decade of independence, the most important legal change reflected efforts to increase production by easing the conditions under which Brazilians could mine, and by establishing the terms for foreign companies to participate in the sector (Chapter 3). After the early 1830s, mining policy commanded little attention.[29] The principle of the state's sovereignty over subsoil resources survived until the Constitution of the first Brazilian republican government in 1891.

Privatizing the Subsoil in 1891

The advent of the Republic in 1889 and the Constitution of 1891[30] introduced the first fundamental changes to subsoil rights in Brazilian history. While the first Constitution of republican Brazil was in effect (1891–1934) subsoil rights belonged to the surface owner, and regulation of mining devolved from the national to the state level.[31] For most of the republican years, mining was not a prominent public issue, and the change attracted little attention at the national level. Gold mining remained depressed throughout the First Republic; only one company actively mined gold by 1930.[32] Industrialization was gaining attention,[33] and the issues of supplying industrial metals to support the production of capital goods gained momentum in the first decades of the twentieth century.[34]

The change in mining rights in 1891 reflected a combination of efforts to unify all property law and ideological commitments to republicanism, with governance devolved to the states (see Chapter 4). Attaching the subsoil to surface rights was attributed variously to a preoccupation with establishing a unified system for treating all property, a narrow focus on individual rights that blocked a perspective of collective goods, or simply as one of many constitutional measures intended to mark a radical shift from the pre-existing imperial law.[35] A small group of Brazilians began to perceive the under-performing mining sector as an impediment to industrialization and debated the best way of remedying the problem.[36] For those concerned with the productive economy, the First Republicans believed that economic liberalization would be sufficient to stimulate modernization.

The theoretical basis of the debate on the legal status of the subsoil hinged on principle of *res nullius*. Some legal scholars pressed the idea that the concepts of *res nullius* property status governed the subsoil.[37] By this reasoning, the subsoil was not a 'thing' that could be owned, because it had not been produced, either by private agents or by any public entity.[38] Rather, a public authority had the responsibility to allocate access to the subsoil, and to establish the terms of access (fees, duration of contract, limitations on ores to be mined, etc). The concept of *res nullius* descended from Roman law, and the Napoleonic Code of 1810 specifically invoked it as the basis of French mining regulation.[39] Advocates of applying the concept of *res nullius* to mines expressed this position early during the republican years: 'Since the mines are *res nullius*, they belong neither to the State nor to private bodies; falling to the State, for general interests, to attribute the property to a chosen individual.'[40]

Theorists typically expected control of *res nullius* property rights to reside at the national level. A minority position in these debates advocated that allocation rights should rest with the individual states, rather than nationally, while accepting that the concept of *res nullius* applied to the subsoil.[41] These arguments also grappled with the logical conflict raised by opponents of *res nullius*: if the state was not the owner of the subsoil, by what right could it transfer to third parties the use of assets that it did not own?[42] These distinctions became important in the context of changing the provisions introduced with the First Republic. In the end, the Constitution of 1891 introduced the *sistema acessão* (or adhesion), which required that secondary characteristics of property 'adhered' to its primary characteristic.[43] Land was the primary characteristic of property; allocation of the subsoil below land that remained in the public domain fell to the states. The commonly agreed principle across all interpretations was that the ore extracted from mines belonged to the party who (legally) mined the veins.

Attaching minerals to land and transferring land in the public domain to local states were not inevitable consequences of republican governance. The committee appointed by the Provisional Republican Government to produce the first draft of a new Constitution reserved both land and mines in the public domain for national, rather than state, sovereignty. Further, at least two reports studied the legal structure of mining and the causes of its slow development during the late 1880s, with diverging conclusions about the desirability of the separation of subsoil from land.[44] A report in 1885 was the most recent one to include the technical perspectives of geologists and mining engineers prior to constitutional reform that advocated maintaining the separation. Another study by mining engineers, commissioned to inform the Constituent Assembly, also did not attribute shortfalls from productive potential to problems of property rights. Both studies recommended that the Constitution keep subsoil rights separate from the surface and retain mining land and law in the federal domain. Nevertheless, anticipating a change to the nature of mining rights, one report highlighted that unfettered rights of individuals to the subsoil existed nowhere in the world, and suggested a pressing need to reconcile inconsistent laws.[45] From a different perspective, a special judicial commission advocated transferring all provisions regarding *terras devolutas*, including mines, to the states in which they fell, as a source of revenue to help the newly federalized states meet their expanded fiscal responsibilities.[46] Doing so promised to open unclaimed mining territories to state, rather than federal, control. While debating and revising the Constitution some prominent constituents advocated that the transfer of land to the states be provisional on their successful development of resources, and others campaigned to keep land and the subsoil at the federal level.[47] The final Constitution differed from all previous technical proposals, with the joining of the subsoil to surface and the transfer of public domain land to the states.

Miners and mining companies were conspicuously apolitical. Most of the prominent mining companies were of foreign origin, and therefore did not have a formal role in organized Brazilian politics. Their political activities were typically limited to informal channels, and were relatively infrequent. Individual miners (*garimpeiros*) were seldom successful or wealthy; they also did not have access to political channels. In Minas Gerais, the concentrated centre of the mining sector at the end of the nineteenth century, mining representation in the constituent assemblies to draft the state and federal Constitutions of 1891 was negligible (see Table 2.1).

Table 2.1: Minas Gerais, representatives to constitutional assemblies, 1890 and 1891.[48]

| | Number of representatives | |
	Total	With mining interests
National Constituent Assembly	39	3
State Constituent Assembly		
Deputies	37	0
Senators	35	2

Inherent contradictions between surface and subsoil remained in the Constitution of 1891 with respect to allocating the first right of access to minerals and to beneficial-use provisions. The Constituent Assembly defined the subsoil as an accessory of the principle property (land), and so it remained with the principle property.[49] By extension, landowners had the first right to use, overturning the previous, strongly held right of first access to the discoverer of mineral veins. Landowners gained control of negotiations with third parties for access to veins. Further, the indivisibility of mineral veins (which remained in effect) conflicted with the physical boundaries of land ownership.[50] Although the joining of land and subsoil created an incentive for miners to own the land that they mined, landowners who were not miners had little incentive or interest in surveying, prospecting or sharing potential gains with miners.[51]

Reflecting developmental concerns, beneficial-use requirements on mineral veins and land remained separate. Unused rights, whether by the surface owner or his/her designee, rendered the subsoil subject to expropriation and return to the public domain. However, the Constitution retained the right of expropriation for the National Congress, while it devolved the regulation of mining to the states. Therefore, no public authority had a clear right to expropriate property in the attempt to encourage mine exploration. One analyst stated in 1911 that

> the old Portuguese legislation, retained in effect with slight modification during the Empire, can also still be applied on occasion, when the ownership, validity or extent of mineral veins, made under the authority of the colonial guarda-mor or the Imperial Government, is questioned.[52]

These reforms did not encourage mining development, at least not to the extent desired (discussed in Chapter 4). In 1901, a federal survey on the problems of expanding mining found the most serious problem to be 'the inertia or caprices of owners and the innumerable complications arising from questions of possession, domain and definition of territorial area.'[53] The change in rights, combined with the practice of common land holdings among small-scale cultivators and grazers, resulted in most small-scale miners having to renegotiate, and often lose, their access to subsoil mineral lodes and water.[54] With landowners in control of contracting for access to the subsoil, many miners with existing claims had to renegotiate their access. Anecdotal evidence and legal treatises suggest that litigation over mining claims increased significantly.[55] Many miners and policy analysts concluded that private subsoil rights accorded to the owner of the surface area impeded, rather than promoted, mineral development as a result of decreased investment and technological innovation as well as increased litigation.[56]

Devolution of subsoil regulation to the state level appeared to respond to decentralizing political interests. The shift required that each state legislate a body of mining law. Perhaps the most dramatic result occurred when the state of Bahia, in defiance of the Constitution, legislated in 1901 to separate the surface and the subsoil within its borders.[57] As early as 1902 the president (governor) of Minas Gerais attributed impaired development of iron ore mining to the absence of consistent, well-defined state-level mining law.[58] These complaints became continual. The state of Minas Gerais did not pass a law allowing the concession of public domain land until 1915.[59] Individual decree and legislation based on individual actions substituted for an organized system.

Almost immediately after privatizing the subsoil, complaints and contradictions surfaced for both ideological and pragmatic reasons. In 1892, the process of granting concessions to mineral veins remained seriously disrupted, as applications to the national authorities dating from prior to the enactment of the Constitution, were left unprocessed.[60] By 1897, complaints about the inability to increase mining output caused the Treasury Ministry to draft the first bill to reverse some of the constitutional provisions. It advocated transferring the right to grant mining concessions back to the Federal Government.[61] This proposal remained under debate for two years, before failing because of the obvious conflict with the constitutional provisions. A subsequent attempt to amend the Constitution, in 1899, based its argument on historical precedent, invoking the 1824 Constitution, and concessions dating from 1857 that granted access to ore veins on privately owned lands as a matter of public utility. The Treasury's draft bill relied on the provisions that 'the mines have always constituted special property, different from surface property'.[62] Initial efforts to clarify mining regulations through inclusion in a proposed Civil Code died when the legislature could not pass a Civil Code in 1902.[63]

In 1904 and 1905, João Pandiá Calógeras published a three-volume study of the mining sector.[64] Calógeras's education as a mining engineer, combined with his high-profile political career (including as a national deputy and as finance minister) gave his opinions on these issues considerable weight.[65] His attention to mining law heightened its visibility as a public interest. *As minas do Brasil* concluded that the most important explanations for the stagnation of mining were the insecurity of property rights to veins and the indivisibility of assets.[66] Calógeras also found that combining the subsoil with the surface disrupted the ability to mine, especially for gold miners, because of increased difficulty in receiving mortgage credit for their endeavours;[67] he further cited over-valuation of land and increased litigation over mining claims.

This report served as the basis for a bill that finally passed in 1915 (the *Lei Calógeras*)[68] reinstating separation of soil from subsoil and the return of national mining regulation for the limited purpose of enforcing beneficial-use provisions. However, enabling legislation remained stalled in the *Câmara dos Deputados* and the Senate because of concerns about reconciling the *Lei Calógeras* with the Constitution.[69] Six years later, the *Lei Simões Lopes* finessed the issue by continuing to define the subsoil as an 'accessory of the soil, but distinct from it'.[70] This differentiation was based on the articulation of the principle that the minerals of the subsoil existed as property separately from the land; therefore, the federal Union could exercise rights over on type of property (minerals) without affecting another type (land).[71] A subtle change to the treatment of mining that the *Lei Simões Lopes* introduced was to articulate the inclusion of iron ore deposits within the parameters of all mining legislation for the first time.[72] The practical effects of the change were minimal, though it brought the issues back to the legislative agenda.

From the first decade of the twentieth century, Calógeras represented concerns that were developmental in nature, rather than ideological. The output of both gold and industrial ore, primarily iron, had not increased immediately with the joining of mining rights to the land and regulation at the state level.[73] The efforts to reform mining from the late 1910s highlighted the shift towards concerns about production, and they emphasized an increasing urgency for developing industrial, rather than precious, mineral deposits.[74] Through the 1910s and 1920s, the state increasingly recognized the need to introduce new technology in order to construct large-scale capacity for extracting industrial ores and for the formation of an industrial manufacturing sector. In the 1920s, the president (governor) of Minas Gerais attributed the slow development of mining to the uncertainty of property rights:

> One of the major difficulties that opposes the development of the extractive mineral industry among us is the uncertainty of property rights. Even the state does not precisely know the lands that belong to it, and relative to those recognized as theirs, cannot determine the extent of the boundaries.[75]

These preoccupations became more pressing as the decade progressed.[76] Reflecting the general insecurity of rights, George Chalmers, the manager of the St John d'el Rey Mining Company – the most influential mining company in Brazil at the beginning of the twentieth century – testified that new mining companies could not open in Brazil with existing public protections and above all, an atmosphere of tranquility and confidence in the acquired rights is essential, save any surprises, not only of the surface property on which they operate, but also in the favours assured by law that make it possible to maintain their services.[77]

As a result, miners and large mining companies did not stand in the way of the changes wrought by the subsequent government regimes.[78] Through the 1910s and 1920s, as the scope of Brazil's endowment of industrial metals (especially iron ore) became evident and ambitions for large-scale industrialization grew, mining rights emerged as an important issue of public policy.

Renationalizing Subsoil Rights in 1934

The renationalization of mining rights occurred in conjunction within a distinct political-economic regime that focused intently on the nature of the Brazilian economy and the possibilities for its industrialization. A coup in October 1930 ultimately ended the First Republic and brought Getúlio Vargas to the Brazilian presidency. One lasting legacy of the regime was to engineer a fundamental expansion of the role of the Brazilian state in the economy.[79] The state, under Vargas, was committed to acquiring control of strategic resources to promote its programmes of industrialization, 'economic nationalism',[80] and centralization of governance. Industrial mineral development, particularly of iron ore, intensified as a concern of Vargas's regime. As a consequence, issues that generated wide attention included the possibilities of federal monopolies, the ability to expropriate private territory and the inclusion of economic security within the rubric of national security. These topics received prominent attention. Provisions to enhance mineral production for export and for industrial development became central to these policies.[81] Within four months of assuming the presidency, Vargas articulated a need to re-separate the subsoil from the surface and bring control back to the national level in the service of 'economic nationalism'.[82] These concepts became hallmarks of Vargas's fifteen-year regime.

Vargas's perspectives on the sovereignty of rights and on state activity were consistently developmental, rather than ideological.[83] His first presidential speech in Minas Gerais, in February 1931, emphasized the centrality of the state's mineral resources for growth and independence, and it articulated a long-term intent to nationalize mining.[84] The overarching perspective of the Vargas regime was that subsoil resources are *different* from other resources, because of their non-renewability, strategic uses and unpredictable geological trajectory.[85] The government quickly backed this rhetoric by moving aggressively to command mineral resources. In December 1931, the federal government first stepped in to regulate mining concessions differently from the republican procedures. A new law required federal authorization of all mineral explorations.[86] Most importantly during the interval from the end of the Republic until the

Constitution of July 1934, mining works (but not the minerals) were explicitly defined to be 'public goods' in November 1932.[87] This designation established the groundwork for redefining subsoil rights.

Reconsideration of subsoil rights did not begin with the ambition of federal sovereignty. The first commission of the Constituent Assembly, in fact, recommended private ownership of the subsoil, though separated from surface (land) rights.[88] Nevertheless, public debate quickly conflated two issues: the perception that the insecurity of mineral veins as property was the major detriment to realizing mining wealth and historical practices that separated the two types of property by virtue of public sovereignty.[89] This conflation shaped the range of resolutions considered. Further, questions of nationality arose early. One attempt to limit foreign ownership included provisions to create a special category of joint-stock companies that could not issue bearer shares.[90]

The new Constitution and a Mining Code, both in 1934, formalized the centralizing and activist policies with respect to minerals by re-establishing federal sovereignty to the subsoil.[91] The wording of the Constitution was very simply that '[t]he mines and other subsoil riches, as well as waterfalls, constitute property distinct from that of the soil for the purposes of exploration or industrial reclamation'.[92] Many legal scholars interpreted the Mining Code and Constitution as applying the concept of *res nullius* property, administered at the national level, to the subsoil.[93] The principles of these changes remained in place for the remainder of the twentieth century and the status of minerals was a subject of importance in each of the Constitutions of that century.[94]

The subsoil's re-separation from land made it possible to return the control of mining rights to the national level while leaving public-domain land with the states.[95] Because the Mining Code grandfathered previously existing concessions, the new code and Constitution affected only a minority of mining activity.[96] By this time, no opposition argued for maintaining the attachment of minerals to the land. General acceptance of the conclusion that the states had failed to motivate mining development facilitated the recentralization.[97]

The Mining Code restricted property rights in the sector more stringently than rights applied to other assets.[98] All newly discovered mineral deposits and concessions declared *devolutas* would belong in the federal domain. The re-separation of subsoil from surface rights allowed the federal government to establish its right to concede access to mineral resources on lands in the public domain. The Mining Code required federal authorization of all 'industrial' mining concessions (whether in the federal domain or not).[99] New mining (industrial or individual) required federal concession. Mining rights for ores considered crucial for national security were subject to expropriation to public ownership. Federal control of mining strengthened for the remainder of the 1930s. Public registration and authorization were required in order to explore for mineral deposits, including on privately owned land protected by the grandfathering of earlier contracts.[100] Authorities at the national level re-confirmed their power to determine whether a concession was in beneficial use, and to set the terms of beneficial use.[101] Beginning in 1938, all companies that contemplated vertical integration into mineral extraction for their own use needed further authorization to operate as a mining company.

The tools for this radical programme relied on definitions of property that derived directly from traditional colonial legal concepts. By the late 1950s, the St John d'el Rey Company, which had been operating in Brazil since 1830, opined that '[c]omparatively speaking, present Mining Legislation differs little from that which prevailed when the Company first functioned'.[102] The most important change in legal principles resulting from the reversion of subsoil claims was the re-separation of subsoil from surface rights. Just as joining them had been problematic, so was separating surface from subsoil rights (or land from mineral rights). As late as the middle of the twentieth century, when

> Mining Concerns had mining rights over 'datas,' as well as water rights and possibly timber rights for the purposes of mining, and the legal situation was quite ambiguous. … It should be noted that the system of concession does not absolutely take away the rights of ownership to the land, but only limits the use that the owner can make of it[103]

Two important changes in specific definitions and practices transformed the implications of the new regulatory framework. The term 'subsoil' took on a counter-intuitive definition:

> The subsoil considered in the face of the mining law, in our accepted use of the vocabulary, is conceived in the sense of mineralized geological beds, *on the surface or underground*, containing minerals subject, by virtue of their industrial utility, to the mining law … The domain of the mining law covers, in reality, all minerals of the national territory[104] [emphasis added]

By this definition, all 'industrial minerals', whether found below or on the surface, were considered subsoil minerals.[105] This definition was necessary to include iron ore and coal[106] (both are normally found on the surface) within the definition of subsoil minerals controlled by the state.

The second departure from earlier principles was the imposition of nationality constraints to limit the participation of foreign individuals and companies. Vargas explained the changes he proposed:

> The law will establish that mines will belong to Brazilians or companies organized in Brazil, and will establish conditions by which they would be explored & exploited – and that other sections of the Constitution assure the public power, in case of national necessity, to occupy the property.[107]

While earlier laws had tinkered with the practices for allowing non-Brazilians to mine, none had a long life or strong enforcement. The 1934 Constitution referred to the 'progressive nationalization of mines, mineral veins and waterfalls or other sources of hydroelectric energy judged basic or essential to national economic or military defense' and it restricted new concessions (but not authorizations) to Brazilian individuals or companies.[108] Foreigners could participate in mining through share ownership or partnership in domestic enterprises.[109] With respect to mining, 'economic nationalization' protected the claims of sovereign domain while it also limited the economic agents who could participate in the sector.

The constraints that the Mining Code introduced were clear. Challenges to the Mining Code's constitutionality began immediately, based on procedural issues, confusion about the distinction between 'authorizations' and 'concessions',[110] the specification of 'industrial mining' that was intrinsic to identifying the minerals regulated, and inconsistencies between the Constitution and the Mining Code.[111] Mining companies perceived opportunities for the state to take control of the subsoil and its minerals. Two provisions within the Mining Code opened this possibility. First, the continuity of existing concessions applied only to veins already under active exploration; veins not in beneficial use would return to the national public domain.[112] Ambiguities about the distinction between 'explored' and 'unexplored' veins (to demonstrate beneficial use) did not take long to surface.[113] The code's second avenue for increasing state involvement was the provision that allowed for expropriation of resources deemed crucial in the defence of national economic and military security.[114] This phrase acquired ever-wider interpretation.

One of the early acts of the Vargas government's extra-constitutional regime, the Estado Nôvo (1937–45), was to legitimate itself with a new Constitution, drafted by two generals (Eurico Dutra and Góis Monteiro) without parliamentary debate.[115] Revisions to the Mining Code made it consistent with the new Constitution. The revised code even more deeply implicated the federal state in mining as it resolved irregularities of the 1934 version.[116] New provisions further limited opportunities in the sector for foreigners.[117] Concessions applied to specific minerals within veins, unless the concessionaire received a charter that specifically covered all minerals. Tight regulation on registration and beneficial-use requirements eased the ability of the federal government to reclaim concessions for the public domain. Finally, in response to complaints that the 1934 code had been 'overly protective' of foreign investment, foreigners could not acquire new concessions or authorizations to mine, and foreign share-ownership of Brazilian-chartered firms was limited to minority status.[118] The 1937 Constitution broadened the state's expropriation rights of mines deemed 'necessary for the public interest' and strengthened national ownership provisions.[119] The Mining Code of 1940 clarified some of the legal ambiguities of the 1937 revisions, but did not change the essential elements established during the 1930s. This version of the Mining Code spelled out administrative details of mining concessions, tightened restrictions that constrained foreign participation, and incorporated natural gas and petroleum into its purview.[120]

After the end of the Vargas regime, changes in mining rights were minimal.[121] The ability of the federal state to allocate mining rights remained in force. The Constitution of 1946 eased general limitations imposed against foreigners and it maintained the principle that the surface owner had exploration preferences for mineral resources. In 1947, mining engineers were still lobbying for such simplifying mechanisms as increased protection for prospectors' first right to any veins they discovered and combining prospecting and extraction concessions.[122] Landowners' first right of exploration remained in effect until 1967, when another new Constitution and restated Mining Code, returned that preference to the discoverer of new veins. Between the Constitutions of 1946 and 1967,[123] the major focus of mining-rights law was to establish federal monopolies in petroleum and nuclear material. The 1967 Constitution more explicitly and expansively enumerated the parameters of legitimate state intervention in private economic activity, while it introduced new limitations on foreign participation in mining.[124] Shortly after the promulgation of the 1967 Constitution, legislation reaffirmed the basic provisions of the Mining Code.[125] This restatement of the Mining Code maintained that the federal (military) government's power to allocate concessions did not challenge the provisions of the earlier code. It attempted to stimulate large-scale private sector development by allowing adjacent miners to join their concessions by forming consortia. However, majority ownership was reserved for Brazilian nationals, reinstating the nationality constraints on investment.[126]

Subsoil rights were controversial in the debates underpinning the 1988 Constitution, which consolidated the return of civilian government from the military. The Constitution explicitly abandoned the application of *res nullius* to the subsoil and declared the federal state its owner.[127] The text of the Constitution identified that 'mineral veins, worked or not, and other mineral resources and hydraulic energy constitute property distinct from the soil, for purposes of exploration and reclamation, and they belong to the Union, guaranteeing ownership of the product of the mine to the concessionaire'.[128] The Constitution assured compensation to surface owners when others mined the subsoil under their land and it restated the application of indivisibility applied to mining by prohibiting the eligibility of mining plant and equipment as collateral on loans.[129] This Constitution also maintained the state monopolies of petroleum and nuclear minerals (subsequently abandoned in 1997). The 1988 Constitution restated the restriction on foreign ownership of all mineral enterprises to minority status. The most important change for the business of mining that this Constitution introduced was not specific to mining. The Constitution 're-modelled' the economic role of the state to include regulation, planning and incentivizing, but not producing. Although still incorporating the caveat of national security, this provision opened the way to privatization of state-owned enterprises (SOEs)[130] (discussed in Chapter 7).

Conclusion

The ambiguities and nuances that followed subsoil rights through Brazilian legal history established the legal foundation for the ebbs and flows of mining development through the nineteenth and twentieth centuries. Most importantly, the one experiment with privately held rights indicated the flexibility of the divide between public and private sectors. To enter into this shift, Brazilians debated the nature of the subsoil as an asset.

Consistency of subsoil rights across political eras was more notable than change. A comprehensive body of law developed early in order to regulate and control mining. The four-century-long trajectory of subsoil rights reveals the very deep entrenchment of their original concepts. Even while privatized, important features of subsoil rights remained constant. Mining veins were indivisible. Concessions remained non-transferable; this chapter has not discussed the transferability of concessions, because it was never up for consideration. A market for mining rights could not develop.

With the re-separation from the surface and the renationalization of subsoil rights, the Brazilian state invoked colonial legal principles for new ends. The reversion consolidated the shift in interest from precious to industrial minerals, and the state claimed control of those minerals. By grandfathering prior claims and by redefining the subsoil to include 'industrial' metals, the Mining Code and Constitution in 1934 signalled that the state was interested in future, not past, mining endeavours. At the same time, the new laws significantly broadened the scope of public control within the private sector.

Nationality constraints for individuals and companies limited participation, the parameters of economic security broadened and bureaucratic procedures increasingly intruded on mining activity.

Through the twentieth century, developmentalist practices proved to be an increasingly strong motivator of subsoil rights, in conjunction with emerging industrial ambitions. Justification within legal theory addressing the definition and allocation of property diminished, but did not disappear from, the political debates to restructure mining rights. Part 2 explores the ways in which subsoil rights intersected with mining practices, economic outcomes, and political economy.

PART II: THE STRUGGLE TO DEVELOP MINERALS

3 IRON AND GOLD IN PRE-INDUSTRIAL BRAZIL

This chapter explores two distinct efforts to develop mining from the end of the eighteenth century and through the nineteenth century. Prior to the onset of industrialization, miners concentrated on the search for gold and precious stones. Nevertheless, provisioning plantations and mines with expensive and scarce iron tools was one of the enduring bottlenecks of the colonial period. Iron ore, forged into implements and machinery, was essential to support the perceived sources of Brazilian wealth: gold, precious stones and sugar. In the twenty-five years prior to independence, the Portuguese Crown attempted to implement Brazil's first industrial policy in order to advance iron mining and forging. This proto-import-substituting-industrialization policy aimed to produce domestically the tools and machinery needed for precious mineral mining and sugar production.

With the return of the Portuguese Crown to Lisbon in 1821, this strategy was abandoned in favour of creating attractive conditions for foreign miners to invest their capital and technology in the search for precious minerals. In response, the St John d'el Rey Mining Company formed in London for the purpose of mining for gold in Minas Gerais. The company's charter dates to 1830, and its mine in Sabará opened in 1834. The unique experience and archival records of this company provide a valuable window into the conflicts and constraints that private enterprise faced in Brazilian mining. The failure of the first industrial policy and the extraordinary corporate practices of the St John d'el Rey Company demonstrate the persistent problems of interrelated institutions, complicated geography and technology challenges, as well as an early attempt to define an economic role for the state. These historical experiences lay the groundwork for the resolutions that Brazilians sought during the twentieth century.

Iron Ore and Industrial Policy

After the first intense period of discovering and extracting alluvial gold and diamonds, from the end of the seventeenth to mid-eighteenth centuries, ambitions of extending these discoveries remained alive, but continually disappointed.[1] Portuguese imperial rule remained constantly concerned with the efforts to extract wealth from Brazilian resources. Therefore, just as mineral extraction motivated the development of legal and colonial administration, it also spurred economic policy. In the middle of the eighteenth century (1750–77), Pombaline policies tried to extract higher rents from producers, with close controls and regulation while also enlarging the perimeter of Portuguese mercantilism.[2] At the end of the eighteenth century, the Portuguese Crown introduced the first policies that were intended to support mineral production, rather than merely extract rents. Policies from the end of the eighteenth and beginning of the nineteenth centuries offer a prism for examining early efforts to refashion a mercantile colonial economy into a modern one.

By the end of the eighteenth century, the Portuguese Crown associated its long-term economic decline, both in absolute terms and relative to the economic growth and political power accumulating in northern Europe, with the decline of Brazilian gold and sugar production.[3] The transfer of the Portuguese court to Rio de Janeiro in 1808 brought the concerns about the colony's productive capacity to the foreground and fundamentally changed the economic strategies of the regime.[4] Since wealth could not, at least temporarily, be repatriated to Portugal, the needs of the colony attained higher importance. With the goal of realizing the potential wealth of Brazil by reinvigorating the output of colonial export products, Dom João's regime (1792–1822)[5] undertook a substantial reorientation of governance and policy. The result was to draw attention to enhancing the productive potential of the Brazilian economy. Opening Brazilian ports to shipping and trade that extended beyond the intra-imperial routes, especially to the direct trade between Brazil and Great Britain, was one of the most important outcomes of this shift.[6] Revoking constraints that prohibited local manufacturing was equally important for the altered economic conditions. A number of important economic advisors, including José Bonifácio de Andrada e Silva (often portrayed as the architect of Brazilian independence) and Rodrigo José de Menezes (a former governor of Minas Gerais) put the problems of mining at the centre of this strategy.[7] Promoting the production of iron ore was a crucial component to garnering wealth from other commodities in the colony. Recognizing the inextricable connection between local development and imperial wealth, the first Brazilian industrial policy emerged from this shift of Portuguese perspective.[8]

The Crown applied two new strategies to encourage the resurgence of the mining sector. Legal innovations targeted increasing mineral production by developing and protecting business partnership structures for mining companies. Secondly, a concerted effort promoted iron ore mining and iron smelting with capital investments as well as production subsidies from the Crown. The attempts to facilitate company formation and to develop local manufacturing enterprises for iron partially owned and managed by the state, in order to provision the local economy were radical, if unheralded, shifts from the previous perspective of Brazil as a potential source of immediate commodity-derived wealth in Portugal.

Mining practices remained relatively stagnant through the eighteenth century. Miners and their slaves worked alluvial deposits of gold (and diamonds). Labour requirements for this effort were onerous.[9] A few miners attempted to use waterpower as a means of separating gold from ore, but refining methods were crude. When alluvial metals were significantly depleted by the middle of the eighteenth century, mines fell dormant. Neither the technology nor the capital was present to develop or import deep-shaft methods.

From the perspective of Portuguese ambitions to have Brazilian minerals provide imperial wealth, the problem was serious by the end of the eighteenth century. Two estimates of gold production for the colonial period are available.[10] Although these estimates vary widely, they concur on the conclusion that gold deposits yielded a significant volume of ore for only a short time (see Figure 3.1). In the first years of the nineteenth century, the preamble to mining laws routinely justified the need for increasing legislation with the 'very grave losses that have reached my [João's] Royal Treasury and the people of the captaincies of Brazil, principally miners ... by the progressive diminution of their veins'.[11] Even so, no recommendation took seriously the possibility that the first years of mining had depleted the minerals available from the Brazilian subsoil. The expectation always remained that the problems were of an economic or technological nature, not problems of resource endowment. One report attributed the ruinous state of mining to the high price of provisioning in Minas Gerais, and specifically cited the price of iron.[12]

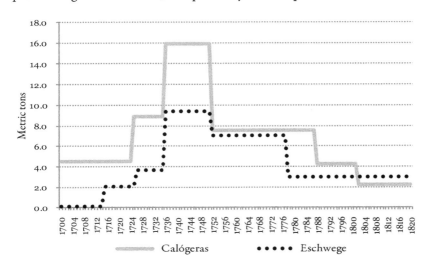

Figure 3.1: Gold production estimates, 1700–1820.[13]

After only slow incremental adjustments to colonial policy in the prior three centuries, the regime of Dom João introduced significant legal and economic change into the Brazilian mining sector. The intention of the reforms was to facilitate capital accumulation, through public and private channels, in order to form enterprises that were large and technologically sophisticated.[14] In addition to focusing on extracting gold and precious stones, Menezes and Andrada turned João's attention to the problem of supplying the inputs necessary for mines and plantations – most significantly, iron ore needed to produce tools and machines.

Despite obviously rich deposits, the story of iron ore was even more moribund story than that of gold.[15] Portuguese settlers had found deposits of iron ore in the captaincy of São Vicente (currently São Paulo) as early as 1554 and the first forges to manufacture iron tools appeared in 1556.[16] Prior to the arrival of the Portuguese court, iron foundries were small and localized.[17] Technological difficulties in providing the necessary power for production remained a constant challenge. African-imported slaves had contributed to their masters' enterprises by introducing air bellows to generate the energy used in refining iron ore.[18] Because of transportation constraints and limitations on trade within the colony, workers and blacksmiths confined their craft to satisfying the immediate needs of their estates, towns and perhaps neighbours.[19] The prohibition on local manufacturing industries within Portuguese colonies removed any incentive to overcome the problems of technology or partnership organization.

Legal reforms (summarized in the Appendix Table A.1A) and extra-legislative activities that attempted to develop the business structure of mining enterprises formed Brazil's first industrial policy attempting to solve the production bottlenecks that impeded the development of wealth.

Organizing Business Enterprise

Dom João's first major attempt to introduce structural reforms into gold, diamond and iron mining was an *alvará* of May 1803.[20] The *alvará* included important administrative and fiscal measures, such as establishing local mints [*casas da moeda*] to monitor production and control distribution,[21] and it halved taxes on gold from 20 per cent to 10 per cent in an effort to increase revenues by lessening evasion. To ensure the mining of known deposits, the *alvará* strengthened beneficial-use requirements to limit idle mining concessions.[22] Beneficial-use requirements returned to the public domain any concession that remained idle for more than three months after its initial grant.[23] This provision reinforced anti-speculative provisions at the same time that it codified the rules for establishing that a mine was abandoned.[24]

More fundamentally, the *alvará* of 1803 also revamped the rules governing business organization in mining partnerships.[25] The *alvará* promoted large enterprises in preference to small-scale individual miners, with the expectation that pooling capital among a wider universe of investors would allow for the acquisition of subsoil-extraction technology. In order to support large endeavours, miners could form joint-stock companies.[26] The resulting provisions specified the structure of mining companies, dividing capital into 128 shares, with each share representing the ownership of between one and eight slaves.[27] The Royal Treasury or (anticipated) miners' savings bank would hold two of the 128 shares in any association, introducing the earliest direct systematic participation of the state in mining enterprise. This attempt to provide incentives to moribund mining at the beginning of the nineteenth century resulted in early corporate partnership laws.

A number of additional provisions of the *alvará* of 1803 reinforced the shift to the company structure from individual enterprise. New discoveries of precious metals and stones entitled the discoverer to a concession encompassing thirty *braças*, thereby requiring a significant slave labour force.[28] Miners also received preferential access to nearby natural resources that were important for mining, especially timber, scrub (*matas*) and water.[29] To reinforce the indivisibility of mining enterprises, the *alvará* prohibited the sale of any concession without the slaves attached to the mining organization.[30] These provisions limited the possibilities for individual miners to exploit legal concessions.

In further efforts to aid mining, the Crown expanded policies with respect to protection from bankruptcy and business partnerships. An *alvará* in November 1813 extended to all miners the 1752 *Lei da Trintena*, which had protected miners with more than thirty slaves against bankruptcy, was one of the attempts to respond to this need.[31] To remedy the shortfall of credit that resulted from the lack of creditor protections, the law also foresaw a savings bank for small miners.[32]

A royal pronouncement (*carta régia*) of 12 August 1817 continued to explicitly recognize:

> The present state of deterioration ... in the gold mines ... not only because they are fully worked ... but also because miners do not have the practical knowledge of mining that is so useful in other countries. ... [T]o animate this most important sector of industry and national wealth, promoting in this captaincy [of Minas Gerais] the adoption of current practices of mining and the use of machinery that serves European mines.[33]

This pronouncement expanded on the provisions of 1803 by expressly articulating the Crown's intent to introduce European equipment and technology through the formation of joint-stock companies in order to support capital-intensive deep-shaft mining.[34] At the same time, it constrained the scope of companies, by stipulating the statutes that would apply to partnerships in which the state participated. New features of the pronouncement (beyond mandating company statutes) gave joint-stock companies preferential access to new mineral discoveries, and provided for the possibility of expropriation if surface landowners did not participate in the enterprise.[35] The Crown maintained its right to participate with two partnership shares allocated to the Royal Treasury and it reserved important roles, including one director's position, to local colonial mine administrators.

Important ambiguities remained in the rules of business organization with respect to share transferability and the ability to unwind (end) partnerships. Although inserting the partnership structure into the complicated mix of asset indivisibility and personal inheritance regulations proved to be a difficult innovation, many miners ultimately used it as a means of preserving the structure of their enterprises across generations. These innovations in partnership provisions occurred long before the Commercial Code of 1850 recognized joint-stock organizations more broadly.

Subsequent regulation prior to independence did not introduce additional innovation, but it granted charters to six companies (gold and iron mining companies) and controlled the monetary use of precious metals. As Figure 3.1 demonstrates, gold production did not increase in response to these legal inducements to promote mining, at least during the remaining years of the colonial regime.

Building an Iron Industry: The State as an Economic Actor

Mining iron ore and processing it into manufactured tools moved to the forefront of economic policy for the first time as the Portuguese faced the problems of economic decline at the end of the eighteenth century.[36] José Bonifácio de Andrada e Silva was a Coimbra-educated mining engineer as well as political advisor. He made a strong case for the state to become involved in the development of iron foundries throughout Brazil to relieve the bottleneck in tools and implements for mining and plantations. Andrada's postgraduate tour of northern Europe beginning in 1790 introduced him to mining engineers and to the industrial manufacturing possibilities for iron ore. He developed a deep appreciation for the contributions of iron, forged and transformed into machinery, to the broad industrialization process that was propelling northern European economies at the time.[37] Rodrigo José de Menezes drew his conclusions on the necessities of iron from his experiences in trying to motivate economic development as the Governor of Minas Gerais.[38] Reinforcing Andrada's and Menezes' perceptions, additional studies identified the lack of iron tools as a principle cause of economic stagnation.[39]

Iron ore is neither glamorous nor precious; it is only an industrial necessity. Easy and inexpensive provisioning of tools and equipment had always been one of the largest problems that commodity producers faced. In a classic problem of industrial development, the activities necessary for the Brazilian economy to grow, iron ore mining and iron smelting, were secondary to the activities that attracted investment. The metal was of interest to the extent that it could provision the more desirable plantations and mines for precious minerals. Iron ore, forged into implements and machinery, became essential to support the conversion of Brazilian natural resources into wealth on a large scale, and therefore, to support the treasury of the Portuguese Crown. Even so, both producers and policy-makers neglected the substance until the end of the eighteenth century.[40] By the beginning of the nineteenth century, Wilhelm von Eschwege estimated that importing iron tools and machinery from Europe to Minas Gerais increased their ultimate cost three-fold, because of transportation costs, merchant commissions and customs duties.[41]

An *alvará* of 1795 (first proposed in 1780 by Menezes, while governor of Minas Gerais) demonstrated the importance of increasing iron production by granting local manufacturing rights to Brazilian foundries at the same time that it abolished taxes on iron ore production. The ability to produce iron locally anticipated the general effort to promote domestic manufacturing by thirteen years. The provisions of 1795 further liberalized the iron sector by removing, for the purposes of supplying iron foundries, the monopoly provisions that governed the importation of slaves and iron.[42]

Having eliminated the prohibition against domestic production, the technical barriers of iron production predominated. The location and transportation hurdles of bringing together factors of production and distributing the output to appropriate markets were, in fact, very high. European iron smelting methods (which Brazilians were trying to emulate) relied on coal for energy. Brazilian iron ore deposits were rich, but energy was inefficiently generated by plant-produced charcoal combined with air-driven bellows. Further, the known deposits of iron ore were in mountainous locations far from the coast, the location of the most concentrated demand from sugar plantations and cities (see Front Map). Prior to railroad construction in the late nineteenth and twentieth centuries, mule trains provided transportation.[43] The options available to producers were to transport ore to the areas where the output was in demand or to establish manufacturing facilities near ore deposits.

The Crown instituted a concerted effort to establish the iron industry in the service of developing other economic activities. It invested capital, offered subsidies and imported technological expertise. João recruited a small group of mining engineers to Brazil in order to survey the mining sector and to develop iron foundries. Between October 1808 and August 1811, the Crown sanctioned the opening of three iron companies and subsidized two of the enterprises. Different engineers applied distinct production methods, factory design, and provisioning strategies to each factory. Three different efforts, resting on different technological resolutions to the problems of geography (transportation and resource location) and technology, represented a range of possibilities by which Brazilians could provide iron implements for themselves. Table 3.1 shows the production (and the scanty financial) data available for these three factories between 1813 and 1821.

The first factory was the Real Fábrica do Morro do Gaspar Soares, familiarly known as Fábrica Pilar, within the mining district of Arraial do Tijico (currently known as Diamantina) in Minas Gerais.[44] The location of iron ore deposits within this rich mining region made a high-volume production here desirable. The Royal Treasury agreed to invest 18 *contos de réis*[45] in Pilar, from 1809 through to 1811, to finance the construction of three blast furnaces and twelve refining forges. Further subsidies included a ten-year tax exemption and purchasing preferences. The potential contribution of the region's diamond and gold mining to Treasury revenues justified the Crown's investment and subsidies. In addition, the labour released from artisanal iron forging would be reallocated to mining precious stones and gold. Pilar suffered long delays in construction while under the initial direction of the Intendente Camara Bittencourt de Sá. When the factory opened in 1815, it was managed by Schonewolf, a German mining engineer, brought to Arraial do Tijico for the purpose of redeeming the project. After initial mis-steps, the factory re-tooled to adopt the small-scale technology that Eschwege had introduced a few years earlier in Congonhas.[46] Fábrica Pilar never produced forged iron on a reliable schedule (see Table 3.1). Schonewolf's failure has often been attributed to managerial and technical incompetence, although scarce surrounding natural resources (brush and water) to generate energy also plagued the project.[47]

The second state-supported effort to introduce industrial production of iron tools brought Swedish mining engineers in 1808, and then the German Fredreich Wilhelm von Varnhagen in 1810, to Sorocaba in the province of São Vicente (currently São Paulo) to manage the Ipanema foundry.[49] Ipanema was also organized as a joint-stock company. The Crown anticipated that it would take thirteen shares of the company, entering into partnership with private investors.[50] The Crown contributed to the factory's construction with land, livestock and one hundred slaves.

Table 3.1: State sponsored iron-processing firms under Dom João.[48]

	Pilar	Ipanema			Congonhas
		Iron production (metric tons)			
		Bars	Shaped	Ingots	
1813					1.5
1814					1.5
1815	0.6				1.9
1816	1.7				1.7
1817	1.2				1.4
1818	1.4				
1819	1.0				2.4
1820	3.7				1.8
1821	0.5				
Total	10.1	23.7	18.5	26.6	
Annual average	1.4	3.9	3.1	4.4	1.7

Operating income statement (*contos*)

	Ipanema			Congonhas		
	Expense	Revenue	Balance	Expense	Revenue	Balance
1815	12.5	4.7	-7.9			
1816	19.4	4.7	-14.8			
1817	16.5	6.5	-10.0			
1818	9.6	4.9	-4.7			
1819	15.7	22.6	6.9	23.8	40.3	16.6
1820	14.5	19.3	4.8	21.2	31.5	10.3
1821	12.2	10.5	-1.7			
Total	100.4	73.1	-27.3			

Varnhagen's ambition for the Ipanema plant was to produce iron on a large scale, providing for a substantial proportion of Brazilian demand for both military armaments and manufacturing needs. Varnhagen relied on charcoal from the local *mata* (scrub) and forests to meet demand for forged iron. The *carta régia* of 4 December 1810 to charter the company also established Ipanema's right to local *mata*. Within a year, João needed to ameliorate the effects of promising the *mata* to Ipanema by requiring an additional survey to justify and minimize its use, as well as to indemnify the landowners of the *matas* for their loss of resources.[51] Recognizing the transportation problems of getting ore from the mines to the refinery and, then, from Ipanema to its consumers, road building was a prominent component of the enterprise's plans. The business partnership and subsidies combined with a loan from Dom João of 100,000 *cruzados*, or 48 *contos*,[52] to build the factory at Ipanema. The loan was almost three times the size of the Crown's capital investment in Pilar and it equated to almost two-thirds of the total revenues earned by the firm while in operation. Ipanema began producing iron in 1815, but continued to do so regularly only until Varnhagen left Brazil in 1821.[53]

The Baron Wilhelm Ludwig von Eschwege undertook the third attempt to build a foundry, in Congonhas do Campo, near the earliest and longest producing gold fields of central Minas Gerais. Eschwege was the most famous of the mining engineers who had come to Brazil. The *carta régia* of August 1817 that reformulated mining company provisions reflected the influences of Eschwege's mining survey and financial observations. Eschwege organized the first chartered partnership for gold mining in Brazil, the Sociedade Mineralógia.[54] His plans for Congonhas reflected the results of his detailed survey of Brazilian mineral deposits and production practices, and Eschwege expected to use the iron company to provision his gold mining company. Unlike the European technologies, which transported ore to the factory, ore refining took place at the site of mining.[55] The Congonhas project also adapted the African-style air bellows to generate energy for smelting iron by introducing waterpower to automatically operate the bellows.[56] Brazilian interest in developing large-scale hydraulic energy to substitute for coal-based energy dates from this effort.

Dom João's approval for Congonhas incorporated a joint-stock partnership with total capital of four *contos*, divided into ten shares.[57] This enterprise took advantage of the 1803 business organization laws for mining companies; but, unlike the facilities at Pilar and Ipanema, this one did not rely on royal investment (as the 1817 *carta régia* might have anticipated), and it did not prioritize the scale of manufacture. Instead, Eschwege introduced a strategy of locating relatively small factories near ore deposits. The potential demonstration effect of Congonhas for other local manufacturers was an important motivation for the partnership.[58] Although this technology was successful enough to introduce into Fábrica Pilar, it did not produce forged iron profitably. Congonhas produced iron only from 1813 until 1820.[59]

None of these enterprises achieved their ambitions, generated profits or continued to grow after João's return to Portugal in 1821.[60] By then, thirty small independent forges were operating in Minas Gerais, producing about 120 metric tons of iron annually.[61] According to this estimate, the state-sponsored factories contributed about 12 per cent of total production. Contemporary analysis of the problems that all three factories encountered was similar. Both fixed and operating costs were very high. Fixed costs reflected the difficulty of building plants with equipment not available locally and the scarcity of skilled labour. Further, organizational structure and João's participation in the investments could not overcome the transportation problem. Royal participation in the construction of the plants responded to the inability to attract private investors who would be willing to participate in the project, given its costs and risks.[62] During the two decades that Dom João invested in, and lent policy support to, these enterprises, solutions to the challenges of making the iron industry viable were not found. Iron production remained largely artisanal and non-commercial.[63]

Importing Capital and Technology: The St John d'el Rey Company

João's departure from Brazil in 1821, followed by independence in 1822, brought to an end the policies of trying to support gold and sugar production by developing local capabilities to supply producers. Throughout the nineteenth century, the major activity of public authorities in mining was to support the training and formalization of engineering.[64] The 1824 Constitution of the newly independent Brazilian Empire offered mining rights to foreign companies.[65] Beyond the statutory tax of 20 per cent (the *quinto*), an incremental tax of 5 per cent applied to foreign mining companies[66] and they were required to offer one-third of both equity shares (in the case of joint-stock companies) and jobs to Brazilians. Nevertheless, as the Brazilians had hoped, the ambitions of mineral wealth attracted Europeans with experience in deep-shaft mining and access to capital.[67] The St John d'el Rey Mining Company was one of the earliest British gold mining companies to receive a Brazilian charter, in 1830.[68] The company's gold mine at Morro Velho near present-day Nova Lima, Minas Gerais (Front Map) established the basis for the longest operating business enterprise in Brazilian history,[69] and Morro Velho was the world's largest, deepest gold mine prior to the 1940s, when South African discoveries expanded considerably. Few mining companies lasted more than a few years, and the St John d'el Rey was the only one to survive beyond the first years of the twentieth century.[70] The company was able to bring capital, organizational capacity and technological innovation to respond to difficult mining conditions and to rebuild after two catastrophic collapses during the late nineteenth century. The experiences of the St John d'el Rey Mining Company during the nineteenth and twentieth centuries offers a case study that demonstrates the litany of conflicts between the needs of large, capital-intensive 'modern' enterprise and Brazilian laws supporting the indivisibility of fixed assets and the familial distribution of personal estates. These institutions that governed property created contingent claims and required constant reconciliation.

The company tried to merge its claims to subsoil and surface land rights; it always made a point of owning the surface above its mines.[71] Between its first acquisition in Morro Velho in 1834 and the sale of its assets to the Hanna Mining Company in 1960, the company acquired sixty properties through hundreds of contractual transactions. Meticulously documented land transactions[72] and legal strategies indicated the possibilities, as well as the costs, of market-based transactions and judicial actions to manage their claims. The company relied on Brazilian law to structure their property acquisitions, define their rights and protect their claims. Detailed records, court proceedings and correspondence serve to document its treatment of property in the forms of renewable resources (land, water, timber, people – slaves[73]) as well as non-renewable subsoil minerals. The example of the St John d'el Rey Mining Company protecting its claims to mineral, land, water and timber rights through the nineteenth and twentieth centuries demonstrates the limits imposed on formal property claims and the implications of these limits for organizational development in Brazil.

The conflicts between indivisibility of real assets (including mines) and mandated division of personal estates resulted in generations of claims and lawsuits against the mining company. Heirs of sellers emerged posthumously, claiming both resources and a share of the company's profits (essentially asserting partnership rights) as their inheritance. Although the St John d'el Rey Mining Company survived until the second half of the twentieth century, its experience demonstrates the disadvantages that impeded businesses when they were confronted with the strength of family-defined property and business networks. In the case of this company, conflicting laws were consistently enforced and effective contracts were difficult to attain.

Property Claims and Challenges

Acquiring the land close to and above their subsoil excavations was one strategy to keep poachers from accessing the same vein while also protecting the water and timber supplies that were crucial to mining and refining. Sufficient water and timber to sustain mining and mineral refining operations were of continual concern to the company.[74] The company not only established its title to land and other resources, it also documented the prior history of title registration to the properties that it acquired. Within Brazil, providing access to the surface resources (timber and water)[75] and protecting its claims were among the major ongoing operational challenges for the company. In the early twentieth century, the company's understanding was that:

> With the confusion that exists in this country resulting from the laws of succession in force for the last century, it is next to impossible to keep entirely clear from lawsuits ... In properties where the Company is part-owner and the other owners will not sell for a fair price, or do not care to sell at all, we are bound to resort to legal division, which is also a slow & troublesome process but unfortunately, in such cases there is no alternative, as it is not in any way convenient that the Company should have property in common with others.[76]

These needs kept the company focused on identifying its rights to resources. One of the company's most perplexing practices throughout its existence was to maintain the geographic integrity and nomenclature of the holdings that it acquired.[77] Doing so required a great deal of effort and multigenerational patience on the company's part. When holdings were adjacent, the company did not consolidate them. For example, as late as 1959, the six adjacent holdings of Bela Fama and California, Santa Rita, Fernão Paes, Honório Bicalhau, and Faria were accounted for as separate properties (see Figure 3.2). The company acquired these holdings in 1883, 1934, 1862, 1901 and 1908, respectively.[78] During the twentieth century, the company often donated land for public works (for such purposes as urban development in the town of Nova Lima, highway construction and laying the electrical network). When these donations came from a variety of holdings, the company registered and documented each tranche of land separately.[79]

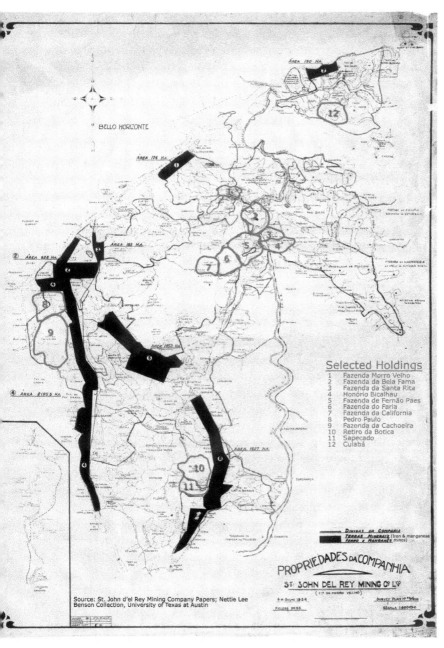

Figure 3.2: Holdings of St John d'el Rey Mining Company, 1954.[80]

Frequently, the company purchased shares of an estate or mine, rather than specific assets (land or mining *datas*). When this occurred, the company later tried to accumulate the entirety of the estate, as it had been configured prior to the company's initial acquisition. Often the company negotiated with multiple generations of heirs in order to re-establish sole ownership of the original property.

These practices began very early in the company's history.[81] The St John d'el Rey Company began its second acquisition in the region, Mingú, in 1834.[82] Two partners had jointly owned Mingú, and the St John d'el Rey initially purchased a share of the partnership from one of them. The final transaction to reconstruct the original holding from the heirs took place in 1898, sixty-four years later. Through one side of the partnership, the company bought land and shares from four generations of heirs, over the course of sixteen transactions. This holding was particularly complicated because the partner from whom the company began purchasing land had as his heirs a wife and fourteen offspring. Among the heirs, some traded their interests in Mingú for other holdings in the inheritance, allowing for some consolidation of ownership in individual land parcels. The heir-partners tended to sell their proportionate shares of the property jointly, either to the St John d'el Rey, other miners or real-estate speculators. The company began acquiring the estate of the second partner in 1862, from an intermediary buyer. Four generations were also required to reconstruct holdings from this side of the partnership. Finally in 1898, the company could assert that it had 'absolute docile and peaceful possession that assures it the right over all of the property now called "Morro do Bonfim or Mingú"'.[83]

The company clearly negotiated many of the transactions jointly to reassemble Mingú. Transactions occurred on the same date, with identical prices, and with multiple heirs. However, a separate contract registered the sale of each heir's proportionate share. The registered transactions denoted that the company bought shares in the estate, rather than specific parcels of property.[84] In another extreme example the St John d'el Rey purchased twenty-five separate 'parts in common' from two couples between 1904 and 1923 in order to gain rights to another holding, the Retiro do Hermenegildo. Finally, in 1931, a legal division and final sale permitted the consolidation of this estate.[85]

The company amicably resolved most of the instances of residual claimants attempting to use company resources. Individuals commonly resided, farmed, logged and practiced other occupations on company land. Sellers and their heirs often retained access rights in ways that did not impede the company's use. However, individual opportunism and the inability to specify completely secure contracts left the company exposed to long and complicated legal cases. Continual challenges to the St John d'el Rey's property claims demonstrate the constraints imposed on the ownership of real property through the nineteenth and first half of the twentieth centuries. Challenges came in forms as simple as having purchased the same land a second time to settling the claims of heirs who emerged subsequent to completed property transactions.[86] Often the company settled these claims in private negotiations; otherwise, the judicial system provided procedures to resolve disputes.

Even the simplest confusions over rights could require decades to resolve. In 1901 the St John d'el Rey purchased the same land twice; this error was not resolved until 1920.[87] In September and October of 1901 the company purchased all of the shares from nine heirs to the Fazenda Gorduras (Pimental). Only a month later, it bought another piece of land that ultimately the courts determined had been part of the earlier acquisition. The confusion arose because, in 1868, an amicable judicial division of land in the *fazenda's* inheritance allowed a widow to sell land that was her half of their mutual estate separately from her deceased husband's offspring. When the widow and her next husband sold land to St John d'el Rey in November 1901, the transaction included a portion that they had previously sold, under the name Pimental (and not properly registered), but had been part of the company's previous purchase in September–October. The resolution of the dispute required the heirs of all previous owners of the land (going back to 1868) to declare that 'they possessed no property denominated "Gorduras"'.[88] More than recouping the financial value, apparently the St John d'el Rey's concern in the matter was to prevent subsequent heirs from reclaiming an interest in the land.[89]

One of the most peculiar cases that confronted the company involved an acquisition in 1911, which they called Morro Velho e Pedro Paulo.[90] Documents registering this land date to 1839, when the then-owners provided for their legacy. Without direct heirs, Dona Antonia Gertrudes da Fonseca specified that her share of her and her husband's estate should transfer to the local church, the Capela de Piedade. However, her slaves and their descendants were to have usufruct rights to the land for ten generations.[91] When he died in 1842, Antonia Gertrudes's husband left his share of the estate to a single heir. The St John d'el Rey acquired the husband's portion, from a subsequent owner, in 1911. In 1920 and 1938, judicial actions resolved challenges to some of the land use. The 1938 case finalized the judicial division of the original estate between the St John d'el Rey and another claimant.[92] The Pedro Paulo property seemed to be incorporated into the company's real estate portfolio without further problems. In 1944 the company ceded water rights and use of portions of the land to the state of Minas Gerais.

During these years, the St John d'el Rey had not purchased Antonia Gertrudes' legacy to the church. The company's original purchase deed included a provision that it held 'half of the *fazenda's* agricultural land, fields, forest, streams and water sources in common with the heirs [*herdeiros usufrutuários*] of D. Antonia Gertrudes da Fonseca who have the other half'.[93] This land holding remained denominated as shares of property, rather than as fully owned, geographically distinct territory. As late as 1936 (when it filed a manifest of its properties under the 1934 Mining Code) the company represented that it 'own[ed] the property in common with the Church'.[94]

Nevertheless, in 1951, forty years after the company acquired its portion of the estate and 112 years after the original inheritance provisions, the company objected to the slaves' descendants violating the *de facto* division of land use.[95] The 'supposed heirs (blacks) of Antonia Gertrudes da Fonseca, which is to say the part belonging to the chapel, invaded the Company's land, and in doing so they destroyed the forest'.[96] After 112 years, although the company did not identify individual heirs, 'blacks' – commonly understood to be descendants of the original slave/usufruct heirs – could still exercise a claim to the land, through their usufruct rights and the Capela de Piedade remained the owner of record. With the dispute in 1951, the company obtained a judicial division of the property.[97] A court order ultimately evicted the 'blacks' in 1954.

Another of the St John d'el Rey's properties had multiple ownership claims that remained problematic through the twentieth century. The lawsuits over claims to land and mining concessions at Cuiabá starkly demonstrated the pulls of competing property rights. During 1877, the company acquired 95 per cent of Cuiabá from the heirs of its British owner, John Pennycock Brown. In 1878, it purchased the small share belonging to Brown's minority Brazilian partner.[98] Also in 1878, the company petitioned to have all abandoned mining *datas* within the geographic boundaries declared *devolutas* (abandoned for lack of use and reverting to the public domain) and re-conceded to its name.[99] The following year, it received an imperial concession for gold-mining rights specifically pertaining to Cuiabá.[100] The St John d'el Rey claimed 797 mining *datas* in the estate.

In 1879, the National Brazilian Mining Association, another British freestanding mining company, challenged claims to 146 *datas* at Cuiabá.[101] The St John d'el Rey won the case, on the grounds that the property had returned to public ownership because its owners had left it idle. Nevertheless, twenty-one years later (1900), the failing National Brazilian continued to appeal the judgment. The company that formed as its successor in 1902, the Rotulo Company, Ltd, pursued the appeal to the Brazilian Supreme Court.[102] Although the St John d'el Rey asserted that it won the appeals, it also agreed to pay the Rotulo Co. a settlement to drop all subsequent claims.[103]

During the course of the case with the National Brazilian, the St John d'el Rey began to purchase the rights of residual claimants.[104] Meanwhile, the heirs of Brown's Brazilian partner and of the previous Brazilian owners who had sold to Brown also tried to exert their personal inheritance claims to both land and mining *datas*. Heirs of the minority partner had shares in the property, rather than distinct holdings, and the long-term possession of property supported their claims.[105] Clear demarcation had not delimited holdings. A large number of heirs and much intermarriage among the heirs of the original holders left specific claims irresolvable.[106] The St John d'el Rey did not believe that the property could be divided, and tried to compel claimants to sell their interests to the St

John d'el Rey. Further challenges emerged in the 1930s and the company entered into agreement with eight additional claimants (members of the fifth and sixth generations of heirs) in 1933.[107] By then, Cuiabá held no gold mining interest for the company; the property's worth lay in its substantial timber resources for producing firewood and charcoal.[108]

In 1936, the company brought eviction proceedings against José Abdo Abjaudi, an aspiring iron miner and steel producer, who resided within Cuiabá and had purchased the inheritance claims of two remaining possible heirs.[109] Abdo insistently pressed the rights that he had purchased. While doing so, he was destroying the remaining natural brush on the estate to make charcoal.[110] The St John d'el Rey pressed for a mandated judicial division of the property. Relying explicitly on the original *alvará* of 1603 'and other legislation in force in Brazil' the company argued that

> [t]wo or more parties having a mine in common or separately any of them who works it must do it in the name of all of them ... hence it follows that he who possesses a just claim to the tenth part of Cuiabá Mine, has not lost his right to this part ... Amongst the indivisible items are (among others) the gold veins[111]

While the company was trying to force a judicial division of the property through the 1940s, Abdo was able to assert claims through inheritance partnerships for more than 50 per cent of the value of Cuiabá.[112] Although Abdo was an opportunist, he clearly invoked claims to partnership with the St John d'el Rey that had legitimate bases within Brazilian property law. The company was aware of seven descendants of the original partners, still living within the confines of Cuiabá, who could follow Abdo's example. Therefore, it refused to negotiate a settlement with Abdo because it feared that a settlement would encourage still more claimants.[113] In 1960, as the company was transferring its assets, it negotiated a settlement with Abdo, and another claim emerged.[114] For nearly a century the constraints on property arising from beneficial-use requirements and familial inheritance principles plagued the St John d'el Rey's access to an estate of decreasing value.

These experiences explain the company's persistent reliance on acquiring 'absolute docile and peaceful possession'[115] of holdings as they had been constituted at their original registration. Doing so was the only means of protecting against subsequent claims. The assertion of prior claims deriving from the principles of indivisibility and familial property imposed strong limits on the sovereignty of private property. The St John d'el Rey owned much of its property in partnership with economic agents not of its choosing. The company was successful in navigating the shoals of property ambiguities, but it required significant attention, time and skill.

Maintaining the indivisibility of real property simultaneously with the mandated partibility of personal estates impeded the formation of extra-familial business partnerships, such as those envisioned by the 1817 pronouncement, in fundamental manners. Complicated ownership patterns, subsequent to estate settlements, rendered it impossible to control, or even to know definitively, the composition of partnerships. The severe difficulties of dividing assets when dissolving partnerships compounded the problem. As a result, invoking legal provisions to regulate private business relationships remained ineffective, or at best, slow and expensive.

Conclusion

From the end of the eighteenth and through the nineteenth centuries, Brazilian mining had stagnated. Remedies based on state activism in the realm of production had failed because of the technological complexities of the project. A strategy allowing private foreign entrepreneurial development could not accommodate the institutional constraints on private businesses. Nevertheless, the efforts to address the stagnation motivated innovation in the organization of the Brazilian economy. Miners and public policy makers, Brazilians attempted two strategies for mineral development. At the end of the colonial period, active statist policies targeted local solutions to the underlying problems, providing capital goods and technology. During the first decades of independence, the approach of opening up private investment channels predominated, with the goal of allowing easy access by outsiders, who could bring their own capital and technology.

Ultimately, statist policies were neither successful nor sustained. Late imperial Portuguese policies were not sufficient to revitalize gold mining or to develop an iron industry. Gold and precious stone deposits existed within the known regions of Brazil, even if they were relatively scarce.[116] Low-cost iron tools remained unavailable; neither did the policies survive João's return to Lisbon. However, the experience was important for the future political-economic experience of Brazil. The royal investment in iron ore enterprises introduced a fundamentally different attitude about the economic role of the state. The iron foundries may have been Brazil's first enterprises with state ownership that had the manufacture of basic industrial inputs as their objective. Further, the experience exposed the difficulties of developing an iron and steel industry despite the easy and plentiful supply of iron ore.

Legal strategies and plans to address mining diminished with political independence from Portugal. Laws that concerned mining addressed specific concessions and fiscal needs, rather than attempting to reform the structure of the sector. The most important change introduced early in the independent empire was to explicitly allow the organization of foreign-capitalized mining companies.[117] The St John d'el Rey Mining Company was the major company to take up that opportunity. Its experiences in protecting its interests in Minas Gerais are instructive for understanding the institutional barriers to industrialized mining.

Contrary to the tone of existing research on tangible real property (primarily land), rights were not under-specified;[118] in fact, they were *over*-specified, and varying provisions for claims were mutually inconsistent, as the St John d'el Rey's experience demonstrates. The particular strategies and property challenges of the St John d'el Rey Mining Company were specific to the attenuated circumstances of a mining company with claims to an exceptionally rich lode. However, all propertied economic agents in Brazil faced the same vulnerabilities to their claims on property from the colonial era through the twentieth century. Clear laws were in place, and when necessary, they were enforced. The conflicts that the St John d'el Rey faced did not involve inconsistent enforcement, unclear requirements or possibilities for coercion or exploitation. Instead, constraints on individual sovereignty created irresolvable claims.

Fixed productive units could not be divided and owners had little flexibility in intergenerational transfers of estates.[119] As Antonia Gertrudes da Fonseca's and José Abdo's cases demonstrated, specific property was not at stake; rather, parties claimed partnerships (and in some cases, a share of profits) in established businesses. Acquiring property brought with it a significant probability of entering into partnerships with the partners and heirs of prior owners. Because of the complexities of inheritance claims the St John d'el Rey could not control (or, at times, even know) the composition of these *de facto* partnerships. Complete and complex contracts could not mitigate these contingencies. The possibility for unanticipated claimants to insert themselves into business enterprises served as an important impediment for large, modern business networks attempting to bring together the capital of otherwise unconnected economic agents in risky endeavours. In these circumstances, the imposition of kinship-based business networks could always compromise the benefits of modern business organization. Small, kinship-based partnerships formed around inheritance structures that worked with, rather than against, established law.

However serious the constraints were, the experience of the St John d'el Rey appears to have been unusual. What explains the differences in the case of the St John d'el Rey? And if this company's experience was unusual, why is it important?

The most exceptional feature of the St John d'el Rey's business was the size and purity of its vein. Other mining enterprises did not sustain their value. Failed excavations and short-lived businesses demonstrated that they could not match the richness of Morro Velho. These mines did not sustain their productive value. Historically, much of the wealth (and expected wealth) in Brazil has been associated with plantation cultivation of export-crops. The most important commercial crops – sugar and coffee – depleted their soils within about twenty-five years, mitigating the need to maintain the physical integrity of a continually 'productive' unit across generations. In short, the property of the St John d'el Rey Company retained its value; whereas, the prevailing experience was for the productive value of property to diminish. The purpose of the property laws protecting the physical integrity of property was to ensure production of wealth; depleted land and empty veins were not of value to their holders or to the state.[120] When that goal remained viable, the legal structure served its purpose.

The relevance of the St John d'el Rey's experience is what it reveals about the *absence* of large innovative firms. Rarely was it worthwhile for private enterprises to undertake the strategies of the St John d'el Rey. Nevertheless, capital formation and technological innovation posed strong barriers to development in the nineteenth century. This chapter argues that these limitations prevented dynamic iron mining and forging. They also played an important role in the early decline of the Brazilian sugar processing and commerce.[121] Similarly, innovation in coffee was slow to occur through the century.[122] In both traditional agricultural business sectors, cultivators usually adopted the extensive expansion through frontier settlement, rather than intensifying production within given properties. Abandoning depleted land proved more reliable than undertaking the production and organizational practices to sustain their physical integrity.

During the second half of the eighteenth and through the nineteenth centuries Brazilian mining had stagnated. Remedies based on state activism in the realm of production had failed because of the technological and organizational complexities of the project. A strategy of allowing private foreign entrepreneurial development could not overcome traditional institutional constraints on private business. Nevertheless, these efforts to revitalize mining motivated important institutional innovation, with respect to business organization and establishing the role of the state, that resonate deeply with subsequent experience.

4 THE SUBSOIL AS PRIVATE PROPERTY

This chapter assesses the abrupt privatization of subsoil property rights in 1891. Privatization offered a third strategy for mineral development, after earlier attempts that relied variously on state participation or the importation of foreign capital and technology, proved unsatisfactory. Legal change occurred at the same time that the interest in minerals shifted from deriving the immediate wealth of precious minerals to the utilitarian metals that provided inputs for an industrial economy. The chapter considers the patterns of mining regulation and the willingness to prospect and mine. It explores the subsequent renationalization of subsoil rights in 1934 in the context of the evolution of the goals for minerals. By examining the commonly accepted proposition that privatization was unsuccessful, the chapter presents the limitations on developing industrial-scale mining derived from a complex mixture of ancillary institutions. It also finds that the change in ambitions for the mining sector transformed institutional inconsistency from a problem for private actors into a national imperative.

The Constitution of 1891 implemented the first fundamental change in Brazilian mineral rights since early Portuguese rule in 1603. Property was redefined to attach the subsoil to the surface. This action privatized the subsoil by removing it from federal sovereign domain. With the intention of liberalizing both economic governance and access to resources, the framers of the Constitution hoped that the private ownership of assets would create an incentive for mineral extraction,[1] although mining engineers were skeptical (see Chapter 2). Simultaneously, the republican regime devolved the regulation of land, along with its subsoil, from the national domain to the states. The transfer of public land and its accessory subsoil to the states supported the decentralizing goals of early republican political orthodoxy and gave the newly federalized states the ability to sell land as a source of revenue to meet their vastly expanded role in providing public services.[2]

While juggling these concerns of political ideology, economic interests shifted from precious minerals to industrial ores. Geologists and industrial entrepreneurs came to recognize that their reserves of iron ore could fuel a dynamic large-scale capital-goods sector to underpin broad industrialization as well as provide a new source of revenues from exports. During the First

Republic (1889–1930), large-scale industrial development emerged as a political and economic goal. Iron ore mining and steel manufacturing were central to technological and political challenges.[3] Against these evolving ambitions, contemporaries judged private-domain mineral rights to be a failure, and re-separated the subsoil in 1934. Renationalization was an integral component of a new effort to achieve these goals.

This chapter focuses primarily on iron ore, because of its subsequent importance in Brazilian political-economic history and in industrial policy. Industrial policy of the period conflated iron ore extraction and its industrial transformation into pig iron and steel when considering the mineral's economic possibilities.[4] The available macro-level data confirm the small size of the mineral sector and its concentration in the state of Minas Gerais. Prior to 1915, neither state nor national authorities collected data on iron ore or pig iron or any mineral production, other than gold. From 1915, through the remainder of the period under consideration, commercial pig iron production in the formal (measured) economy was undertaken entirely in Minas Gerais.[5] Iron ore became a prominent political issue in the twentieth century. The efforts to develop industrial mining exposed barriers for iron ore extraction that derived from a wider range of resource and institutional constraints. Institutions that created barriers to the organization of large enterprise appeared as the binding constraint for iron ore, and they help to explain the limitations of privatization. The experience of developing iron ore deposits in the region became one of the galvanizing political controversies in Brazil during the 1930s and 1940s.

This chapter offers an opportunity to better understand the institution of subsoil rights, and the institutional conflicts that limited wealth creation and economic growth. A detailed assessment of the effects of changes in subsoil rights sheds light on the intersection between institutional change and industrial development. Limitations and failures of institutional change may have been more common than their successes and they deserve more attention than they have received to date.[6]

In the case of subsoil minerals, the right to a specific resource was important, politically contentious, and could not be disentangled from a complex endowment of interrelated institutions and resources. In the locales and years under consideration here, neither factor endowment nor technology changed significantly. Liberalized subsoil rights directly addressed one asset of concern, but did not serve the evolving ambitions of transforming a dormant mining sector into a dynamic industrial activity. Other important institutional constraints limited the effectiveness of a seemingly crucial property right, and by extension, constrained the support that capital markets could give to mineral extraction and the related infrastructure requirements. The malleability of institutional innovation reflected the increasing importance of ambitions for industrialization while also preserving entrenched practices in other endeavours. These attempts at the beginning of the twentieth century in Brazil highlight the importance of identifying institutional change within the contexts of exogenous constraints and interactions with other institutions. The case of developing Brazilian iron ore mining required mediation with capital markets, business structure practices and the economic role of the state.

If institutional change is to succeed, new arrangements must produce higher returns than the previous ones, concord with other institutions, and the benefits need to accrue to those economic actors who incur the costs of change. From this perspective, the failure of privatized mineral rights to achieve its larger goals can be explained by the high and asymmetric distribution of the costs of change. Privatization alone could not overcome this problem. This explanation invokes concepts from Olson's classic consideration of the nature of collective action and from recent economic development theory.[7] The renationalization of mining rights places this interpretation within the contexts of political economic theories about externalities, collective action and path dependence. It also explains the backdrop against which activist industrial planning emerged, with the state at the centre of the productive sector in subsequent years.

Changing Subsoil Rights and Exploiting the Subsoil

The analysis of subsoil privatization proceeds in two steps. First, it uses patterns of regulatory activity targeted toward the mineral sector to examine the rules that governed the extraction of minerals and the consequences on the behaviour of actors. Then, the record of investors' efforts to acquire access to the subsoil (as connoted by mining concessions and land purchases) suggests that changes to subsoil rights affected the behaviour of actors within the mining sector. The empirical data for exploring this change of property rights are: 1) the detailed laws and decrees that governed mining rights issued by regulating authorities at the national level and in the state of Minas Gerais, categorized by its target: all actors within the mining sector generally or a specific beneficiary (numbering 108 general and 48 specific regulatory actions); 2) the concessions granted to prospect for and to extract minerals (with or without ownership of the land) throughout Minas Gerais;[8] and 3) sales of land designated as 'mining land' in two mining-intensive *municípios* within Minas Gerais, Sabará and Itabira.[9] Concessions allocated prospecting and extraction rights separately, and they were not transferable. The concessions and land-transfer registrations are ordinal, rather than nominal, data; they do not yield information on size or quality of mineral deposits and land. The data cover the period from 1880 until 1940, from the decade prior to the privatization of rights and devolution of regulation until shortly after reversion to substantially pre-republican arrangements.

Because the data refer to different geographic units,[10] they are not directly comparable. However, their patterns indicate whether prospectors and miners (as a proxy for all potential investors) responded to changing rights with actions that increased their future capacity to extract minerals through land acquisitions or concessionary rights. The Data Appendix offers further details of the sources and limitations of these data.

Pattern of Mining Regulation

Three important legal changes defined the institutional environment for minerals between 1880 and 1940.[11] The Constitution of 1891 joined the subsoil to the surface and devolved regulation to the states. A partial mitigation of state-level sovereignty over the subsoil in 1921[12] returned the enforcement of the beneficial use[13] of mines (separately from the land) to the federal government in response to perceived bottlenecks within the states. A separate Mining Code and new Constitution in 1934 formalized the renationalization of the subsoil. Importantly, the Mining Code explicitly defined the subsoil to include all industrial minerals, whether found below or on the surface[14] (see Chapter 2 for a fuller discussion). Surrounding these major changes, an array of regulatory actions structured the practices of mining.

The pattern of national and *mineiro* (within the state of Minas Gerais) mining regulation that targeted mining generally (see Figure 4.1) follows the trajectory of regulatory debate in a straightforward manner. Clusters of new regulations (defined as at least five new regulatory actions within one year) coincided with the three major changes in the structure of rights. Of the 108 regulatory actions that affected the mining sector from 1880 to 1940, thirty-nine of them (36 per cent) occurred in the periods of these innovations. The regulations enacted during these years specified the changes necessary to implement institutional realignment. Much of the regulatory change for privatization occurred during 1890. The Constitution of 1891 consolidated and codified the changes introduced by the provisional government. The changes in 1921, when the enforcement of beneficial-use provisions on public domain land returned to the national level, remained concentrated within that year. However, the twenty-six changes (24 per cent of the total) in mining and mining-related regulation from 1931 through 1934 reflect the increased importance of mining and the significance of renationalization.

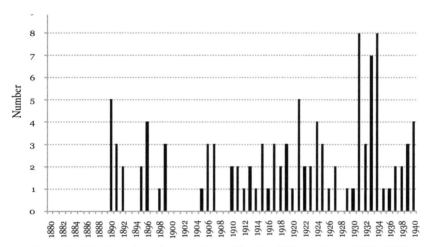

Figure 4.1: Number of regulatory actions, federal and Minas Gerais, 1880–1940 (generally applicable actions).[15]

Clustering of regulatory activity did not occur at other times. Mining entered the regulatory agenda of the federal or *mineiro* authorities only sporadically. No regulatory measures were put into place during the decade of the 1880s. In fact, the last generally applicable mining-related regulation put into place prior to 1890 occurred in 1871. This gap of nineteen years demonstrates the disinterest into which mining had fallen. Reflecting the growing preoccupation with the supply of industrial ore, regulation passed *mineiro* and federal legislatures steadily from 1910 and throughout the remainder of the period under study.

Beyond its timing, we can explore the cumulative trajectory of mining regulation. Each of the 156 national and *mineiro* laws and decrees directed at mining from 1880 to 1940 has been further categorized to indicate whether the provisions removed or enacted constraints for miners and prospectors. Faced with the methodological infeasibility of estimating the economic value of regulatory change, each action has been assigned a value of +1, 0, –1 signifying regulations that removed constraints to mineral access, had a neutral effect or increased constraints, respectively. Regulations that removed constraints to mining and production included such actions as loosening specific conditions of beneficial use or registration on privately owned land, tax and tariff incentives, incentives to the closely related endeavours of steel production and coal, easing the participation of foreigners, etc. New constraints imposed by regulation included registration requirements, tighter provisions for demonstrating beneficial use, limits on foreigners, mortgage collateral restraints and provisions against transferability. Providing for regulatory bureaucracy or administration and laws that confirmed previous arrangements were neutral in their impact on accessing the subsoil. The sum of the assigned direction of the effect from enacting each of the regulations in any given year represents the net direction of constraints on investment in the future productive capacity of minerals created by the change. To compare the trajectory of regulation with its impact on access to the subsoil, an index of change accumulates the annual number of new regulatory actions and their net change for generally applicable and specifically targeted regulatory actions (see Figure 4.2).

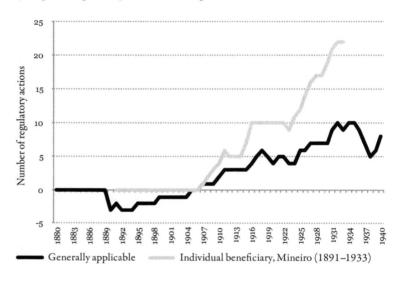

Figure 4.2: Accumulated net change in number of regulations relaxing access and benefits of mining rights, 1880–1940.[16]

Regulation, nationally and within Minas Gerais, was slow to loosen constraints on access to the subsoil in a sustained pattern. 45 per cent (forty-nine of 108) of the mining and mining-related actions were neutral with respect to their impact on access and production. Of the remainder, from the beginning of regulatory activity in 1889 until 1940, a net accumulation of eight regulations positively affected the mining sector. For the time period (full years) during which mineral rights were privately held, from 1891 until 1933, a net positive accumulation of twelve laws served to ease mineral access. As with the overall pattern of regulation, steady increasing regulatory encouragement for mining did not begin until late in the first decade of the twentieth century. Federal and *mineiro* laws and regulations began after a long delay, but they accumulated a positive trajectory of reinforcing incentives to access mineral veins in Minas Gerais.

Even so, from 1902, the annual reports of the presidents (governors) of Minas Gerais noted the persistent inability to enact mining legislation.[17] The data corroborate their observations. While governance rested with the state (1891–1933), thirty-five of the eighty-three (42 per cent) of the regulatory actions came from federal authorities, and only three state laws addressed the underlying structure of the mining sector. These were the initial instructions with respect to mining, a provision to regulate explorations and finally a law to regulate mineral extraction.[18] Indeed, the state of Minas Gerais did not pass a law that specifically authorized the state government to issue mining concessions on land in its public domain until 1915, twenty-five years after gaining the authority to do so. The state of Minas Gerais did not grant any new mining concessions on land in the public domain after it acquired the regulatory mechanism until that right transferred back to the federal government. Much of the legislative and regulatory debate directly focused on mining concerned the administrative mechanisms, criteria for regulating beneficial use and the constitutionality of state-level expropriations (which they did not invoke).[19] Twenty-eight of the forty-eight actions (58 per cent) taken by *mineiro* officials did not seem to include provisions that would alter the incentive to mine; this proportion compared to 45 per cent (eleven of thirty-five actions) at the federal level, during the same period.[20]

These findings suggest that the effectiveness and depth of regulation did not match the accumulating trajectory to support accessing the subsoil. Although the authorities of Minas Gerais had difficulty regulating access to minerals, the need for such legislation may not have been clear. With minerals attached to the soil and with the state able to dispense land in the public domain as it pleased, existing land laws, rather than mining law, governed access to minerals. Nevertheless, the resulting perception of inadequate governance by the states eased the recentralization of mining rights in the 1930s.

In contrast to the relative dearth of effective legislation to open the mining sector, companies and individuals engaged in mining learned to pursue regulatory favour from the state of Minas Gerais to their own benefit.[21] They achieved benefit by seeking legislative or executive decrees that offered tax relief, granted land that could be cleared for charcoal production, extended the time period for demonstrating beneficial use on a concession, and (most numerously) granted the ability the extend railway trunk lines. Individual actors did not seek regulatory favour until the first decade of the twentieth century, nine years after the initial change in subsoil rights. By the 1910s, when the mining of iron ore emerged as a political controversy, regulation targeted to individual beneficiaries had become a routine practice. While in command of regulating the subsoil from 1891 to 1933, thirty-two actions applied to individual beneficiaries, with a net accumulation of twenty-two actions serving to enhance access (see Figure 4.2).

In a highly codified legal system that was slow to generalize procedures, it is not surprising that expansive mining regulation and incentives occurred through the expedient of specifically targeting beneficiaries.[22] Neither is it surprising that the accumulated net change of accessibility for regulatory actions targeted to individual beneficiaries should be much more positive than for general regulation. Any benefit bestowed by individually targeted actions that did not come to fruition did not require remedial action in order to negate the effect.[23] These findings, however, highlight two important features of the business environment that miners and prospectors faced. First, state-level regulation did face difficulty in easing access to the subsoil to potential participants on an equal basis. Secondly, absent effective regulation of the sector as a whole meant that actors could reasonably anticipate that individual, rather than collective, action was an effective business development strategy.

Access to Minerals

How did changing the legal structure affect access to mineral deposits? The few scholars who have addressed this question have drawn exclusively from Calógeras's contribution, which determined the privatization of mining to be an unmitigated failure.[24] Further, as late as 1926, Nelson de Senna, another prominent mining engineer in Minas Gerais, continued to attribute the confusion surrounding the allocation of assets in the public domain and litigious procedures for claiming subsoil and surface rights as major obstacles to mining development, while also citing the lack of investment capital and technological expertise as additional impediments to iron ore.[25] The available data are less categorical than this assessment. The willingness to prospect and mine reflect the value and credibility that the sector's participants attached to the new regulations.[26] The patterns of granting concessions to prospect or to mine and the notarial registrations of sales of mining land indicate the expectations of miners and prospectors with respect to their future ability to benefit from their activities (see Figure 4.3).[27] Without indicating an immediate transformation of the sector, these data suggest that slowly increasing activity took hold in the mining regions of Minas Gerais during the First Republic.

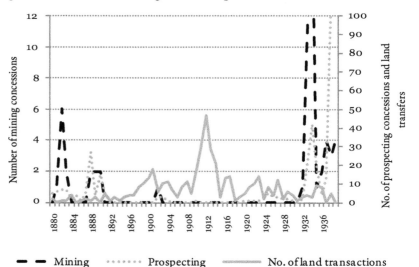

Figure 4.3: Indication of mining activity, 1880–1940.[28]

During both of the redefinitions of subsoil rights, aspiring miners responded with increasing activity in Minas Gerais. Between 1890, as it became more certain that the principles controlling mining would change, and 1892, when federal authorities cleared the backlog of applications (which were grandfathered), miners undertook a short burst of concession-seeking to prospect for minerals. Similarly, notaries registered an increasing, if uneven, trend of land transfers for mining land in Sabará and Itabira that began slowly in the years after the Constitution joined the subsoil to the surface in 1891. Few mining lands changed ownership between 1880 and the end of the century. Though remaining slow and uneven, by 1899, land sales had become the mechanism for accumulating access to mines in both Sabará and Itabira. Two separate development efforts, one by the St John d'el Rey Company (see Chapter 3) and another by foreign consortia of steel producers hoping to mine iron ore in Itabira (discussed below), explain the concentrated peak in land transfers during the first half of the 1910s. The pattern of land sales in Sabará, where many miners explored for both industrial minerals and gold, more clearly indicates the trend of accepting land ownership as the instrument for acquiring mining rights trend than in Itabira (with its sole focus on iron ore by a small number of foreign mining syndicates, as discussed below; see Figure 4.4). Land transfers diminished with the end of the Republic. The prospect of re-separating subsoil rights from land rendered ownership a less secure means of claiming minerals. Indeed, an increase in federally issued mining concessions followed an initial burst of concession-granting in 1934.[29] The increasing importance of industrial metals introduced major tensions for mining policy and the claims of sovereignty over mineral rights at the same time that it spurred the efforts of business enterprises.

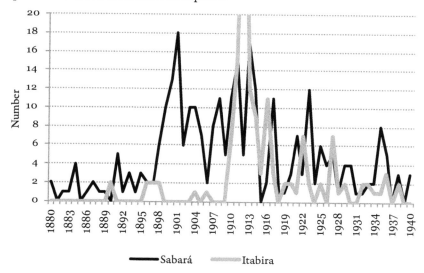

Figure 4.4: **Number of mining land transfers, Sabará and Itabira, 1880–1940.**[30]

Politicization of Iron Ore

Global attention turned to Brazilian iron ore deposits and domestic political-economic interests began to coalesce to promote industrialization simultaneously during the first decade of the twentieth century.[31] European steel producers, concerned about the prospect of dwindling known reserves of iron ore, discovered the untapped deposits of Brazil. For Brazilians, slowly accumulating interest in developing the output of industrial metals gained momentum, but faced daunting obstacles.

The coordination problems created by institutional and resource endowment constraints that had impeded mining in the eighteenth and nineteenth centuries re-emerged in the twentieth century.[32] Despite its generous endowment of iron ore, the capital requirements for two essential components impeded ambitions for large-scale ore mining and steel production during the first half of the twentieth century. Transportation infrastructure and fixed investment in plant and equipment were binding financial constraints for Brazilian ambitions in ferrous metals.[33] Iron ore deposits in the mountainous interior of Minas Gerais (the *Quadrilátero Ferrífico* – Iron Quadrangle; see Front Map) were far from the most robust demand for iron and steel products, in the coastal regions of São Paulo and Rio de Janeiro. These were the locations of industrialization, large-scale export-agriculture, and the ports for ore exports. The land transportation most suitable for iron ore was the railroad, with enhanced capacity and capability for heavy freight across mountainous terrain. The engineering and technological requirements for the railways were complicated, but solutions existed.[34] The second constraint imposed by resource endowment was that coke (the mineral form of coal), useful for refining iron ore and necessary as an input for transforming iron into increasingly complex steel products, was not available in sufficient quantities within Brazil.[35] Coal deposits in the southern states of Rio Grande do Sul and Santa Catarina remained under-explored, transportation facilities were insufficient, and plant-based charcoal continued to substitute for coke. By the early 1920s steel and coal received the same favourable policy support for their development.[36] Britain also supplied coal imports, which Brazilian financial authorities regarded as a drain of hard currency.[37] The transportation needs (railroads and ports) of imported coal were the inverse of the requirements for iron ore.

Itabira Iron Ore

In 1908, a consortium of British mining engineers first acquired land in the otherwise sleepy Itabira region of the Rio Doce Valley in Minas Gerais (see Front Map).[38] The British Hematite Syndicate, later renamed the Itabira Iron Ore Company, organized in 1910, for the purpose of mining iron ore and exporting it to Britain.[39] Also in 1910, a report prepared for a conference of steel producers in Stockholm to consider the problem of international iron ore reserves identified Brazil as the location of the world's largest unexploited ore deposits.[40] By 1922, industry officials estimated that Brazilian deposits accounted for 23 per cent of known global iron ore reserves.[41] Further, much of the Brazilian ore was of exceptionally high quality (high iron and low phosphorous content in the ore's chemical composition).[42] International demand for Brazilian iron ore intensified with time and with the disruptive supply conditions of world wars (see Chapter 5). The Itabira deposits were the jewel-in-the-crown; the extent and purity of these deposits were unrivalled for decades.

Exploiting the Itabira deposits became a technological, bureaucratic and political struggle as the company encountered the array of coordination problems that plagued iron efforts. The infrastructure development and government licenses required to export the Itabira ore proved too cumbersome for the British syndicate. They did not complete the first contract with the Brazilian authorities until 1920, and the contract encountered significant difficulty.[43] As a result, the syndicate sold options to the company to Percival Farquhar, a would-be baron of Brazilian mining and infrastructure development from Pennsylvania.[44] Farquhar organized a consortium of investment partners and assumed the planning and negotiating responsibilities.

Extracting ore from the ground was the easiest part of the project. The Itabira deposits were 22 km from the nearest rail connection. The railroad (the Estrada de Ferro Vitória a Minas, the option to which Itabira Iron Ore had acquired)[45] to the coastal port of Vitória, through approximately 500 km of difficult mountainous terrain, was inadequate for large volume transport of heavy freight, and it required extended routing. Vitória did not have facilities capable of shipping ore, and sufficient freight shipping did not service Brazil. Farquhar expected to provide all of these facilities; he planned to rebuild the railway,[46] construct a port and operate a shipping line. Further, he planned to import coke using the return routes of his newly constructed shipping and rail lines. For these facilities, Farquhar needed railway, port and shipping concessions, as well as export–import licenses and eventually mining authorization from the federal government. He also needed tax agreements and operating licenses from the state of Minas Gerais. Even with the subsoil in the private domain, these complex requirements opened several possibilities for state and national interests to inject their goals into the project.

As iron moved toward the centre of domestic industrial ambition, political intervention plagued the Itabira Iron Ore Company from its first appearance in Brazil.[47] The earliest and most effective opposition to the project came from Artur Bernardes. As governor of Minas Gerais (1918–22), he instituted a state export tax on iron ore of three *mil-réis* per ton, which both critics and advocates described as prohibitive.[48] To gain exemption from this tax, the Itabira Iron Ore Company agreed to construct and operate an integrated steel plant in the state.[49]

As president of Brazil from 1922 until 1926, Bernardes's continual objections to contractual arrangements prevented agreement. The theme of national control of natural resources emerged as the central argument in the debates about the Itabira contracts.[50] In the late 1920s, opponents framed the controversy as an effort to prevent the formation of a foreign-owned monopoly. The company attempted to obtain profit guarantees on its railway investment, as other lines had received for decades.[51] Farquhar insisted on being able to restrict transport on its lines, which railway-guarantee policies prohibited. If successful, this privileged arrangement for transportation effectively would grant the Itabira Iron Ore Company a monopoly in the industrial-scale mining and export of iron ore, at least for a considerable time period. Further complicating the endeavour, the contracts that the state and national governments finally negotiated with the Farquhar group in 1927 and 1928[52] remained in dispute until 1939, owing to Farquhar's inability to raise capital in the London and New York equity markets within the two-year period specified in the contract.[53]

The history of the Itabira Iron Ore project became a galvanizing controversy in national politics that persisted for two decades, and it was intricately intertwined with Brazilian economic ambitions and institutional development. Leaders divided over the desirability of developing ore deposits for export. Analysts at the time and subsequently have attributed the change in subsoil rights in 1934 directly to this case.[54] Many saw the Itabira project as ceding a monopoly to foreigners for a valuable resource, with little benefit for the Brazilian industrial base. The first provisions that limited the presence of foreigners in mining arose from this perspective. Still others objected to foreign presence in a core industry that became strategically important to the economic standing and military defence of Brazil.[55] Local producers with expansionary ambitions, tried to promote the argument that a focus on ore exports would delay local steel development. Some were reluctant to export Brazil's non-renewable natural resources if they could be used to promote rapid local industrialization. Among the opponents, some simply anticipated that they could maximize potential for revenues from iron ore by delaying its development, awaiting the diminution of alternative sources.[56] Proponents of the plan saw the opportunity to benefit from the presence of foreign capital and technology, as well as the substantial public revenues that iron ore exports would generate through tariffs and fees. Some also favoured the Itabira project for the demonstration effects it offered to Brazilian enterprise.[57]

The project to develop the ore deposits at Itabira in order to supply global demand for iron amplified Brazilian interest in minerals and the rights attached to them. The interest of foreigners in iron deposits only encompassed their export potential. The efforts to tie ore exports to domestic steel production contributed to the conflation of these two activities in Brazilian policy for two decades. Controversy surrounding the project gave potential Brazilian miners, industrial entrepreneurs and their political representatives a venue for voicing their ambitions.

A formal industrial policy that targeted large-scale iron and steel began to take shape in the 1920s, including such measures as transport subsidies, tariff exemptions, tax exemptions to iron ore miners who also produced pig iron and steel, and preferential access to mineral coke. These measures (and perhaps undocumented production improvements) brought the cost of producing pig iron for the major companies in Minas Gerais to levels comparable to the US experience in the early 1930s (see Figure 4.5). Private sector efforts to develop domestic mining and steel production jointly involved important enterprises from Minas Gerais (such as Companhia Siderúrgica Belgo-Mineira and Usinas Queiroz Júnior). These enterprises benefited from domestic incentive policies and ultimately became successful large firms; but they remained small during these years. By the middle of the 1920s, the extent of the Itabira deposits, the difficulties of developing them and their potential for international trade and domestic industry gave rise to powerful new reasons to reconsider mineral rights. In light of the new perspective, ambitions for mineral rights escalated.

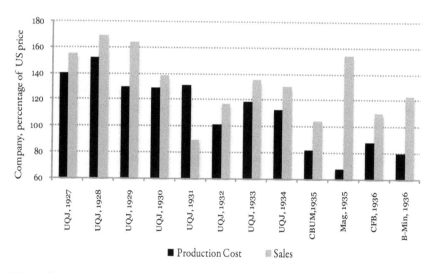

Figure 4.5: Pig iron; company production costs and prices as percentage of US price, selected companies.[58]

Iron Ore and Renationalizing the Subsoil: 'Outside of iron there is no salvation. Only iron enriches'[59]

The new political regime in 1930, led by Getúlio Vargas, established centralized governance and 'economic nationalism' as the cornerstones of economic policy.[60] Shifting the relative capacity of the Brazilian economy from agricultural export products toward industrially produced goods for domestic consumption emerged as an explicit goal of the regime. Industrialization, based on a large, advanced and domestically owned iron and steel industry that vastly expanded the nascent private efforts of the first decades of the twentieth century, became compelling national policy. Vargas clearly communicated the prospect of the reversion of subsoil rights in order to service industrialization in his first presidential speech in Minas Gerais, three months after the coup that brought him to power.[61] In the view of the new regime, 'without iron and steel it is not possible to assure the sovereignty and progress of a nation'.[62] Vargas intended the development of iron ore exports to generate the capital necessary for steel production, without need for public subsidy.[63] This strategy reflected the expectation that 'steel is one of the consequences of extractive industry in iron ore'.[64] It was also an audacious attempt to pursue new avenues of traditional export-orientation in order to support simultaneous import-substituting growth. Both subsoil property rights and the Itabira iron ore deposits were central to the strategy.

The Constitution and Mining Code, both enacted in 1934, firmly transferred mining rights and regulation back to the national government, motivated by the prospect of developing industrial-scale iron ore mining.[65] The argument for this change was that private rights, subject to varying state-level regulations, were incapable of maximizing national development. With the subsoil and surface separated, control of land in the public domain remained with the states. That arrangement ensured that state governments did not object to the transfer. By removing decisions about the subsoil from the landowner above which minerals might be found, prospectors had greater security that they could benefit from their discoveries. Further, the specification of the principles governing subsoil minerals in the Constitution and the Mining Code brought a uniform body of law to the field and made it difficult to repeal without substantial constitutional and legislative reform. The result was that earlier prospectors and miners could exploit their discoveries with greater confidence of garnering the gains. Political debate and opposition to renationalization were minimal. More pointedly, Juarez Távora, the Minister of Agriculture and main architect of the Mining Code, expected the re-separation of the subsoil to 'guarantee the federal government the tools necessary to avoid and annul assaults such as those of the Farquhar Group'.[66]

Even with stronger regulation and constraints, mining concessions increased and companies clamoured to register for mining rights. From 1934 to 1940, national authorities issued 318 mining authorizations (the instrument that replaced concessions to prospect) and thirty-three mining concessions; eighty-five companies received authorizations to operate as 'mining companies' from 1938 to 1940[67] (see Figure 4.3). These responses suggest that the mining sector understood the changes as a remedy for the confused arrangements of the First Republic and a commitment to develop mining, in preference to maintaining a specific interpretation of republicanism.

Failure? No and Yes

The commonly accepted proposition that the privatization of mining rights had failed reflected the inability to resolve confusions over access to the subsoil as well as a shortfall in mineral output from heightened ambitions.[68] Assessed by the level of output, indications of production increases after the privatization of mining rights were impressive. Commercial output of pig iron during the nineteen-year period, from the beginning of data availability in 1915 until the introduction of the Mining Code in 1934, increased 35-fold, an average annual rate of 15.1 per cent (see Figure 4.6). Further, local business publications often recognized the increased capacity of existing producers.[69]

However, the return of mining rights to federal authority coincided with an even more rapid increase in output than occurred under the regime of private ownership and state regulation. Output increased at an average rate of 20.5 per cent annually between 1934 and 1939 (see Figure 4.6). Although the causal connection was very dubious, the coincidence of timing served new policy well.[70]

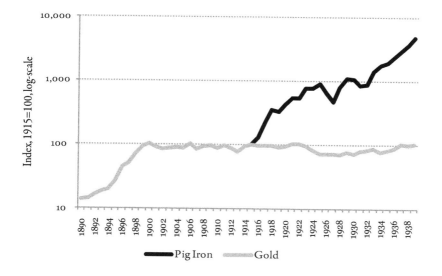

Figure 4.6: Pig iron and gold output; index, 1915 = 100.[71]

Institutional and Resource Constraints

Iron and steel were highly capital intensive because of the investment requirements dictated by its coordination problems for transportation and resources. This capital intensity contrasted sharply with the institutional biases in favour of small enterprise. Indivisibility provisions continued to introduce contradictions in all aspects of economic life, such as sustaining the system of legally mandated partible inheritance, unwinding or transferring business partnerships and loan collateralization. By 1904, analysts believed that conflict between indivisibility of veins and conjoined subsoil-land rights was a major impediment to the sale of mineral properties.[72] The inability to control the composition of partnerships, because of partible inheritance laws, contributed to the small number and size of partnerships and firms operating within the mining sector. Consequently, indivisibility privileged prior capital accumulation while inhibiting future accumulation on a scale sufficient to build large mining enterprises.[73]

Many authors have noted the small size of Brazilian enterprise and the slow development of formal capital markets.[74] Metallurgy companies, in particular, remained small. In 1907, the average Brazilian foundry (or other metal-working company, whether of iron ore or other mineral) had capital investment of 136 *contos*, increasing to 206 *contos* in 1919 (the equivalent of approximately US$43,000 and US$55,000 in 1907 and 1919, respectively), with average value of production increasing from 182 to 185 *contos* (US$57,000 declining to US$50,000)[75] according to the scant data available through the 1907 and 1919 industrial censuses (Table 4.1).[76] Small size was especially pronounced within the state of Minas Gerais, where the iron ore was. *Mineiro* metallurgy companies were about one-third the size of the Brazilian average (by capital) and about one-quarter the national average by production. Among iron forging and laminating companies (those concentrated in the use of iron ore) the difference was even more pronounced: *mineiro* companies were, on average, 20 and 17 per cent the size of the Brazilian average, by capital and production, respectively. Transport costs as a share of total expenses for *mineiro* metallurgy companies[77] were more than triple the national average. Larger, but still relatively small, enterprises located in the states of Rio de Janeiro and São Paulo, close to demand and far from ample resources. Tellingly, mining and metallurgy companies also remained organized as unincorporated sole proprietorships or partnerships. The limited-liability joint-stock organizational structure was slow to permeate the sector, and the slow trend was more pronounced in Minas Gerais than elsewhere (see Table 4.2).

Table 4.1: Size of metallurgy companies, 1907 and 1919.[78]

	1907			1919		
	Total Brazil	Minas Gerais	Minas Gerais, % total Brazil	Total Brazil	Minas Gerais	Minas Gerais, % total Brazil
Total metallurgy						
Average statutory capital (*contos*)				132	42	32.1
Production (*contos*)	427	148	34.7	204	51	25.0
Expenses, transportation % total				2.8	9	316.7
Iron forging and laminating						
Average statutory capital	136			206	41	20.0
Production				285	48	16.8

Table 4.2: Corporate structure of metallurgy companies, 1919 (number of companies).[79]

Total metallurgy	Total	Unincorporated	Limited-liability joint stock	Joint-liability partnership	Other
Brazil	509	479	22	4	4
Minas Gerais	76	72	1	2	1
Iron forging and laminating					
Brazil	116	102	9	2	3
Minas Gerais	32	na			

In contrast, the first Itabira Iron Ore Company plan for investment in 1911 was for 214,000 *contos*. Further, a survey of the rail transport requirements for a similar hypothetical expansion to service iron ore development in 1923 projected railway investment costs of 375,000 *contos* and four years to meet the needs.[80] Beyond its comparison with the size of existing Brazilian metallurgy, the scale of this one enterprise was very large relative to Brazilian access to capital markets. Through the 1920s and 1930s, the plans that Farquhar produced for his proposed project required capital (or combination of capital and long-term debt) that varied from almost ten times to more than thirty-five times the capital of the largest private company then listed on the Rio de Janeiro stock exchange (see Table 4.3 and Data Appendix).[81] The scale of the capital requirements was one of the reasons that Farquhar planned to issue equity in London or New York.

Table 4.3: Plans to develop Itabira Iron Ore Company deposits, relative size of projects.[82]

	IIO	PF	PF	PF	PF	Vale
year of plan:	1911	1921	1928	1930	1938	1942
Itabira Iron Ore, Capital, as % largest companies on Bolsa de Valores						
Largest company without govt guarantee	3560	3511	2939	1907	956	133.33
Largest company, not RR or bank	356	843	490	763	1594	133.33
Largest company	305	602	294	763	956	na

When the Companhia do Vale Rio Doce opened in 1942 to mine ore at Itabira (see Chapter 5) it and the companion integrated-steel project (Companhia Siderúrgica Nacional, both with a majority of the capital held by the national government) each had statutory equity that was one-third larger than the next largest firm on the Rio de Janeiro stock exchange. Earlier plans, without public sector investment, would have created a company of much larger size differential (see Table 4.3). All indications support the conclusion that the capital-intensity of infrastructure requirements and of industrial mining increasingly rendered sole-proprietorship or small family-centred partnerships infeasible business structures.

The mechanisms that allowed for large-scale capital accumulation were in place by the beginning of the twentieth century. The Commercial Code of 1890 permitted the free formation of limited-liability joint-stock companies, and local debenture and equity markets existed to facilitate the acquisition and exchange of financial assets. These tools offered opportunities to mitigate the problems of asset indivisibility and the need for personal ties to cement partnerships. Many enterprises actively benefited from them.[83] However, change was slow. For example, among the innovations that Farquhar sought (and did not receive) for the Itabira project had been an amendment to the 1890 Commercial Code allowing for preferred equity shares, in addition to common stock.[84] Business practices had evolved to invoke financing tools to an extent that was much smaller than necessary for unproven and capital-intensive industrial iron ore endeavours.

Foreign enterprise offered a manner of escaping the problem of capital accumulation. Practices and procedures for establishing large-scale joint-stock companies, not subject to the constraints of local custom, could permit capital accumulation for endeavours within Brazil. Such activities also offered the potential of transferring incremental capital into the economy. During the first half of the nineteenth century, this approach had brought European mining companies to Brazil (see Chapter 3). At the end of the nineteenth century in an open international financial atmosphere, and with the strong hold of classically liberal ideologies within the political economy of newly republican Brazil, foreign capital held strong attraction.[85] By the 1920s, the political implications of importing capital had become very complicated with respect to developing industrial minerals, with the Itabira Iron Ore Company at the centre of the controversy.

Public versus Private Interest

In contrast to the large demands of the Itabira project on capital markets, the immediate first-order impact on Brazilian macroeconomic measures remained small. The Itabira Iron Ore Company presented its first full proposal to exploit the Itabira deposits, in order to export ore to Britain in 1921. Figure 4.7 uses the projections from this unrealized enterprise to estimate counterfactually the first-order impact of the project on export revenues, import expenditures and national production, under the most favourable assumptions for project implementation. The scale of the project would have transformed iron ore mining and metallurgy in Brazil. If expeditiously and successfully developed according to this plan, Itabira Iron Ore Company exports would have reached a level almost 250 per cent above the actual volume of total iron ore exports in 1942, and the company's production of pig iron would have exceeded annual actual Brazilian consumption until 1939 (Appendix Table A.11). However, this potential early success would have increased export revenues by less than 1.5 per cent through the 1920s and 1930s, while reducing import expenditures (for pig iron) by as much as 2.2 per cent (see Figure 4.7). The relatively larger impact on imports than on exports substantiates the importance of the import-substituting possibilities that had been the focus of Brazilian authorities. Increased exports and decreased imports, combined (one notional measure of the opportunity costs of not undertaking the project), could have accounted for a maximum of 0.15 per cent of national production.

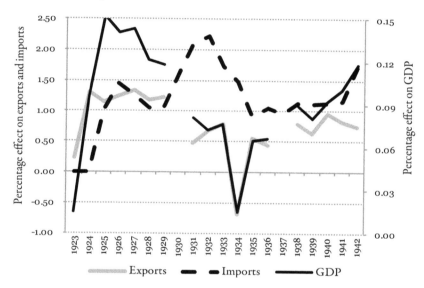

Figure 4.7: Itabira Iron Ore Company; contribution to macroeconomy, as of 1921.[86]

Simply put, the large demand on capital markets would have been asymmetrical and disproportionate with the small impact on macroeconomic measures for the first-order effects of the Itabira project. Although Itabira Iron Ore profit expectations may have been sufficient for its private investors, the importance of the project for the Brazilian economy lay in its externalities, not its first-order effects. These disparate results for public and private sector considerations suggest an explanation for the inability to develop domestic industrial-scale iron ore projects.

The traditional dreams of wealth derived from precious minerals had been firmly allocated to individual mining interests, with the sovereign as the residual beneficiary.[87] While privatized, access to the subsoil by miners (individuals as well as companies) required either becoming a landowner or sharing the gains, but not the risks, of mining with landowners. This chapter has demonstrated that some miners accommodated these rules and their mining proceeded, if often complicated by onerous constraints. Simultaneously, iron ore and pig iron output increased impressively. It is not possible here to estimate the opportunity costs of exploration and production that did not occur because of the constraints.[88] Given the scope of iron ore deposits and the increasing interest in developing them, the opportunity costs of foregone mining must have been very high.

For the national economy, the importance of minerals changed and escalated in significant manners that differed from the interests of private actors. Industrial minerals, and specifically iron ore, became crucial to the emerging ambitions for a large prosperous and modern industrial economy. Mining policy, an indispensible aspect of these ambitions, faced the complicated problem of aligning new demands with institutions rooted in four centuries of accepted practice.

In attempting to understand disparities between private and public interests, economists focus on the special difficulty for a private entrepreneur to provide goods and services that generate externalities (costs or benefits to economic actors who do not participate directly in the activity).[89] When economic activity generates externalities the incentive for any individual or enterprise to engage in that activity diminishes, because of the benefit that actor cannot capture (or external cost that actor will incur). The schematic in Table 4.4 summarizes the transactions benefits and costs of industrialized iron ore mining that extended beyond the immediate actors. Olson further theorizes that small, tightly defined groups have important advantages relative to larger, more disparate groups in effectively representing their interests. Smaller, cohesive groups can more easily coordinate action and identify higher marginal benefits to its members from collective action. These concepts point to the disadvantage of those attempting to innovate by industrializing mining relative to traditional activities.

Table 4.4: Externalities of industrial iron ore mining.

	Internalized by mining	External to mining
Benefits		Declining industrial prices
		Larger and more dynamic capital markets
Costs	Technology and infra-structure development	Transactions costs of changing institutions (indivisible assets and mandatory partible inheritance) – family inheritances, business structure

Two benefits of domestic industrial-scale iron and steel would accrue broadly across all economic sectors: declining industrial prices resulting from lower costs of iron and steel and increasingly dynamic depersonalized capital markets. In this case, collective action theory predicts that the large, indistinct group of beneficiaries from these factors would be difficult to identify, and would hinder the consolidation of a group to support the development of the mining sector and of capital markets. The full potential benefits of expanded capital markets and deeper industrial capability remained external to mining and metallurgy. While the potential gains could accrue widely throughout the Brazilian economy, the entrepreneurs taking the full risks of innovation and investment could not realize the full gains. In other words, these risks[90] remained internalized, while the gains were externalized. In consequence, and as we have seen, business practices and the legal system during the early twentieth century favoured individual action over the collective actions of widespread transformation of capital markets and business practices.[91]

By the same token, other transactions costs incurred by changing the fundamental institutions of indivisible real assets and mandated partible personal estates fell on those, small in number and easily identified, with entrenched property interests. Whether seen as an interest group or an entrenched elite, property owners had constructed a system to accommodate deeply embedded rules that had become their norm for structuring and sustaining their commercial affairs.[92]

The observable gains of modernizing the institutions that governed mining and metallurgy were relatively small compared to the costs required of other economic sectors. Just as the full costs of developing mining and metallurgy could not be externalized, the full gains could not be internalized. The outcome was exactly as economic theory would predict: privatizing subsoil rights did contribute to developing the mining sector, but could not do so beyond narrow limits because of additional constraints for which economic solutions did not reside within the domestic private sector.

Conclusion

The subsoil carried heavy baggage and the attempt to privatize and devolve the Brazilian subsoil offers an important caveat to studies in institutional change. Studying the effects of specific changes within the contexts of a wide range of additional factors, such as other institutions, resources and the path dependency of historical experience, allows for a fuller understanding of large-scale change and for the many cases of failure to realize the expectations of change. The barriers to capital investment and infrastructure development remained in place as long as the related institutional barriers prevailed. The factors favouring small enterprise in preference to large organizations reflected deeply embedded institutions that governed property and business structure. Specific practices and legal redefinition attempted to work around, rather than change, those institutions.

When attempting to apply liberalizing concepts, policy-makers of the First Republic faced the messy realities of reconciling countervailing claims that had originated in the same long-term trajectory from which subsoil rights emerged. Although privatized rights attached to land supported the acquisition of mining property, it was slow to occur, and policies did not effectively ease access to the subsoil. Measured against its own history, privatization successfully supported new ownership practices and output expansion. However, policy-makers were aiming at a moving target, as their goals for the mineral sector evolved. The narrowly constrained 'success' of private ownership rights did not support the industrial transformation of the mineral sector. The inability of private investors to raise capital and to overcome infrastructure and ancillary resource constraints reflected the limitations on entrepreneurship. This inability and that of the states to develop effective regulatory regimes for mining that could remove constraints to develop mines resulted in characterizing the privatization as a failure. 'Failure' is a reasonable description of the privatization, when measured against the formation of successful and very large-scale capital-intensive iron ore mining that became the ultimate goal of the Brazilians and that began shortly after the consolidation of renationalized mining.[93]

While the subsoil was privatized, institutional inconsistency had become obvious, and minerals had become economically and politically important. Renationalizing the subsoil was a very strong indication of shifting interest-group strength. The logical difficulties of attaching subsoil to land rights during the First Republic had complicated mining efforts. Goals to expand iron ore extraction for export and for domestic manufacture of steel gathered force during the 1920s. The interest groups promoting these ambitions increasingly prevailed with pragmatic developmentalist policy, in preference to the ideologies of a specific interpretation of economic federalism.

Global focus on Brazilian ore deposits imposed another dimension of complexity onto mineral policy. Foreign interest in gaining access to ore generated controversy about how to develop the potential of this non-renewable resource and who should benefit from it. This controversy took place within the context of the Itabira Iron Ore Company and Percival Farquhar's plans because institutional barriers prevented other entrepreneurs from stepping forward with alternative projects of similar scope.[94] The proposed project at Itabira presented a range of logistic, financial and political complexities that remained unresolved for years.

Attempts to resolve these complexities domestically revealed that at least two of the three earlier criteria for successful institutional change – that it must concord with other institutions and that the benefits need to accrue to those economic actors who incur the costs of change – were not met through the limited means of privatized rights. The experience with mineral rights highlights one of the important characteristics that scholars have recognized as a difficulty in Brazil, and in 'late-developing' economies more broadly: the difficulty in accumulating capital from sufficiently broad sources to form large-scale and inherently risky enterprises.[95] Individual action in accumulating access to minerals, in contrast to developing effective regulatory procedures and collective action for the sector remained the most effective way for miners to secure their interests. Further, the indivisibility of real assets left mining partnerships uncertain. The unpredictable extent of subsoil veins exacerbated these concerns.

Indivisibility and the efficacy of individual action reinforced traditional practices of small close-knit groups to form enterprises, rather than larger depersonalized groups that could come together through capital markets.

As we will see in Chapter 5, during the second half of the twentieth century, Brazil emerged as one of the world's largest producers and exporters of iron ore, as a result of constructing the edifice for strongly interventionist federal industrial policy. This occurred within the property rights regime put in place in 1934. Brazilians applied a traditional structure of rights, originating during Portuguese rule, to a new goal.

5 INDUSTRIALIZING IRON ORE

In the middle of the twentieth century, increasingly influential political and business interest groups invoked long-entrenched traditional practices in order to pursue dynamic industrial policies. This chapter explores the formation of a state-owned enterprise (SOE) for iron ore mining in the context of coordinating complex institutional and material requirements. The Brazilian government reverted to earlier property definitions that established its sovereignty over the subsoil and mineral resources, and it used the global strategic circumstances of World War II to great advantage. As a result, the state promoted large-scale industrial development in the twentieth century by consolidating a strong entrepreneurial role for itself within the productive sectors of the economy. Much historiography addresses the early formation of the capital-goods industries.[1] The National Steel Company (Companhia Siderúrgica Nacional, CSN) was the lynchpin of that effort. The iron ore story is less well known; but its institutional implications were as profound as the efforts to produce steel. The transformation of the British-owned Itabira Iron Ore Company into Companhia Vale do Rio Doce (Vale), an SOE, demonstrates the expansion of the concept of the public domain that was crucial to institution-building of the period.

Defining the domestic iron ore mining and steel manufacture as strategic industries hinged on the large important externalities of enhancing both national military security and rapid, broad-based industrialization. The chapter argues that the formation of SOE for iron ore production and export successfully accomplished these goals of the Brazilian government. Although state ownership was not necessary to their original plans or ideologies, this experience (along with the companion state-owned CSN) transformed the state into the largest industrial producer and defined the future of 'state-capitalism' within Brazil. The emergence of the state as an entrepreneur solved multiple organizational problems of capital accumulation and technological coordination, without challenging deep-seated institutional arrangements with respect to asset indivisibility, partible inheritance and nationality sensitivities for entrenched holders of private property. The implications for future development of economic institutions extended to important consequences for capital-market development, industrial and resource allocation policies and the economic role of the state.

Absent a domestic private sector means to institute mining and manufacture as efficiently as projects pursued by outsiders, the state ultimately took advantage of a particular set of exogenous circumstances that allowed it to substitute for private providers. Industrial policy emerged that accepted arguments in favour of public sovereignty over subsoil resources and public participation in iron mining as well as steel manufacturing during the 1930s. The state resolved financing and organizational problems in both mining and production by constituting SOEs. Vale's formation as a state-owned iron ore mining company relied on a statist solution to two long controversies: industrialization and the domain of mineral resources. The Brazilian government anticipated the beneficial externalities from iron ore production and steel manufacture. Strategically, they foresaw contributions to industrialization, independence from global market fluctuations, development of a disciplined technologically sophisticated labour force and increased material well-being.[2] Externalities associated with capital markets development also affected the value of the project.

Economic Role of the State and Evolution of Interest Groups

Economic Nationalism

Economic nationalism, defined as the development of a self-sufficient, modern and industrial domestic economy, was at the centre of goals for political governance during the regime in place from 1930 until 1945, led by Getúlio Vargas.[3] Industrialization and economic nationalism were also linked goals for a combination of increasingly successful interest groups in Brazilian politics. The military found common cause with leading industrial entrepreneurs.[4] Much of the business community explicitly associated the development of industrial-scale mining and steel production with the 'political and economic sovereignty of the nation'.[5] Both groups understood secure access to mineral resources and large-scale steel production as the first steps towards economic modernity and independence. They constituted powerful interests to ensure that the state perceived iron and steel as a sector that generated important externalities not captured by private entrepreneurs, thus motivating state participation to ensure their provision.[6] In order to effect this fundamental transformation, the political regime hoped to rely on the exploitation of iron ore and (in its expectations) petroleum. These resources promised both important inputs for production and export earnings to finance steel manufacture, which in turn would provide the basis for industrialization.[7]

The military and industrial sectors successfully built a strong platform in the Vargas regime that equated economic and military security.[8] The connection between these forms of security first arose during the War of the Triple Alliance (1864–70) when the backwardness of Brazilian military technology and equipment became apparent. With the cessation of international trade during World War I, protection against war-related supply disruptions became defined as a significant security issue. This concern was not exaggerated. Although the effect of trade disruptions on the economy has been the subject of debate, Brazilians at the time were acutely aware of the need to avoid further disruptions.[9] Blockades halted the ability to trade. The annual average value of total imports (measured in pound-sterling and composed primarily of industrially manufactured goods) from 1914 to 1918 was 75 per cent of the five years preceding the war; the value of imports declined by one-half between 1913 and 1914 alone.[10] The inability to provision themselves with imported manufactured goods reinforced Brazilian intentions to diversify the domestic economy.[11] These issues remained at the core of policy motivations.

The increasing importance of the military in political governance (including its crucial role in installing and maintaining Vargas in office) and economic development issues ensured that their opinions carried considerable weight. Frank McCann paints a very stark picture of this relationship: 'The arrangement was straightforward. They [the military] were to give Vargas internal peace and security, and he [Vargas] would get them the arms and modern industries that would support continued military development.'[12] Concerns about provisioning the military joined the interests of the military with the attempts by entrepreneurs to build a capacity in iron and steel manufacture that could ultimately be independent of imported capital goods.

Recentralization of governance and the emergence of strong political ambitions for industrialization ensured the influence of this coalition of interest groups. State participation in these goals was a way to finance economic development, protect against foreign dominance of strategic sectors and enhance the chance of domestic entrepreneurial success.[13] Both the army and industrialists maintained active presences in all of the federal commissions studying iron ore strategy and for reviewing the Itabira Iron Ore contract. Any plan required the army's agreement that their needs for modern materiel would be satisfied.

The experience of business interest groups with influencing government policy was largely rooted in mercantile commerce.[14] Industrial groups began forming during the First Republic.[15] Industrial entrepreneurs participated in many realms of policy formation. For example, as Brazil's first Minister of Labour, Roberto Simonsen (a pre-eminent industrial entrepreneur from São Paulo) laid the framework for the close nexus between state and industry in shaping labour and unionization policies.[16] The active pressure of such entrepreneurs as Alexandre Siciliano and Guillherme Guinle[17] to formulate an iron and steel policy fell squarely within this tradition. Aligning with military interests offered stronger opportunity for success and laid the foundation for a tradition of high-level military presence within strategic enterprises.[18]

Immediately upon assuming executive power, Vargas began constructing the bureaucratic apparatus that would allow the structuring and management of strong economic and industrial policy, thereby redefining and extending the limits of state sovereignty in the economic sphere.[19] As a consequence, a wide range of legal codes and regulatory agencies were instituted. The Mining and Water Codes of 1934 and the National Department of Mining Production (Departamento Nacional de Producção Mineral or DNPM) were the integral components of the approach that connected natural resources with industry and state.

Economic Role of the State

Property rights and industrial policy of the 1920s and early 1930s supported increased iron ore extraction, pig iron and steel production, and capitalization of private sector producers of pig iron and steel. But they proved insufficient to advance the larger industrial ambitions that were central to economic nationalism. In order to address these ambitions, another fundamental institution – the state – came into play.

Returning the subsoil to federal domain and controlling access through individually granted concessions were the first steps to consolidate the federal state's presence in mining. Increased federal activism in mining appeared in the forms of nationality constraints and ever-broadening definitions of national security.[20] The abilities to mandate access to the subsoil attached to privately owned land, to allocate concessions and to coordinate concessions with additional preferences became tools that the national government actively used to promote mineral extraction and to select participants within the sector. Authorization was required for all exploration on private or public domain lands and for companies engaging in mining as one activity within vertically integrated enterprises. Annual reporting of investment, output and operating data for individual veins to the National Department of Mining Production established close oversight of the sector.[21] Expropriation provisions became more expansive, as the definition of national security (the strongest argument for expropriation) expanded to include economic security. Regulations increasingly limited foreign participation in mining.

Control of the iron ore deposits at Itabira was the defining issue for economic nationalism.[22] The first order of business for implementing economic nationalism was to address the Itabira Iron Ore project both because of the political controversy already attached to the effort and because it offered the most immediate prospects for export earnings and steel production. The increasing constraints against foreign ownership in the mining sector through the 1930s addressed concerns about the ability to direct sectoral development of the domestic economy.[23] Some historians have attributed the increasingly tight provisions against foreign participation in mining as a reaction against Farquhar's attempt to control the Itabira ore deposits and targeting them solely for export as a private enterprise.[24]

Review commissions and renegotiations prolonged uncertainty surrounding the Itabira contract. The National Steel Council received the mandate to review and search for alternative organizational arrangements that could provide for both iron ore exports and large-scale integrated-steel production. The Council's review in 1931–2 recognized that, since projected exports from the Itabira deposits accounted for only 4 per cent of total Brazilian iron ore reserves, sufficient alternative sources were available to meet domestic military and industrial needs into the foreseeable future.[25] Unable to resolve the problems of financing, coal supply, plant location or transportation more economically with local ownership than the Itabira project (see Chapter 4), this Council recommended renegotiating the original contract. They proposed denying the railroad and port monopolies, requiring that the company make available its (specifically designed) iron ore freighters to import heavy industrial equipment on return trips, reducing tax preferences and imposing an export tax. They also recommended that the contract require, rather than permit, a steel plant.[26] By allowing for the possibility of meeting their goals through either a foreign-owned steel plant at Itabira or through other arrangements, the military appeared neutral on the question of the nationality of ownership. However, reflecting its broadening role in public policy, the Army Ministry also opined that the contract was 'monstrous' in its allocation of benefits and control of the 'public wealth' to the Itabira Iron Ore Company.[27]

Percival Farquhar, head of the investment group holding Itabira Iron Ore Company options and planning the project, was willing to accommodate many Brazilian concerns through the decade. He reorganized the company to charter the operational components in Brazil, with majority Brazilian ownership, and he was willing to commit to building a steel plant, giving the military priority claims to its output.[28] However, irresolvable disagreement surrounded the physical infrastructure. Farquhar was not willing to relinquish complete ownership rights to the infrastructure, and he was willing to forego any externalities of additional uses for the rail and shipping facilities. In keeping with its attitude that the Itabira project offered significant externalities, the Brazilian government was intent on capturing those generated by the physical infrastructure.

Simultaneously with additional constitutional and Mining Code reform in 1937, the Brazilian government reopened the search for alternatives for developing a modern steel industry separately from its iron ore ambitions.[29] Industrial and political factions began debating the merits of an SOE to ensure politically crucial steel production by the mid-1930s. Iron ore exports remained an integral strategic component, with the intention that its hard-currency revenue would provide financing. Private Brazilian investors were not able to raise the capital or incur the debt needed for the size and risk incumbent on enterprises of sufficient scale to transform the economy.[30] Alternative proposals for the joint development of industrialized iron ore mining and steel manufacture, reviewed by the Technical Council of Economy and Finance in 1938, again failed to offer viable solutions to the organization and financing problems without either significant federal involvement or foreign capital. However, foreign borrowing (as opposed to capital investment) was not an option because the Treasury had suspended payment on existing international debt.[31] One of the alternative plans advocated for outright expropriation of all iron ore veins.[32] In the end the commission again found the Itabira Iron Ore project more economically efficient than the alternatives.[33] Expressions of the military's industrial interests strengthened in 1938. The government insisted on linking the construction of a steel plant at Itabira to the shipbuilding demands of the Navy.[34] In the 1938 review of the Itabira contract, the army once again explicitly endorsed the development of large-scale iron ore exports as the means to finance the steel industry.[35]

Prominent Brazilian industrialists took an increasingly active role in pressing for domestic steel production to supply their needs, and were willing to work with the Vargas regime to develop mixed public-private schemes toward this end. Guillerme Guinle (who later became the first president of the national steel company), Henrique Lage and Alexandre Siciliano, among the most prominent industrialists in Rio de Janeiro and São Paulo, were the most active proponents to suggest alternative solutions to the Brazilian 'steel problem'.[36] Although their plans differed with respect to the preferential protection they might require, the location of facilities and organizational dynamics, all of the alternatives prominently featured substantial financial assistance from the national Treasury. Nothing suggests that either ambitious industrialists in other sectors or small-scale steel producers already operating in Brazil believed that they could undertake the expansion of steel production on a scale sufficient to meet national aspirations without significant government participation for capital and technological-organizational support. Further, Guinle formulated his concerns about the iron ore project in terms that resonated with economic nationalism, extending well beyond entrepreneurial concerns. He complained that if ore exports as well as port and railway facilities were to become the domain of the Itabira Iron Ore Company, then:

> nothing would be left for the Brazilian economy other than manual labor and a small tax revenue ... a representing a small percentage of the enormous commercial value of this desirous export ...
>
> And thus is the particular character of extractive industry when exercised by foreign individual or enterprises who are owners of mines. It turns, from a national point of view, into an industry in which everything leaves the country and almost nothing remains commercially.

So, knowing that the richest Brazilian ore deposits are in the possession of foreign enterprises, would it be suitable to the national interest to disregard the disposition of this export?

Evidently not.[37]

In 1939, Vargas adopted the logic of this argument, ignored the findings of the previous reviews and revoked the Itabira Iron Ore Company contract. Instead, the state committed to direct involvement in industrial development.[38] The revocation, combined with the strengthened Mining Code of 1937, constraining foreign access to the subsoil and tightly regulating authorizations to concessions, rendered the probability of privately owned large-scale iron ore mining very unlikely. Accepting the inevitability of state participation, another special commission recommended that the export of iron ore and manganese be the monopoly privilege of the state, that concessionary mining was against the public interest, and that state-supported steel enterprise would give preferential accessibility to the military. They further recommended the formation of a Metallurgy Institute to regulate both iron ore mining and steel production.[39] Pursuing an avenue to separate the iron ore and steel production projects, the national Ministry of Infrastructure attempted to entice the US Steel Corporation, in association with US Export-Import Bank loans and technical assistance, into an arrangement to develop an integrated steel plant in Brazil.[40] At this time, Treasury officials also began to explore the possibility of issuing foreign debt, but not accepting foreign equity, as a stratagem for funding the endeavours.[41] Initial negotiations with US Steel for technical assistance fell apart with the beginning of World War II.[42]

World War II

None of these developments required that the state become a major industrial entrepreneur. The outbreak of World War II provided the Brazilian government with a windfall opportunity. British demand for wartime equipment increased its need for iron ore simultaneously with serious shortages resulting from the shutdown of its traditional peacetime supplies from Sweden.[43] Further, the war-diplomacy goals of the Allies sought to limit German presence in the Brazilian economy[44] and to strengthen allegiances in the western hemisphere. These circumstances created new international economic dynamics for Brazil.[45] At the same time, the war reinforced earlier concerns about trade disruptions impeding the supply of capital goods within Brazil.

Allied interest in Brazilian resources offered the possibility of separating the steel production and iron ore export ambitions of the Vargas regime. In 1941, technical assistance and financing ($20 million) from the US Export-Import Bank enabled the Companhia Siderúrgica Nacional to organize and build a large integrated steel plant. The agreement permitted the US military to build a base in the north-east of Brazil in support of war operations in northern Africa.[46] The CSN plant was to be located in Volta Redonda (within the state of Rio de Janeiro) and it would rely on imported coal. The Volta Redonda project established the precedent for similar technical assistance and Export-Import Bank loans (initially $14 million) for a state-owned iron ore mining company at the Itabira mines in 1942, the Companhia Vale do Rio Doce.

The Washington Accords of March 1942 between the governments of the US, Great Britain and Brazil[47] tackled the war-related iron ore supply problems simultaneously with Brazilians's continued desire to export ore. The British government bought the shares of the Itabira Iron Ore Company and transferred them to the Brazilian government.[48] The Export-Import Bank loan and technical assistance ensured the upgrading of mining, railway and port facilities, and provided commitments for coal imports from the US.[49] The agreement committed the Allies to purchase 750,000 tons of Itabira ore annually, for three years, and provided for production plans for 1.5 million tons per year of ore (more than three times the volume of production nationally at the end of the 1930s; Appendix Table A.10).[50] Given the difficulties of private Brazilian ownership, the formation of a privately owned enterprise was not considered.

The transfer of Itabira stock had important implications in Brazil beyond the implicit subsidy of the value of the equity shares in the capitalization of Vale.[51] In order to comply with its commitments in the Washington Accords, the British government expropriated property from its citizens in order to transfer it to Brazilian ownership. For the British government to transfer the shares of the Itabira Iron Ore Company to private Brazilian owners, even for crucial war-related purposes, would have defied legal practices. Even without the serious complication of nationality, expropriating private commercial property for the purpose of transferring it to a different private commercial enterprise is not a practice that falls easily within standard legal parameters for expropriation. This transaction may have ensured that a majority share of the company would remain with the state.

Two important characteristics differentiated the organization of Vale and the enterprise that Farquhar had proposed for eighteen years: state ownership and the elimination of the ties between iron ore and steel production strategies.[52] With the establishment of Vale, both control and ownership of the largest contiguous reserves of Brazil's most important mineral resource in the middle of the twentieth century resided firmly with the sovereign state. Ownership of these enterprises qualitatively transformed the role of the state in the Brazilian economy, firmly establishing state participation within the system of production. In earlier decades, SOEs facilitated the organization of railroads and other physical infrastructure and extended to banking.[53] In 1942, the state, through Vale and CSN, became the largest industrial entrepreneur in Brazil.

Production and Exports with State-Owned Enterprise

Although the level of output is not a relevant measure in assessing the change in subsoil rights (see Chapter 4) it is useful for considering the impact of SOE. As early as 1945, the US Department of Commerce judged Brazil's iron ore project as a success[54] and its trajectory was set. Early growth was rapid; after beginning operations at the Cauê mine in Itabira, Vale expanded in 1954, when it opened the adjacent mine of Conceição. Adapting to important changes of political regime and policies, state-owned iron ore production and export remained a priority for the Brazilian industrial sector for the remainder of the twentieth century.[55]

From 1934, with the renationalization of the subsoil and codification of mining regulation, until 1997, when Vale was privatized, the growth of total production of iron ore, pig iron and crude steel by all Brazilian producers was exponential: averaging 9.7 per cent per year for both pig iron and crude steel; for iron ore the average annual growth rate was 18.1 per cent from 1934 to 1990 (subject to data availability considerations). From 1942, total production grew at rates of 13.0 per cent, 9.7 per cent and 10.0 per cent per year for iron ore (through 1990) pig iron and crude steel (both, through 1997), respectively (see Figure 5.1; the Data Appendix discusses the underlying data).[56] The diminished growth rate for iron ore using the later base year suggests that substantive impetus to industrializing iron ore successfully occurred during the period between the privatization of subsoil rights and full production at Vale. Nevertheless, growth at 13 per cent per year resulted in a 250-fold increase in iron ore production between 1946 and 1990. By 1973, 8 per cent of global iron ore production took place in Brazil. (see Figure 5.2; the increase to 12 per cent in 1974, which continued to a maximum of 21 per cent in 1985, reflected the successful operation of the Carajás reserves, an even larger deposit of iron ore discovered in the Amazonian state of Pará in the late 1960s).[57]

The growth of iron ore production exceeded the production of pig iron and crude steel, reflecting the dual purposes that ore served: generating export revenues and down-streaming to pig iron and crude steel. The emphasis on iron ore also became very evident in Brazilian export trends.

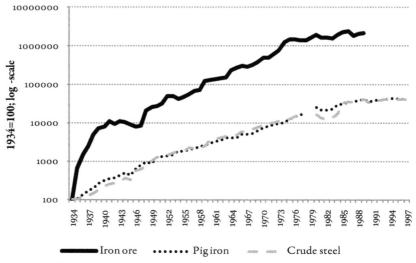

Figure 5.1: Production in Brazil, 1934–97; 1934=100 (log scale).[58]

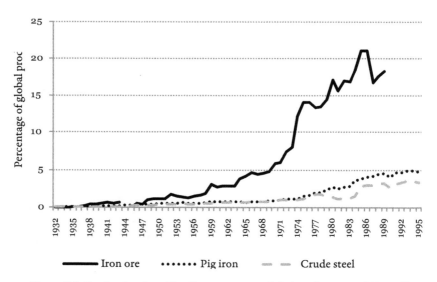

Figure 5.2: Production from Brazil as percentage global production, 1932–97.[59]

In 1967 (the first year that the United Nations reported aggregate trade value) Brazil accounted for 6.7 per cent of global iron ore exports, increasing to about 30 per cent by the time of Vale's privatization in 1997 (see Figure 5.3). Brazil became the world's largest exporter in 1979. In its early years, Vale remained committed to exporting iron ore; for twenty of the forty-three years for which consistent data are available (1947–90) the company exported at least 95 per cent of the enterprise's ore production (see Figure 5.6).[60] In keeping with the original strategy of import-substituting industrialization, pig iron exports did not begin until 1962 and the company did not sell its ore into the domestic market until 1968. Because of the rapid rate of growth generated during the initial years of export (beginning from zero) pig iron exports increased at the rate of 18 per cent per year from then until 1997. Nevertheless, both the share of the world's trade in pig iron and the share of domestic production exported have remained significantly lower than, and uncorrelated with, the rates experienced by iron ore (see Figure 5.4).[61]

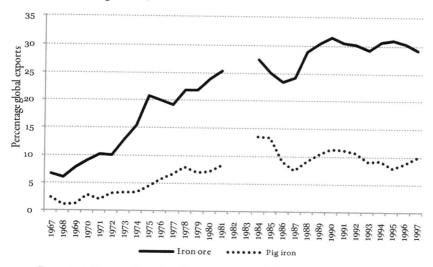

Figure 5.3: **Exports from Brazil as percentage of global exports, 1967–97.**[62]

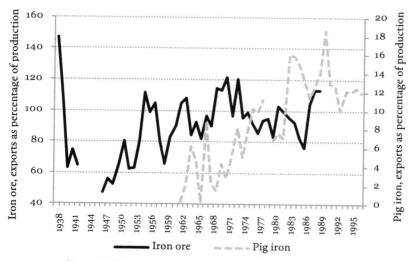

Figure 5.4: **Exports as percentage of production, 1938–97.**[63]

The Vargas regime did not begin with a commitment to bring industry into the public sector,[64] and the Companhia Vale do Rio Doce was not a monopoly. Nevertheless, the company overshadowed, without eliminating, private sector production. A large, centrally controlled and vertically integrated enterprise emerged simultaneously with relatively small firms in the private sector. Other firms in Brazil mined iron ore during the 1920s and 1930s, largely for the purpose of commercially producing their own steel, and this practice continued.[65] Within Minas Gerais, some of these companies included such early entrants as Belgo-Mineira, Usinas Queiroz Júnior, and the St. John d'el Rey Mining Company, as well as smaller operators such as A. Thun and J. A. Abdo. CSN also mined its own ore. Nevertheless, Vale quickly dominated iron ore mining and exports (see Figure 5.5). Although its dominance never disappeared, Vale's market share for both ore and pig iron diminished as other firms entered production. Achieving the goals for iron ore proved easier than for steel.[66] Vale maintained its commitment to mining ore solely for export for more than twenty years (see Figure 5.6); domestic sales did not begin until 1968. With time, the company evolved into a complex web of subsidiaries that participated in some of Brazil's most wide-ranging mining (iron ore and other minerals) and transportation infrastructure projects.

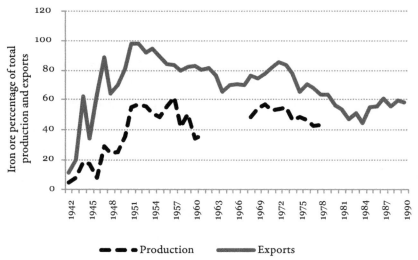

Figure 5.5: Companhia Vale do Rio Doce, as percentage of total Brazilian iron ore exports and production, 1942–78.[67]

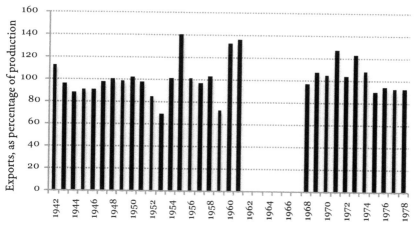

■ Vale, iron ore exports as percentage of production

Figure 5.6: Companhia Vale do Rio Doce, iron ore exports, as percentage of production.[68]

Financial Institutions

Establishing a large SOE in basic industry had a strong impact beyond the levels of production and exports, as opponents to foreign ownership had insisted would be the case. The railways and ports built in conjunction with Vale and CSN production facilities were available for use by other developing industrial companies. Infrastructure was always an important component of the company's operations and investments, accounting for 67 per cent of total assets in 1955, declining to 15 per cent in 1963.[69] The new state enterprises offered demonstration effects from their subsidized imported technologies. These externalities were among those that the Vargas regime anticipated. In the early years, the beneficial externalities also extended to important financial institutions.

US Export-Import Bank financing of the iron ore and steel manufacturing projects separately rendered moot the argument that externalities of the iron ore enterprise would underpin large-scale integrated steel.[70] However, in the face of the windfall available to Brazilian iron ore ambitions, capital flows from the loans, technical assistance and the acquisition of Itabira iron ore fields, the state captured and redirected wide-ranging financial opportunity as well as the externalities associated with industrial production and the expansion of railway, port and freight infrastructure. Many of the financial institutions that came to bear on the formation of Vale and CSN combined important features of both public and private enterprise. Externalities for capital-market development quickly became evident. The results often differed from those predicted by financial theory.

Capitalizing Industrial Iron Ore

Substantial foreign credit and technical assistance became available for the industrialization of mining through the US Export-Import Bank. The original $14 million loan from the bank, equated to about 137 per cent of the original equity (Cr$200 million, or approximately US$10.2 million).[71] The new firm could represent itself as being fully 'Brazilian', even as the value of the long-term foreign loan exceeded the equity invested in the new company.

The Export-Import Bank loans that provided long-term credit for Vale and CSN incurred sovereign, rather than private, risk. After the first loan to Vale of US$14 million in 1942, additional loans from 1943 to 1954 brought their total principle value to US$27.4 million.[72] Beyond the conditions attached to the loans,[73] the Brazilian state committed its future international financial reputation to the project. Financial literature identifies the state's creditworthiness, with its increased capacity to capture revenue and to realize lower interest rates in capital markets, as one reason for organizing state enterprise.[74] In an inversion of normal experience, these loans helped to recreate, rather than risk, the future reputation of the Brazilian government in international capital markets. Brazil was in arrears and/or suspension of its international debt servicing obligations from 1932 until rescheduling in 1944; the sovereign state had no international creditworthiness to apply to the loans.[75] Exogenous events leading to the diplomatic accords, as well as tight conditionality, made the loans possible.

Export-Import Bank financing presented Brazilians with the opportunity to obtain technical assistance and substantial foreign credit at a favourable cost, while maintaining domestic ownership. The terms of the Vale loan strongly subsidized the costs of forming the company. The loan's interest rate, 4 per cent, was significantly lower than the cost of the restructured sovereign debt from 1945 until 1957 (see Figure 5.7). The notional value of the benefit conferred by the low interest rate can be assessed by two counterfactual alternatives: Vale either would have had to increase its earnings to meet additional interest requirements or the company could have increased its borrowings by the accumulated compounded value of the interest rate subsidy. The benefit of the interest rate subsidy from 1942 until 1945 cannot be calculated. The debt payment suspension meant that the special circumstances of the loan gave Brazil access to credit, rather than lowering the price of borrowing. (Strictly, the benefit for the first four years was infinite.) Nevertheless, in 1945, the first year after the debt rescheduling, the interest rate differential applied to the principle amount of the Export-Import Bank loans represented 28 per cent of Vale's gross revenues in that year, or alternatively, 4 per cent of the company's net liabilities.[76] From the debt rescheduling until the interest rate differential between Vale and Brazilian debt turned negative in January 1957, the interest rate differential declined with improvement in the perceived creditworthiness of Brazil, but still accounted for 4 per cent of the company's accumulated gross revenue. Although the interest rate subsidy associated with Export-Import Bank financing was not a determining factor in either the availability of the loan or the negotiation of its terms, it contributed a significant benefit to Vale during its early years when incurring operating losses (Appendix Tables A.7 and A.7B summarize Vale financial statements).

Figure 5.7: Cost of borrowing sovereign and Companhia Vale do Rio Doce. [77]

Capital Markets

Vale was organized as a limited-liability joint-stock company, and was not fully state-owned. The Brazilian Treasury held 56 per cent of the company's original equity; public-sector agencies (small-account savings banks) held 16 per cent, and 29 per cent of the equity remained in the hands of the private sector (see Table 5.1).[78] The state's share of equity increased to 65 per cent with a capital increase in 1944, and to 85 per cent in 1948.[79] Increased long-term debt of US$5 million from the Export-Import Bank (bringing its loans to 124 per cent of equity) in 1945 and Cr$300 million in domestic bond markets, issued from 1944 to 1946, demonstrated the state's ability to leverage its investment in Vale. With further gradual transfers, the state ownership reached approximately 95 per cent by the end of the 1950s. The small portion of Vale equity held by the private sector is a feature seldom recognized by analysts.

Table 5.1: Companhia Vale do Rio Doce; distribution of statutory capital.[80]

	Statutory capital (Cr$ millions)					
	Initial	Increase		Total capital		
	1942	1943	1948	1943	1948	1964
Brazilian treasury	110	83.7	350	193.7	543.7	33,219.6
Public sector agencies	32.8	3	0	35.8	35.8	21,49.14
Privately held	57.2	13.3	0	70.5	70.5	3,631.3
Total	200	100	350	300	650	39,000.04
	Percentage distribution (%)					
	Initial	Increase		Total capital		
	1942	1943	1948	1943	1948	1964
Brazilian treasury	55.0	83.7	100.0	64.6	83.6	85.2
Public sector agencies	16.4	3.0	0.0	11.9	5.5	5.5
Privately held	28.6	13.3	0.0	23.5	10.8	9.3
Total	100.0	100.0	100.0	100.0	100.0	100.0
Total capital (Cr$, mln)	200.0	100.0	350.0	300.0	650.0	39,000.0

The Rio de Janeiro and São Paulo stock exchanges listed and traded the company's equity shares.[81] The purpose of public listing was not to accumulate capital from, and share the gains among investors, as financial historians would typically hypothesize. The decreasing minority proportion of the company available to public investors and the division of the original equity into shares with a par value of Cr$1,000 signalled that small investors were not invited to participate in the company.[82] Allowing for the transfer of equity on the exchange was a side effect of the organizational form.

If accumulating capital from a wide range of investors was not its goal, why did Vale organize as a publicly traded joint-stock corporation? Doing so enabled Vale to issue bonds on the Brazilian financial exchanges. From 1944 through 1946, Vale issued bonds in three tranches, for a value of Cr$300 million. This operation doubled the long-term financing of the company without diluting equity control. Further, as a joint-stock company, Vale committed to meet the requirements of the Brazilian Commercial Code. These requirements included publishing audited financial statements and annual reports, holding annual shareholders' meetings, making routine public filings with the *Bolsas de Valores* (the stock exchanges) and its regulatory bodies.[83] Anyone with access to a newspaper could follow the evolving market value of the company, by keeping track of both share prices and (unexecuted) quotes for Vale shares. Making its financial statements available to public scrutiny committed Vale to the same criteria of accountability and transparency that applied to private corporations who competed for capital in the open market.[84] Finally, incorporation as a joint-stock firm preserved important options for the enterprise. One obvious benefit of a joint-stock company was that the government preserved the ability to privatize Vale easily. The Treasury could simply sell the equity shares that it held. Vale did, in fact, foster such expectations long before privatization actually occurred in 1997.[85]

Although its corporate organization conformed to private market structures, Vale was established explicitly as a 'dependency of the Brazilian government, interested not in profit goals, but primarily in developing ... Brazil's natural resources, ultimately, to better attend to the interests of the country and of other American republics.'[86] The small amount of capital in private hands and the reduced trading population resulting from the large share size relieved the firm of the profit-maximizing pressures that market-oriented firms faced. Vale did not report a profitable year until 1950, according to their financial statements (Appendix Tables A.7A and A.7B). The company did not reach its original export plans of 1.5 million tons of iron ore until 1951, six years behind target. Using one of the most accepted measures of financial strength, when equity exchanges actually occurred, share prices declined from about 95 per cent of book value in its first trades (during 1943) to below 50 per cent of the statutory book value in 1950 (see Figure 5.8).[87] Price quotations by market-making brokers for the company's shares, in the years sampled, did not surpass Cr$700, or 70 per cent of statutory par value, before the end of 1955 (see Figure 5.9).[88] One of the state's important subsidies to large-scale iron ore mining was to relieve the company of shareholders clamouring for profitability and dividends while maintaining losses in its early years. The persistently low market/book price ratios (actual and quoted) of Vale and CSN, relative to other metallurgy enterprises, support the assertion that these enterprises had developmental goals as their primary consideration, rather than profit maximization.

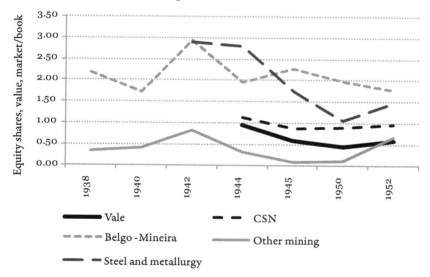

Figure 5.8: Average market-to-book values of shares traded (selected years 1938–52). [89]

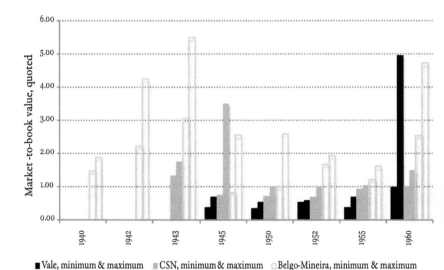

■ Vale, minimum & maximum ▨ CSN, minimum & maximum ▢ Belgo-Mineira, minimum & maximum

Figure 5.9: Major mining and metallurgy companies' range of quoted market-to-book ratios on Rio de Janeiro Bolsa (selected years).[90]

A related, untested, hypothesis is that low but actively quoted share prices lent credibility to public capital markets at the same time that they indicated the ability of the new firms to forego immediate gains in the price of equity shares. Financial agents were quick to use the presence of both CSN and Vale on the public securities exchanges for important developmental purposes. Private equity markets had emerged slowly and unsteadily through the second half of the nineteenth and first half of the twentieth centuries. The dynamic willingness to 'make a market' in the shares of the earliest SOEs (Vale and CSN) contributed significantly to establishing private sector financial markets in Brazil.

When first listed on the Rio de Janeiro stock exchange, Vale and CSN (in 1943 and 1942, respectively) had the highest levels of statutory capital on the exchange.[91] Their presence occurred simultaneously with a significant upsurge in both the number of mining and metallurgy companies listed on the exchange and their total statutory value (see Figure 5.10). Because the actual trading of equity shares (the secondary market) remained quite limited, data on brokers' price quotes (for which they would be willing to engage in an exchange) adds important information to the impact of Vale and CSN on the equities market. Mining and metallurgy companies became among the most actively quoted industrial firms on the bolsa (see Table 5.2).[92] A third metallurgy company, Companhia Siderúrgica Belgo-Mineira, was also heavily quoted (and traded) from 1938.[93] The actual equity price quotations demonstrate that mining and metallurgy companies experienced a sharp upsurge in quotes with the appearance of Vale and CSN. Further, on days when brokers issued price quotations for mining and metallurgy companies, firms in this sector accounted for 34 per cent to 55 per cent of the companies quoted, peaking in 1942 and 1943 (when Vale and CSN appeared). The company that led in the volume of share trading and quotations was Belgo-Mineira, rather than the SOEs. Both the number of days that traders quoted prices for Belgo-Mineira and the firm's quoted (though not actually executed) ratio of market-to-book price increased significantly during 1942 and 1943, when the state enterprises were organizing. Data are not available to test the causal relation between market-making for these two companies and a general increase in financial market activities. Nevertheless, the parallel timing, their dominant presence on the exchange and the very rapid increase in the number of smaller privately owned mining and metallurgy companies helps to support the earlier claims about externalities of industrial entrepreneurs, the military and Getúlio Vargas.

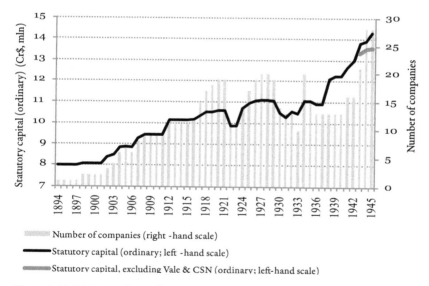

Number of companies (right-hand scale)

Statutory capital (ordinary; left-hand scale)

Statutory capital, excluding Vale & CSN (ordinary; left-hand scale)

Figure 5.10: Mining and metallurgy companies on Rio de Janeiro Bolsa, 1894–1945.[94]

Table 5.2: Price quoting of mining and metallurgy companies on Rio de Janeiro Bolsa de Valores (selected years, 1930–60).[95]

| | Mining and metallurgy companies quoted | | Number of industrial companies quoted | |
	# of days quoted	% companies, mining and metalurgy	minimum	maximum
1930	0			
1931	2	30.6	2	9
1934	12	34.0	2	6
1940	145	44.4	1	7
1942	246	54.7	1	9
1943	275	52.8	1	15
1945	270	45.5	1	13
1950	210	34.3	1	17
1952	216	28.0	3	17
1955	234	27.8	3	18
1960	222	33.6	5	43

For later periods, the 1960s and 1970s, analysts have concluded that the predominant role of SOEs hampered, rather than furthered, capital-market development. The reasoning for this hypothesis is that as relatively low risk firms, they crowded out other investments (see Chapter 7).[96] No systematic testing of any hypotheses on the subject has been undertaken for the 1940s and 1950s.

Money

The Brazilian Treasury looked to Vale as a source of hard-currency export earnings; the firm ultimately became successful in that regard. Beyond generating hard currency,[97] additional gains derived from the combination of Vale's export orientation and monetary controls. In 1945, as Vale began significant ore exportation, the monetary authority (Superintendência da Moeda e do Crédito, or SUMOC) introduced a policy of managing foreign exchange.[98] From then, the Brazilian *cruzeiro* was persistently over-valued. In consequence, a black market for hard currency developed immediately. Exporters earned their revenues in international markets and incurred expenses (mostly) domestically.[99] Translating earnings into domestic currency, at an artificially high rate, resulted in lower local-currency-denominated earnings. Dutra Fonseca identifies iron ore and petroleum as the products at the core of the Vargas currency management strategy.[100] The mechanisms of exchange control varied over time, and became quite complex. From 1953 through 1957, SUMOC and the Banco do Brasil instituted a regime of multiple exchange rates, with as many as a dozen rates being in effect at any given time. Administering multiple exchange rates was a tool to offer price relief on the importation of capital equipment that could jumpstart industrialization, while preserving the Treasury's gain from the company's undervaluation of export earnings.

Vale did not receive consideration in monetary policy that distinguished the company from others. However, as one of the largest Brazilian exporters, Vale hard-currency revenues were important to the national Treasury.[101] As a notional approximation, the annual scope of this benefit between 1945 and 1964 reached maxima of about 180 per cent of the company's revenues in 1963 and 5 per cent of the money supply (M^2) increase in 1952.[102] Exchange controls, untied to a fiduciary commitment to maintain the hard-currency value of domestic currency (as demonstrated by the sustained presence of a black market for currency), emerged in the middle and late twentieth century as a tool that the state increasingly used to generate financial resources. The exchange controls constituted an 'inflation tax' imposed on the Brazilian population. For Vale, the controls generated foregone earnings (as reported in local currency terms) that escaped accountability.

The full impact of Vale on financial institutions was unexpectedly profound. Pulling together the pieces needed to develop iron ore exports could not have succeeded without the national government as the majority equity partner. The state became comfortable with owning large commercial enterprises. Subsequent capital increases were fully subscribed by the federal treasury. The interest-rate subsidy on the company's initial loans further aided its formation. The presence of these companies on the securities exchanges seems to have underpinned the securities markets for other mining and metallurgy companies. The experience with extracting immediate gain from exchange rate controls provided powerful demonstration effects for future policy.

Conclusion

Percival Farquhar and his adversaries were both right. The iron ore enterprise, and its attendant transportation activities, held the opportunity to unleash vast economic forces in Brazil. Focused on harvesting that opportunity to accommodate a specific vision of industrialization and economic modernity, industrialists and the military found a willing ally in the Vargas regime for controlling mineral development.

State entrepreneurship in the service of industrialization occurred almost two decades before the formal articulation of structuralist (or dependency) economic perspectives and policies predominated throughout Latin America.[103] Nevertheless, it clearly anticipated the ideologies and goals of import-substituting industrialization policies that took strong shape during the 1950s and 1960s. In the cases of iron mining and steel manufacturing, state economic activity did not displace domestic privately owned industry. Rather, a broad range of interest groups and public opinion were determined to keep this sector within the domestic sphere, and to displace foreign entrepreneurs while transforming its scale. Brazilian industrialists looked to the state to support their efforts. The SOE became a substitute for foreign business interests, when private domestic capital, technology and organization could not meet the needs. The insistence on domestically owned strategic enterprise and the concept of 'economic nationalism' did not represent withdrawal from the global economic arena. Rather, they redefined the terms of participation.

Ultimately, the establishment of industrial-scale iron ore mining responded to the confluence of three important factors: subsoil rights in the public domain and controlled at the national level, the windfall gain offered by World War II, and the state's willingness to become an industrial producer. In this regard, World War II was an exogenous shock that the government manipulated skilfully. Mining rights and the entrepreneurial role of the state required significant changes in fundamental economic governance during the 1930s and 1940s. These changes drew heavily on deeply rooted precedents in property rights and centralized governance from the colonial and imperial periods of Brazilian history. Further, they did so without challenging deeply embedded institutions that governed the control of property in other activities. Institutional practices of state capitalism emerged to reconcile a complex set of goals.

The path of exogenous historical events brought all of these factors together and led to the formation of state-owned iron ore mining and steel behemoths the Companhia Vale do Rio Doce and Companhia Siderúrgica Nacional. Both firms could represent themselves as being fully 'Brazilian', even as the value of the long-term foreign loans exceeded the equity invested in the new companies. Domestic ownership may have been an attractive political outcome for the steel company, but it was not a legal condition of its existence, as the Mining Code made increasingly likely for the iron ore mining enterprise. Vale and CSN transformed the state into the entrepreneur behind the two largest companies in Brazil. This experience qualitatively changed the scale and nature of the state's role in the economy.

Brazilian industrialists and the military constituted powerful interest groups, and they kept the state focused on important externalities of iron and steel that were not captured by private entrepreneurs. A large-scale and technologically sophisticated integrated steel plant supplied new downstream industries with a necessary input. It also contributed to developing industrial labour skills and organization. Iron ore mining for export, also on a large scale, provided similar demonstration effects in industrial organization and labour skills.[104] More importantly, export earnings from iron ore subsidized industrial development through the effects of capital markets and monetary mechanisms. The mining project further offered important benefits from the externalities generated by physical and financial infrastructure. In short, the Brazilian state, military and industrial sector met their long-term goals.

State ownership offered crucial advantages through protections and subsidies offered to Vale (and CSN) with respect to capitalization as well as railway and port development. Policy makers and entrepreneurs anticipated the transport externalities more clearly than those of financial institutions. Organizing the firms as limited-liability joint-stock companies, in which the state was the majority shareholder, inextricably tied public and private interests.

The Vargas regime viewed iron mining and steel production as basic infrastructure, offering benefits that extended beyond those that producers could capture, and requiring financial resources beyond their command. However, separating the effort to develop industrial-scale iron ore mining from steel production dramatically changed the justification for the iron ore project. Rather than applying the externalities directly to steel manufacture, they reached wider targets by providing hard currency, transportation infrastructure and demonstration effects for overcoming coordination problems. The major impediment to the superordinate goal of developing a large and independent capital goods sector was the need to organize and finance a large technologically sophisticated capital-intensive company; exogenous circumstances provided a solution to this problem.

Subsequently (and beyond the scope of this research) a vibrant iron and steel sector developed within Brazil. The oldest firms from Minas Gerais, such as Belgo-Mineira and Queiroz Júnior, were among the most successful. Because of its rich availability, steel producers generally mined their own iron ore. They also took advantage of the same import-substituting policies that benefited Vale and CSN, at the same time that they received impetus from the enhanced infrastructure network, skilled labour and technological-organizational expertise that the state-owned firms contributed. In the shorter term, this experience moved the state into production and commerce on a scale much larger than prior public or private endeavours, setting a precedent for further economic participation.

PART III: UNDERSTANDING BRAZILIAN INSTITUTIONS AND MINERALS

6 MINERALS AND THE FORMATION OF ECONOMIC IDEOLOGY

Minerals offer an unusually clear venue for understanding the history and application of economic ideas in Brazil. This chapter demonstrates the path dependency of economic ideas and the importance of ideology for conditioning economic governance within Brazil by focusing on the long course of often competing debates about import-substituting industrialization, export promotion and foreign economic involvement. The strong hold of structuralist theories during the middle of the twentieth century; the role of foreign individuals, capital and technology; the divide between public and private sectors in the economic sphere and the emergence of the state as an industrial entrepreneur have been prevailing themes in Brazilian debates about governance and ideology. As we have seen in Chapters 3 to 5, they have also been the themes that dominated the institutional conflicts in developing industrialized iron ore capacity for three centuries.

The emergence of structuralism and of economic nationalism examined in this chapter makes three important points. First, the debates and developmental efforts of the second half of the twentieth century were not new; they have roots in ideologies articulated as early as the colonial era. Secondly, competing (and evolving) definitions of property were central to the formulation of the economic role of the Brazilian state in the twentieth century. Thirdly, the abstract ideas of economic ideologies were important factors that shaped the manner in which industrialized mining emerged within Brazil.

Beyond the exigencies of actual production, and separately from the legal/regulatory choices with respect to subsoil property rights, the entry of the state into productive sectors of the Brazilian economy in the middle of the twentieth century was an important outcome of a very long debate about the appropriate economic role for the state. Two cornerstones of this debate were the sustained history of underachievement (or 'backwardness' and 'falling behind' in the language of economic historians[1]) in material well-being for Brazilians, and the role of foreigners within the domestic economy. In the eyes of many, these conditions were related to each other through the mechanisms of resource extraction by outsiders, whether imperial marauders, would-be robber barons or monolithic multinational corporations.

Economic Ideology and Minerals

The most important economic ideologies to gain political representation through the nineteenth and twentieth centuries were liberalism, positivism and structuralism. Although these bodies of ideas had European origins, their selective transmission to Brazil responded to local needs and interests. Structuralism is the field in which Brazilians had made their strongest contribution to the global history of economic thought. At the end of the twentieth century, Brazil became one of the emerging economies to adopt neo-liberal globalism most strongly (this is beyond the scope of this study, but briefly surveyed in Chapter 7). The economic position of minerals required distinct attention under each of these political-economy regimes.

Liberalism

While the Portuguese Court resided in colonial Brazil and immediately after independence in 1822, many of the advisors and administrators in the colony were among the most responsible for introducing liberal economic ideas into Portuguese governing circles, for the purpose of transforming a mercantile economy into an industrializing one. These advisors, including José Bonifácio de Andrada e Silva and Rodrigo José de Menezes, were both prominent in introducing liberalism to Brazil and intimately involved in the projects to mine iron ore and construct forges at the beginning of the nineteenth century. Both were well educated in mining issues and political philosophy. Andrada was a mining engineer and had undertaken projects to understand the emerging industrial affluence of north-western Europe. These administrators shaped their interpretations of liberalism to accommodate the interests and positions of their circumstances and their peers. Definitions of citizenship (claimants to the rights and privileges of liberal society) remained constrained and the sanctity of property (including slaves) trumped many other liberal principles. Constitutional boundaries introduced with independence may have constrained monarchical government, but monarchy and hierarchically organized society continued to prevail.[2]

Anticipating concerns that re-emerged in the twentieth century, the transfer of the Crown to Rio de Janeiro emphasized the vulnerabilities of relying on overseas supplies for basic capital goods. Following classical liberal economic principles, state intervention to aid iron ore mining and forging into tools, machinery and weapons fell within the parameters of infrastructure and national security, collective goods appropriate for state provision. The official response was a set of policies that resembled later measures promoting import-substituting industrialization within activities that supported private wealth creation in export agriculture and precious metals.

Investment in local production capacity coexisted with a reliance on easily recognized comparative advantages in the export of primary commodities (primarily sugar and gold, at the turn of the nineteenth century), similar to the dual strategy that prevailed in the middle of the twentieth century. In accord with Brazilian concepts of liberalism, foreign capital and technology were actively sought to remedy bottlenecks, and the state's role extended to policies that supported development and provided for its own material needs. These policies included increased state economic activity and incentives in favour of iron ore mining and forging. The policies did not achieve their ambitious goals. After independence, and for most of the remainder of the nineteenth century, mining remained outside of the concerns of the state. The major government policies affecting mining included tax exemptions and universally available subsidies for railway construction. The concerns of the early nineteenth century re-emerged with the transition of economic interest from precious to industrial metals and the attempt to introduce industrial practices.

Positivism

The mining-rights debates during the First Republic uneasily juggled liberal ideas with the precepts of the newly influential positivism. The ideology (or religion, as its Brazilian adherents fashioned it) of positivism prioritized positive, empirically verifiable scientific knowledge as the basis for organizing all material, social and cultural aspects of society.[3] In its Latin American interpretation, positivism asserted that a modern, wealthy economy would emerge through 'order and progress'.[4] While different interests and individuals may have advocated varying policies in specific instances, their common underlying principle was to allocate to the state (at either the national or local level) the role of organizing society and economy in the service of producing progress, order and modernity. The social role of the individual was to participate in this larger project. Positivism, as a social and developmental ideology, coexisted, often inconsistently, with continued expressions of liberalism during the First Republic. Attempts to maintain aspects of open liberal economic policy persisted, especially in the realms of money, banking and capital flows, even if they were severely compromised.[5]

Positivists argued for constraining the property rights of individuals in preference to the public well-being. For example, Pedro Calmon, a prominent jurist and legislator, advocated for the effective use of economic assets as a legitimate selection criterion in their allocation that could trump ownership.[6] In 1892, another jurist and legislator, Américo Werneck called for protection for domestic manufacturing, in the forms of credit, exchange rate and infrastructure policies.[7] Werneck and Calmon explicitly considered mineral exploration as a public good that could justify expropriation. Innocencio Corrêa Serzedello, the economic writer and legislator, argued in 1903 against the traditional division between 'natural' and 'artificial' industries (those that did and did not, respectively, benefit from comparative advantage) in order to expand the range of activities to which protectionism applied.[8]

Positivism gained its strongest foothold in the military. After a disastrous showing in the War of the Triple Alliance (1864–70) foreign training introduced engineering and organizational concepts into the military, accompanied by European positivist belief structures that reinforced traditional hierarchies. Engineering, education and other 'modern' professions (such as accounting, management and public health) addressed important needs in the military at the same time that they offered the tools of economic modernization. The ideology served as a platform propelling the military into civilian and political realms.[9] By 1930, the military was the strongest institution of national scope in Brazil and assumed an increasing role in the political system, in pursuit of political stability and the imposition of order.[10] Military support of the coup that brought Getúlio Vargas to power left him beholden to the armed forces. In addition, Vargas had intellectual and political roots deeply influenced by positivist ideology. His advocacy of economic nationalism envisioned an anti-liberal and anti-individualist economy that comported with positivist precepts.[11]

As a consequence of the military's strategic and intellectual roles in Vargas's political position and in promoting basic industries, high level officers held prominent positions throughout the industrialization of non-renewable natural resources and retained veto power on development plans. Most notably, Juarez Távora, the Minister of Agriculture from 1932 to 1934, designed the Mining and Water Codes and oversaw the formation of the mining regulatory framework. He and other officers advanced the military's interest in industrialization and established authority in mineral development.[12]

Structuralism

The debate among Latin American economic policy-makers and historians about the nature and origins of persistent poverty took a new turn during the second half of the twentieth century. Structuralism was an economic argument[13] that challenged the basic core of classical liberal theory that societies attained their best economic outcomes by maximizing production of the goods and services in which they held a comparative advantage (resulting from natural resource endowment or from the accumulation of financial or human capital) while trading for other desired goods and services. With time, structuralist interpretations emerged in contrast to classical ones in nearly all fields of economic policy and theory, including capital controls and monetary, fiscal and labour policies.

Developed economies of North America and Western Europe remained the reference against which Latin Americans compared their material well-being. The basic tenet of the structuralist position was that the deep entrenchment of their economies within global trading networks, with a comparative advantage in primary goods, left Latin Americans in a condition of continuously falling behind. The terms of trade of primary goods (exported by Latin Americans, with prices that were both low and vulnerable to fluctuation) relative to expensive, 'advanced' manufactured goods (imported by Latin Americans) was the mechanism through which their structural disadvantage operated.[14] In keeping with observation and widespread belief, Latin American structuralists saw that countries with large industrial manufacturing capacity seemed to prosper. Proponents of structuralism with a historical perspective traced these patterns to earliest Iberian colonial expansion, when the extraction of natural resources for European use began.[15] Much of the bias against foreign ownership of domestic resources and favour of decisive government intervention to aid 'infant' industrial development arose from these observations. Despite its many variants,[16] the common conclusion of structuralists was that shifting comparative advantage away from primary goods, by giving incentive to industrial manufacturing and domestic ownership/control of domestic assets, offered the keys to broadly based prosperity. Structuralism provided the theoretical justification for promoting the state as the major force in economic development; it could provide leadership that 'market signals, feeble or distorted by monopoly in backward economies, could not'.[17] The inability to move economic structure from reliance on primary goods exports to domestic manufacture (industrialization)[18] and consumption within the private sector added powerful impetus to structuralist policy recommendations for state intervention.

Structuralism has a long history. Joseph Love's research demonstrates the roots of Brazilian structuralism in the early twentieth-century economic writings of the Romanian, Mikhail Manoilescu.[19] Nícia Luz was among the early historians to identify the continual tension in practice and in policy within Brazil beginning in the middle of the nineteenth century between the arguments for developing a strong industrial base, as opposed to realizing the benefits of Brazil's comparative advantage in producing primary good for export (such as sugar, cotton, coffee and rubber).[20] Other scholars have identified the consolidation of an emerging 'national industrial discourse' in Brazil during the 1920s.[21] As Love observed, '[i]ndustrialization in Latin America was a fact before it was a policy and a policy before it was a theory';[22] but theorizing was seldom far from practice.

Within Latin America, the theory predominated in economic policy and thought in the middle of the twentieth century, under the aegis of a dynamic mixture of academics and policy makers, many of them associated with the United Nations Economic Commission on Latin America (ECLA or CEPAL, its Portuguese and Spanish acronym). These figures included Raúl Prebisch, André Gunder Frank and a large contingent of Brazilian academics, among them were Celso Furtado, Caio Prado Jr, Fernando Henrique Cardoso and Florestan Fernandes.[23] The import-substituting-industrialization policies that structuralists advocated focused on supporting infant industries.[24] Specific policies included tax and tariff preferences, allocation of credit and production inputs (such as coal, iron ore and steel), price management and exchange controls. The policies also extended to state capitalism (or entrepreneurialism). Although subsequently challenged on the bases of both empirical evidence and theoretical reasoning, structuralism offered Latin America's strongest contribution to the history of economic thought, and it retains strong advocates.

Furtado, in particular, emphasized the importance of control over natural resources as the initial spark to break the constraints of structuralism.[25] Brazilian experience with iron ore and forged iron and steel from the early nineteenth to the twentieth century informs three crucial aspects of structuralist ideas. First, it demonstrates a longer and more complicated historical trajectory for the tension between domestic manufacture and primary product production than has been previously articulated. The goal of the early nineteenth-century proto-industrialization policy combined many of the tools and concepts later articulated by structuralists while promoting domestic manufacturing of capital equipment to serve domestic producers of commodity exports – gold and sugar. Its tools were remarkably similar to those that the Vargas regime brought to bear on the same problem of domestic capital-goods manufacture (see Chapters 3 and 5). Secondly, the ore and steel experiences were the most important and the earliest targets of structuralist policy in the twentieth century. Thirdly, the resolution adopted in Brazil highlights the dubious nature of the dichotomy between export-production and import-substitution. In the eighteenth and nineteenth centuries, proto-import-substituting-industrialization was intended to service export-oriented production; inversely, in the middle of the twentieth century, the Vargas regime and its successors viewed export promotion (of iron ore) as crucial support for import-substituting industrialization.

The State as an Economic Agent

'Economic nationalism', the term that Brazilians applied to their policies in the 1930s and 1940s, connected positivism and structuralism. Economic nationalism's goal of a self-sufficient, modern and industrial domestic economy anticipated structuralist import-substituting industrialization policies. The rhetoric, if not the form, of economic nationalism espoused in Brazil in the middle of the twentieth century often explicitly juxtaposed domestic modernization against foreign interests.[26] Its superordinate purpose was to lessen the importance of the comparative advantage in primary-good production by providing incentives for industrial manufacture, with Brazilians in control and ownership of production processes.[27] To effect this transformation, the Vargas regime relied on a complicated strategy of enhancing the export of new primary products, iron and (hopefully) petroleum, in order to support import-substitution.[28]

Bradford Burns and John Wirth have emphasized the importance of natural resources, and especially the iron ore conflict, in the development of economically nationalist policy.[29] Some Brazilian legal scholars and mining engineers provided the precedent for this view, by citing the arrangements for mineral exploitation as the major problem of industrializing nations, and promoting the re-separation of subsoil from surface as the key to unlocking the major impediment to realizing the nation's natural wealth.[30] Industrial-policy makers, such as Eduardo Soares Macedo and Juarez Távora recognized the early Vargas policies towards iron ore as the precedent for subsequent claims to the subsoil rights in 1934.[31] Control over water had parallel overtones; the Water Code of 1934 (enacted in conjunction with the Mining Code) provided the legal context for state control of hydropower.[32] These policies subsequently broadened to include the monopolization of petroleum[33] and to more expansive import-substituting industrialization.[34]

The idea of the state owning business enterprises, as developed in the Brazilian case, that operate in conjunction with the private sector, is not natural, inevitable or even obvious. Galambos and Baumol suggest that the motivations to establish state-owned enterprises (SOEs) have typically been the failure of markets or market-oriented capitalism to provide collective goods.[35] Some of the common justifications for state intervention have included the presence of information asymmetries, externalities or systemic synergies.[36] The choice of establishing an SOE to satisfy a demand for a good or service that private markets do not otherwise provide also requires an ideological willingness of the state to assume a direct role in production and commerce. Further, state ownership had precedents in Brazil. It had coexisted with private enterprise in infrastructure (for example, railroads, urban transportation, telegraph, etc) and banking – sectors that were widely perceived to provide significant value as collective goods.

From a very pragmatic perspective, SOEs enjoy intrinsic advantages over those of private entrepreneurs.[37] They spread the business and investment risks across the wider population who benefit from the externalities, rather than limiting risk to private investors. The state's creditworthiness can contribute to lowering the cost of capital. For large, risky capital-intensive projects these advantages can be considerable. When information asymmetries render regulation unreliable, the state's role as the major investor implies that relevant regulatory information is available, even while setting up a conflict between regulation and market participation. Finally, profit maximization may receive lower priority in public enterprise than in private sector efforts. All of these considerations are relevant to the mining and metals sectors.

Embedded ideas about one of the fundamental concerns of property rights – the distinction between the public domain and private property – underpin the organization of SOEs. By forming a business enterprise, the state enters into an activity in which it interacts in business transactions with other economic agents. Its partners, customers and competitors do not have the same powers as the SOE to command resources, benefit from explicit or implicit subsidies, regulate practices, set prices or allocate output.[38]

In the case of iron ore in Brazil, intervention took the extreme form of the state becoming the entrepreneur to produce and commercialize ore. The justification for this action was that, after the two-decade-long effort to find a domestic private sector solution, state intervention would allow for the creation and capture of benefits that accrued far beyond the realm of the enterprise that produced iron. The transition to this perspective began with the rhetoric surrounding the Mining Code, which placed its justification within the framework of the collective welfare of Brazilians.[39]

The Vargas regime was very careful and deliberate in establishing SOEs in the productive sector of the Brazilian economy. Much of the hesitation rested in the presumption that the 'the State is a bad industrialist'.[40] During the first Vargas regime (1930–45) government remained wary, and it imposed three tight strictures on the firms that it established.[41] Although control and ownership would predominantly rest with the state, these enterprises were to be of mixed ownership, with some private sector participation. The companies would not receive direct subsidies from the federal treasury,[42] and any public sector benefits they received would be through programmes also available to other domestic firms. Finally, state-owned firms would not be monopolies within their sectors. The Companhia Vale do Rio Doce met all of these conditions.[43]

Definitions of Property and Minerals

In a seminal piece presenting ideas about the distinction between 'public' and 'private,' Hirschman suggests that the boundaries between the two realms of activity shift with time and circumstance.[44] In the middle of the twentieth century, the widespread introduction of SOEs responded to a prevailing hope that 'enlarging public properties and activities would open the way to a fundamental change in the distribution of power within society; thus engendering a new socioeconomic equilibrium'.[45] Creating employment, industrialization, improving industrial relations and addressing other social goals (such as income distribution) were among the public goods that often provided motives for establishing SOEs. The ends that the Brazilian state sought for mineral development fell squarely within these parameters.

The principles for managing the allocation of property have remained remarkably consistent for four centuries. Even so, property was not an immutable concept in Brazil; it received a great deal of consideration. Limitations on individuals' rights to property, the balance between a right to property and constraints on its use, and the means by which economic actors could transform property into private wealth were concerns that animated the debates surrounding mineral rights.[46] Various categories of property have shifted between private and public domains. The legal regime structuring subsoil rights has changed from personal property of the Portuguese monarch to the state as the sovereign institution, then to individuals, later to the state as regulator and administrator for *res nullius* rights, and finally returning to the state as owner of the subsoil (see Chapter 2). The specific regime, with the notable exception of private subsoil rights for individuals who owned the surface area, had little practical importance for the business or economics of miners. Rather, the indivisibility of fixed assets and the mandated partibility of personal estates remained principles that continued to define the structure of businesses and to constrain the potential for economic growth and innovation. The intersection of these principles with the exigencies of mining was uneasy, and through the twentieth century the constraints on foreign participation in the sector exacerbated the difficulties of transforming the economy.

Property, State, Minerals and Capital

In contrast to the relative lack of importance for miners, ownership of the property has offered an array of possibilities for the state in their ability to influence the economic use of minerals. Economic and legal principles played roles in all of the debates and changing practices that affected access to the subsoil. Reliance on varying institutions changed from time to time. When legal principles did not reconcile with economic goals, practices evolved to accommodate both, as with the incompatibility of indivisibility of real assets and partible inheritance. These accommodations held even as the economic goals of new interest groups ascended. In response, different institutions were put into play to compensate for the limitations of earlier, entrenched practices. First, property gained new definitions that transferred assets from one jurisdiction to another within the public domain and then moving public domain assets to the private realm, by attaching the subsoil to the surface. With the interest in minerals shifting from the precious to the industrial varieties, and with the newly found strong coalition of industrial entrepreneurs and the military, property that had been transferred to the states came back to the federal level, and the economic role of the national state was substantially transformed.

Sacrificed in this approach was the evolution of behaviour and methods among private individuals that could have encouraged the accumulation of small increments of private savings to build private sector industry. The SOEs that formed in the 1940s supported the structure and form of capital markets; but listing and quoting prices for equity shares on the stock exchanges had only indirect effects on investor behaviour. Vale continually traded at a large discount to the par value of its shares through the 1950s, a clear demonstration of the implicit subsidy provided by state ownership. The most dynamic public trading of a privately owned company was for the shares of Companhia Belgo-Mineira, a steel producer also engaged in iron ore mining for their own use. An (untested) hypothesis that bears consideration is that investors viewed Belgo-Mineira as a more secure company, as a result of the increased state activity within the sector. Nevertheless, without dynamic capital markets, private enterprise mostly remained smaller than could have been the case, and SOEs were heavily represented among the largest firms listed through the middle of the twentieth century (see Table 6.1B).

Foreign equity investment in Brazilian mining was a catalysing topic in the effort to industrialize iron ore, given its emphasis on extraction and export of a non-renewable natural resource. Opposition to foreign capital extended to ownership (equity), but not to long-term foreign loans, as we have seen in the cases of Vale and CSN. The relationship between foreign and domestic finance remained complex. Further, opposition was not as monolithic as it appears in retrospect. Some influential legislators of mining continued to support foreign investment as a source of incremental capital within the Brazilian economy, even as it became increasingly unviable for political reasons.[47]

Table 6.1: Brazilian state-owned enterprises.[48]

A	Total number of SOEs by year of creation	
	1940–49	10
	1950–59	15
	1960–69	39
	1970–75	88
	1976–85	33
B	Ownership distribution (percentage) of 30 largest non-financial firms, selected years	
	Public*	Private
1962	12	18
1967	13	17
1971	17	13
1974	23	7
1979	28	2

*   Public includes all SOEs at the federal, state and municipal levels.

The state substituted for both foreign investors and dynamic capital markets when it established Vale and CSN. Replacing foreign investors with the state addressed the concerns about continued outside 'exploitation' of Brazilian resources. Concern about the effects of foreign enterprise has never disappeared.[49] Substituting for larger and more dynamic capital markets allowed the state to avoid reforms that would challenge fundamental institutions of property, and to preserve the structures that encouraged close networks of partnerships in private sector business formation. Reforms to encourage small or foreign investors willing to participate in 'Brazilian' firms, and enterprises defined by depersonalized ownership structures proceeded very slowly. Potential reforms included the issuance of preferred equity shares, clear bankruptcy provisions, and transparent and open managing boards.[50] Instead, in the realm of capital markets, in parallel with the treatment of property, the preservation of existing arrangements coexisted with new interests by the mechanisms of state economic intervention.

SOEs remained tightly constrained under the first Vargas regime. The only new federal SOEs after the iron ore and steel companies during the 1940s were the Companhia Hidroeléctrica do São Francisco and the Fábrica Nacional de Motores (to manufacture aircraft engines, a national security goal that later expanded its industrial reach).[51] The commitment to state-led developmentalism increased notably in the second Vargas regime (1951–4) in the pursuit of industrial capacity.[52] By abandoning such constraints as forbidding monopoly and by introducing increasingly strong interventionist policy, the Vargas regimes set the stage for rapid expansion of SOEs that occurred during the 1960s and 1970s, the years of Brazil's military rule[53] (see Table 6.1A). This shift in approach gave rise to the characterization of Brazil's policy as 'state capitalism' in pursuit of import substitution. The timing is paradoxical because the political-economy rhetoric of the military government was heavily oriented towards the liberal free market. The common feature of state-owned commercial enterprises during these years was that they were large firms in basic industries (such as steel, petroleum, chemicals, concrete and paper)[54] down-streaming to other production. Managing the output and pricing of these firms was sufficient to affect the price structure for other Brazilian firms and consumers. Through at least the 1970s, state-owned enterprise continued to dominate activity in Brazilian capital markets.[55]

These were also the years when Vale expanded its operations both horizontally and vertically to include new iron ore reserves (principally deposits in Carajás, Pará), other industrial minerals[56] and to sales in the domestic market. By 1976, SOEs completely dominated the mining sector, largely attributable to Vale's expansion (see Table 6.2). The company also expanded beyond its mineral-based businesses (and related infrastructure of ports, freighting, railroads, water and technological research) to enter other resource-based industries, such as fertilizers and cellulose/paper. These industries previously resided totally within the private sector.[57]

Table 6.2: State-owned enterprises in mining, 1976.[58]

	SOE as percentage of total
Capital	
Statutory	68.5
Fixed	65.6
Earnings	76.8
Employment	55.7

Conclusion

Brazil was not unique in adopting the goals and policies that it followed.[59] Rather, they corresponded to standard post-World War II economic development practices, which fell into disfavour during the last decades of the twentieth century. Recent economic theory and history have subjected the ideas and efficacy of import-substituting industrialization to still another re-examination, and have revised the negative conclusions.[60] Some have suggested an explanation for the logic and timing of protectionism, such as that provided by SOEs, based on the time-value of capital and the ability of different economic agents (foreign or domestic, public or private) to wait for the positive effects of economic innovation. Gómez-Galvarriato and Guerrero-Luchtenburg find that, if the state has a longer time-horizon for return on its investment than private agents and has lower borrowing costs, the cost of protection can be balanced against the benefits of the protected activity (with externalities internalized for both costs and benefits).[61] From a different perspective, Colistete finds that import-substituting-industrialization policies and improved industrial productivity occurred together in many Brazilian firms and sectors, rather than being in conflict with each other as earlier analysts concluded.[62]

In the scope of actual experience, economists and historians have long recognized that in the years during and after the Great Depression, economic policy 'turned inward,' away from global openness.[63] Trade protectionism, industrial subsidies, capital constraints, financial bailouts, complicated management of exchange rates, interest rates and other prices were among the policies that contributed to turning inward. These policies have, at times, been invoked counter-cyclically to lessen the impact of the global depression on large Latin American economies, as well as for long-term developmental purposes.[64] Policies approaching 'economic nationalism' have historical precedents. Economists and economic historians have characterized these policies as a means by which late developing countries could 'catch-up', or alternatively as a very common, longstanding strategy of economic development.[65] If state capitalism in Brazil developed stronger roots and subsequently spread more extensively than in many other national economies, the difference was a matter of degree rather than substance.[66]

State-owned enterprise is one specific policy, which is not necessarily specific to ISI, but has been widely applied for that purpose. Moving the state into industrial production, these enterprises set the tone for state capitalism in other endeavours. By 1942, the US highlighted, and recommended, Brazilian protectionist policy as a conscious tool of industrialization, particularly with respect to iron and steel.[67] Following iron ore and steel, petroleum became defined as a strategic industry; tight concessionary control over all mining of industrial minerals and state enterprises for aircraft construction and shipbuilding followed upon Vale and CSN. The initial entry into industrial production opened the gates for expansive interpretations of appropriate endeavours within the public domain. Because their goals of changing comparative advantage of production within the Brazilian economy superseded the more usual entrepreneurial goal of profit maximization, these enterprises simultaneously supported and were free from the constraints of the marketplace. Chapter 7 considers the SOE experience in Brazil, through the lens of subsequent privatizations in the 1990s; the history of Brazil's largest and most enduring SOEs informs that topic.

Finally, the original strategy to which the state committed to the iron ore mining and steel production projects belies the dichotomy of import-substituting-industrialization in opposition to commodity export production. The goal of the Vargas regime was to develop a new commodity export in order to underwrite the construction of basic industry for the capital goods sector. In other words, the state relied on its comparative advantage in iron ore to shift long-term economic structure. The special circumstances surrounding the US Export-Import Bank loans severed the direct connection between iron ore development and steel. However, the strategy was applied in the more general support of industrialization.

Although functioning in unanticipated ways, neither the economic liberalism of export-oriented growth nor the structuralist quest for economic independence with a modern industrial sector operated without the other. Similarly, the economic ideologies of liberalism, positivism, nationalism and structuralism interacted dynamically with economic policies and practices. As each set of ideas gained strength, they found expression far from the realms in which they were originally formulated, within the ongoing efforts of mineral development.

7 IRON ORE AS PRECEDENT AND EXAMPLE

The experience gained from creating a large-scale iron ore exporting business, and doing so as a state-owned enterprise (SOE), set a precedent for economic governance through the second half of the twentieth century in Brazil. It offers important insight into the use of natural resources, in general, and on state economic intervention. This chapter identifies two of the issues that can be understood more fully in light of the iron ore case. It briefly reviews the subsequent and related history of petroleum development and the influence of the iron ore experience on economic governance. The chapter then explores the widespread privatization of SOEs since 1988, identifying continuities and discontinuities with historical experience. In conclusion, this chapter identifies (without analysing) other examples of current controversies regarding sovereignty and natural resources in Latin America in which the institutional debates about natural resources covered in this study may have a conspicuous role.

The role of minerals within the Brazilian economy remains controversial and frustrating for some economic analysts. In 1995, one mining economist referred to the 'Brazilian mineral question as one of the central dilemmas of the economy'.[1] Although Brazil's mineral endowment is the richest in Latin America, the extraction of other minerals has not attained the success of iron ore. At the beginning of the twenty-first century, geologists have estimated that, with one-third to one-quarter of global reserves of all minerals embedded in about 42 per cent of its national territory, Brazil has sufficient reserves to produce commercially up to fifty-five different minerals.[2] With the notable exception of iron ore, the development of large-scale mineral extraction has proven disappointing (at least to its advocates). Other minerals remain mired in the contradictions and difficulties of insufficient domestic investment, insecure rights and uncertainty for foreign capital that plagued iron ore for centuries. Low levels of domestic demand discouraged domestic investment.[3] In the jargon of neo-classical economics, existing demand is not sufficient to overcome the financial and transactions costs (risk, time-value, institutional conflict) associated with developing the potential supply, with the result that the relative value of untapped reserves has not merited the investment. The argument for bringing investment in other minerals into the public sector, by virtue of their externalities, has not succeeded. Nevertheless, the precedents set by the iron ore case extend to the sovereignty of other natural resources, especially with respect to the development of the petroleum industry and economic governance.

Petroleum and Sovereignty of Natural Resources

Petroleum is the substance for which the case of iron ore provided the most direct precedent and the point of departure for the expansion of state capitalism.[4] Vale and CSN anticipated further incursions by the state into core resource industries. State-owned iron ore mining informed Brazilian petroleum exploration.[5] The legislative and regulatory trajectory of petroleum development also paralleled that of iron ore. Petroleum fell within the same rules and administrative department (the DNPM) that regulated minerals under the original Mining Code.[6] Responding to the perception that the Mining Code created barriers to petroleum exploration, regulation of petroleum was separated from minerals in 1938.[7] The Constitution and Mining Code reforms of 1937 recognized ownership of extracted minerals by the concessionaire. Proponents of petroleum nationalization made the case for the petroleum itself to be the property of the state; this distinction would remove petroleum from private ownership claims.[8] The status of the state-owned petroleum firm, Petrobras,[9] as a state monopoly, became embedded in Brazil's Constitution in 1967. Petrobras was the most notable exception to the policies formalized in the Constitution of 1988 to encourage both privatization and liberalization. In this Constitution, petroleum, natural gas, other hydrocarbons and nuclear minerals remained state monopolies[10] until the hydrocarbon sector opened in 1997.

Petroleum first arose as a national issue in the early 1930s, about the same time that efforts to develop iron ore intensified. The problem with petroleum, however, was somewhat different than the iron ore problem. Early exploration and prospecting did not identify commercially viable deposits, though they often found enough evidence that geological conditions supported the likely presence of petroleum to keep expectations high.[11] Getúlio Vargas quickly associated petroleum with iron and steel. In 1939, he announced that '[i]t remains for us now to industrialize petroleum and install large steel, which we will do soon ... Iron, coal and petroleum are the mainstays of any country's economic emancipation.'[12] Early in the debate, many analysts agreed that '[i]t falls to the Government to legislate access, facilitate exploration and guarantee rights. To private initiative – all else, from locating the drilling to the distribution of refined products.'[13] The first effort to form a petroleum company (the Companhia Petróleos do Brasil) in 1932 failed two years later, when the DNPM issued a statement that nothing substantiated the expectation of finding petroleum reserves in the area under exploration. The Technical Council of Economy and Finance (the same body that issued the opinion in favour of renegotiating the Itabira contract in 1938) signalled the federal Treasury's unwillingness to participate in a venture;[14] private investors could no longer justify the investment. Geologists first verified deposits of petroleum offshore near Bahia in 1939. However, by 1940, analysts for the Serviço Geologico determined that the quantity of deposits was insufficient to merit extraction.[15] After new finds in 1951, production began in 1954, when 2,500 barrels per day were produced in the Recôncavo of Bahia (onshore, but close to the coast).[16]

Framing the importance of petroleum in terms of national defense and economic security, the debate about government participation in the sector emerged in terms and actions very similar to those of iron ore. The Brazilian military and industrial sectors, the same interest groups that successfully brought iron ore mining to the public domain, sought a means to finance petroleum exploration. In the absence of proven reserves, state intervention in petroleum meant supporting its continued exploration as well as developing the ability to refine petroleum and to distribute its products. As with iron ore, the formation of an SOE was not inevitable. The nationalization of petroleum in 1938 referred to the requirement for majority ownership by Brazilian nationals. At the same time, the National Petroleum Council was commissioned to explore options for developing an oil industry.[17] The earliest projects presented to the Council in 1951 estimated that the required capital investment would be triple the volume of the largest previous state undertakings, those of Vale and CSN.[18] Capital constraints that were similar to those impeding the development of iron ore continued to hamper domestic exploration, refining and distribution of petroleum products

The individuals associated with early petroleum explorations were many of the same private sector industrialists and senior military officers who had engineered the iron ore endeavour. These included José Bento Monterio Lobato, Henrique Lage, Guilherme Guinle, and such military officers as Júlio Caetano Horta Barbosa, Juarez Távora and Goís Monteiro.[19] Former Brazilian President Artur Bernardes, the earliest and strongest antagonist of foreign-owned iron ore deposits, also fought foreign presence in petroleum. Monteiro Lobato was a writer and would-be iron and oil entrepreneur, who had been involved in organizing the Companhia Petróleos do Brasil. He accused the DNPM of supporting foreign petroleum companies in contravention of the Mining Code. Monteiro Lobato spearheaded the campaign advocating the continued exploration for domestic reserves until his death in 1948. In 1941, he was the first to publicly advocate an SOE for petroleum. In his public advocacy, Monteiro Lobato explicitly invoked the case of the Companhia Vale do Rio Doce as a precedent and example of state involvement.[20]

By the late 1940s Juarez Távora understood both that continued exploration would require large-scale state intervention (he phrased it as 'monopoly')
and that a state monopoly was politically infeasible.[21] The arguments transferred
the debates of iron ore to petroleum, and they became even more intense. The
economic nationalism and national security issues that premiered in the iron ore
debate evolved further with their application to petroleum. The polemic against
foreign control of petroleum escalated during the 1940s and 1950s into a politically sensitive public campaign, with the catalysing slogan '*O petróleo é nosso!*'
('The petroleum is ours!').[22] Without having identified significant reserves of
petroleum, the slogan referred to hoped-for but still undiscovered oil, and it
extended to refining and distribution capabilities within the country. This campaign, based on intense expressions of nationalism, galvanized public opinion
against 'imperialist invasion of the Nation'.[23] Standard Oil-New Jersey and Royal
Dutch-Shell were the specific targets of the campaign against foreign petroleum
companies. These companies were trying to establish distribution networks in
Brazil. Nationalists believed these companies were impeding domestic exploration and had developed undue influence in the mining administrative bodies
(DNPM and its section, the Serviço Geológico).[24] Influential rhetoric against
foreign oil companies tended to invoke such tones as the following, from General Horta Barbosa, the Army's Director of Engineering at the time:

> without petroleum our military potential is low; without petroleum, sadly, the con-
> stant, uninterrupted penetration of Standard Oil, Royal-Dutch Shell, Mexican Eagle
> into the tiniest nooks of our nation. I urge, therefore, the substitution of all of these
> names for Brazilian names.[25]

Horta Barbosa made the same connection as he argued for the federal government to maintain a strong equity and management position in the sector.

In response to the gathering momentum and the continuing lack of private
sector capacity, President Vargas (recently returned to the presidency and more
willing than previously to expand state economic intervention) submitted a bill
to Congress in 1951 to provide for the formation of Petróleo Brasileiro S.A.
(Petrobras), including federal capital and mandatory national control. Petrobras
opened in 1953, based on its claims to property rights and the firm-ownership
model of Vale. In a significant departure from the experience with Vale, the legislative actions forming Petrobras established the company as a state monopoly in
the exploration, drilling, refining and distribution of petroleum.[26] Eleven years
after the formation of Vale and CSN, the prohibition against SOEs operating
as monopoly firms had fallen. As with the other basic-industry SOEs, Petrobras
management remained relatively free from state interference in its daily operations,[27] even while its political importance and economic contributions built
upon the precedent set by the earlier companies.

With federal capital and control, Petrobras's initial mandate concentrated on building a capacity to refine imported crude oil. The company acquired its first two refineries (expropriated with compensation) from foreign companies, but began building its own facilities shortly afterward.[28] In the 1970s, under the military regime that took power in 1964, exploration gained higher priority as the cost of continued reliance on imports increased in the light of global petroleum embargos. Petrobras found reserves and was able to bring new wells into production; extraction increased at exponential rates in two distinct time periods (see Figure 7.1): during the second half of the 1950s (a very low base level of extraction resulted in high growth rates), and after significant discoveries in 1974, extraction more than tripled from 1979 to 1987. Reliance on domestically extracted petroleum reveals a somewhat different pattern (see Figure 7.2). The Brazilian economy did not begin to reduce its reliance on imported oil on a sustained basis until the 1980s. The combined increases of extraction and imports[29] fueled rapid industrialization in the third quarter of the twentieth century. Extraction did not exceed imports until 1990 (see Figure 7.1); and Brazil became self-sustaining in petroleum for the first time in 2007.

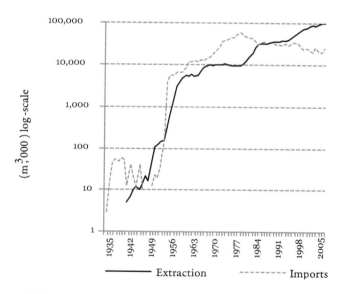

Figure 7.1 Petroleum extraction and imports, 1935–2007 (m³, 000, log-scale).[30]

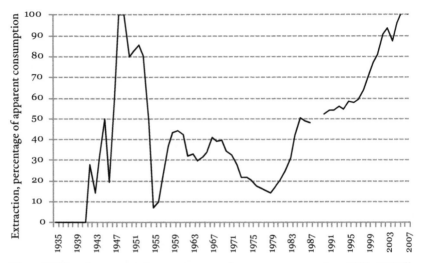

Figure 7.2 Petroleum extraction, percentage of apparent consumption, 1935–2007.[31]

Brazilian oil deposits have proven richest in offshore locations. Since Petrobras began producing from offshore wells in 1970, the proportion of offshore production rose from less than 6 per cent in 1971 to 90 per cent in 2007.[32] Also in 2007, Petrobras confirmed deep-sea deposits that the company estimates could increase their reserves by 50 per cent. Production from these deposits began in 2009.[33] To reach these levels of exploration and production, Petrobras created one of the most advanced research and development capacities in the global petroleum industry, which has required continuing large injections of capital. The company was, until August 2010 (when it was surpassed by Vale), the most highly capitalized firm in Latin America.[34] Beyond high levels of capital, with control by the state – although with an array of private shareholders – Petrobras has also entered into partnerships with other national governments, including the US and China, to develop the technologically advanced offshore operations. Foreign-government-financed participation is in the form of long-term loans, rather than equity. While Petrobras's monopoly in the Brazilian petroleum market ended in 1997,[35] provisions regarding the ownership and access of petroleum, as with minerals, remain in the national domain. The largest equity share and control of Petrobras remains with the state and nothing threatens the company's national dominance.

Economic Governance

Mid-Twentieth Century

The same arguments that initially justified state intervention to produce iron ore applied in other cases. In addition to the political rhetoric, many of the theoretical characteristics that have supported state intervention also were present in the efforts to develop a Brazilian petroleum industry: long-time frame, high risk, capital intensity and asymmetric information. Petroleum, the first and most important extension,

> came after previous attempts to convince domestic and foreign enterprises to launch exploration of petroleum within the rules established by the State. With respect to petroleum, the sensitivity to foreign extraction remained. Foreign companies only demonstrated an interest in large concessions, for almost unlimited time periods, as they had been given in other Latin American countries.[36]

Nevertheless, by the end of the regime of Getúlio Vargas, the general parameters of development policy were in place for most of the remainder of the twentieth century. These included central planning, widespread state intervention, and the state acting simultaneously as an economic actor and the mediator/regulator in selected sectors.[37] The expansion of state economic intervention, begun during the second Vargas regime (1951–4), set the stage for comprehensive efforts to build physical infrastructure. The National Development Bank (BNDE) was created in 1952 to finance large projects in the energy, transportation, steel and chemical sectors. The bank became a major platform for development policy, and it built a base of strong influence during the presidency of Juscelino Kubitschek (1956–61), which expanded formal state-centred developmentalism. Five-year development plans, slogans such as 'fifty years in five', the articulation of import-substituting industrialization policies and building Brasília as a new modernist capital city signalled the intensity of the push towards a 'modern' Brazil. The ambitions and goals of the interest groups that prevailed in the iron ore controversy had become core components of national policy. In retrospect, many attribute the sustained and high inflation that followed to the inability to balance fiscal, monetary and development policy that resulted from this escalation.[38]

Privatization and Globalization

Vale was privatized in 1997. As a brief digression from the major themes of this book, this section outlines the changes of economic regime and ideology that led to the privatization of most Brazilian SOEs.

Even as the formation and expansion of SOEs came to dominate many sectors of the economy,[39] deep reservoirs of ambivalence remained. Opposition to state-capitalism was always present, and its policies were subject to ebbs and flows.[40] By the 1970s, the global macroeconomic environment, and its effects on Brazil, rendered increasingly infeasible the maintenance of large, growing, capital-intensive firms that relied heavily on national fiscal policy for financing and subsidies. The oil shocks of 1973 and 1978 and attendant high interest rates focused attention on the link between macroeconomic policy and the state's role as an entrepreneur.[41] Brazil was the largest international debtor among all developing nations, and the burden of financing its enterprises was extremely high.[42] Some analysts have identified the 'lost decade' of the 1980s as inciting a profound re-examination of ISI policies.[43] Government studies began to explore the possibilities of privatizing firms, giving voice to those who had remained, or became, sceptical about the state's role in import-substituting industrialization.

Between the almost twenty years from its first expression to its adoption as active policy in the early 1990s, many arguments favoured privatization.[44] Concerns resurfaced about removing from the private sector those activities that it could perform more effectively (in the view of market advocates). Some expected greater efficiency through privately owned enterprise. Still others believed that restructuring capital markets for wider participation among private participants carried the greatest potential for development. Further, import-substituting industries proved to be import-intensive, creating additional stress on financing and hard currency requirements.[45] One argument inverted the earlier advocacy for state capital to replace private investment by suggesting that capital-intensive industries created intermediate goods that ultimately satisfied demands of upper-income consumers, ignoring the needs of the impoverished.[46] In addition, the fiscal windfalls offered by the sales of state-owned firms proved attractive.[47] Not only would ongoing costs to the state be diminished, but the revenues from sales could offset large ongoing federal budget deficits in the short term.

Capital markets offered some of the strongest empirical evidence and ideological arguments for privatization. Research showing that equity trading was concentrated among SOEs (again generally mixed enterprises, if only with small amounts of private capital) raised questions about the ability of private firms to raise capital ('crowding out'), as well as the potential returns they offered to investors. The hypotheses of increased efficiency and productivity from privately owned enterprises, generated expectations of increased value of privately owned firms (measured as the ratio of market-value to book-value of equity prices).[48] Other studies, examining specific cases and actual equity price patterns, revealed more complicated results. Vale and Petrobras were often held up as successful efficient and well-managed, to demonstrate that SOEs could be successful financially.[49] Based on the trends of equity prices, the risk-adjusted return-on-equity for Brazilian SOEs was higher than that for private firms from 1975 to 1984. However, three firms – Vale, Petrobras and the Banco do Brasil – accounted for all of the positive contribution of SOEs, relative to private firms.[50]

Policy to privatize SOEs advanced slowly, beginning with the first commission to study the subject in 1975. The slow implementation demonstrated inconsistent political enthusiasm for privatization; but other complications also arose. Very high rates of inflation and unpredictable economic policy during the 1980s created unfavourable conditions for attracting private investment. Although the terms of the 1988 Constitution removed the decision from the realm of economic decision-making by mandating privatization of federally owned enterprises, economic and administrative obstacles still required resolution.[51]

By the 1990s, decisive support for privatization came from one of the strongest theorists of structuralism in the 1960s. As Minister of Finance and then President of Brazil, Fernando Henrique Cardoso advanced the ideology and the policy that, given the return to a global macroeconomic environment of open markets, the strongest avenue for permanent escape from underdevelopment was for private firms to compete in global markets, in areas of their comparative advantage. The role of the state, by this reasoning, would be to create conditions that socialize (distribute) some of the economic gains associated with externalities, thereby contributing to dynamic conditions for private domestic markets.[52] Implicit in this argument was the idea that responding to the degree of openness of the global macroeconomic regime, rather than ideological commitment, represented the best outcome for the Brazilian economy.

In the rhetoric of globalization, one of the arguments in favour of SOEs, which could also reconcile with privatization, remained unexamined. If state intervention supported 'infant industries', then the successful maturation of those enterprises argued for privatization. Fifty years of state capitalism may represent a longer 'infancy' than expected. Nevertheless, the longer history of failed efforts to build an industrial scale mining and steel sector suggests the difficulty of the ambition.

The National Development Bank (renamed, with the new acronym of BNDES) continued to manage industrial policy by shifting its efforts to the privatizations. BNDES oversaw the valuation and offering procedures, and at times issued long-term loans to Brazilian investors.[53] Between October 1991 and March 1999, 115 SOEs were privatized, and minority shares in other firms were sold.[54] Many of the privatizations, such as the eight firms that had been consolidated into the steel conglomerate Siderbrás in 1974 (including CSN) reflected the inability of the state to invest in the firms sufficiently to make them competitive in global markets that reshaped worldwide production trends. The steel firms were sold into the private market from 1991 to 1993.[55]

The mining sector attracted particular attention in the development of privatization policies. At the same time that the 1988 Constitution mandated privatization, it prohibited a majority share of foreign ownership in the mining sector.[56] Vale's was the most difficult of the privatizations undertaken. It was often portrayed in emotional terms, as an assault on national sovereignty and an important step towards dismantling the Brazilian state.[57] Vocal press and political campaigns energized proponents and opponents alike; 217 lawsuits (more than one-quarter of all privatization-related suits) required resolution before the public offering could take place. The argument against the sale tapped into the remaining strands of economic nationalism: it was 'wrong' to sell access to non-renewable natural resources, a crucial part of the national patrimony. Further, many opposed selling one of the state's most profitable enterprises. Proponents of the sale saw the opportunity to greatly increase the scale of the company.[58] In 1997, the majority purchaser of Vale shares was the federal employees' pension fund, financed with a loan from the national development bank (BNDES).[59] The Banco do Brasil and Petrobras remain the major state-owned Brazilian companies. In 2010, the federal government remained the majority shareholder of the Banco do Brasil, and although the majority of Petrobras capital is in private hands, the federal government remains the largest shareholder.[60]

The unwillingness of the Brazilian government to divest of Petrobras demonstrates the limits of the privatization programme and of the reshaping of the Brazilian state that the Constitution of 1988 formalized.[61] The Constitution retained a caveat in support of state economic activity as a matter of national interest, invoking the political and strategic importance of petroleum and energy independence, and ensuring the infeasibility of Petrobras's privatization. In an interesting twist, opponents of privatization recognized the complaint that during the military regime 'state enterprises existed for the purpose of amplifying the profits and benefits to the private sector'.[62] Without picking up on the observation that the originators of the SOEs would have considered that description as a sign of success, this circumstance served as a reason for reform, if not abandonment, of the SOE strategy.

The debate about privatized industry in the Brazilian economy continues. Diniz and Boschi point out the essential contradiction of the state acting as an economic agent and its position as a potential tool for special interest groups. They observe that the non-ideological approach of industrialists, as an interest group, invoking the state to act on their behalf, has been one of the characteristics that contributed to their success.[63] Under this line of reasoning, and assuming the continuing predominance of the interest groups that had successfully aligned for state intervention in iron ore and petroleum, then the logic of privatization for iron ore, but not for petroleum, can be explained by the continuing combination of risk and investment requirements attached to oil exploration, drilling and marketing.

However, the fluidity of the interests of distinct groups also points toward another consideration with respect to privatization: the process is neither linear nor necessarily permanent. Rather, a continuum may best represent the process and extent of privatization, and political-economic conditions may not support continued privatization. Evidence suggests such a possibility in Brazil at the beginning of the twenty-first century. During the 1990s, until 2002, 133 SOEs were privatized; afterwards, the number of SOEs grew from 108 in December 2002 to 137 in December 2005.[64] Despite the global attention to (and expectation of) privatization, a cross-national literature has emerged on the continuing strength of SOE in developing nations.[65] These authors hypothesize that 'policy makers in the average developing country are more skeptical' than its enthusiasts about the potential of privatization. They further find that

> [i]n most countries, the SOE sector consists mainly of firms operating in four sectors: public utilities, heavy industries, financial services, and extractive industries. These firms tend to be large and monopolistic or oligopolistic. They all entail either high risks or present opportunities to earn high rents. Neither the theoretical nor the empirical literature suggests unambiguously that such firms will perform better if privatized.[66]

Yarrow also makes the points that successful privatization (from the perspective of the enterprise) requires an institutional structure that aligns with the changed structure of principle and agent, and that state divestiture of the control it had exercised through ownership can be offset by regulatory controls.[67] These findings put the Brazil squarely within the norms of privatization experiences. Vale, faced with high risk and the possibility of high rents as well as significant externalities in its early history, became the object of particular controversy during the privatization programme because of its success.[68] Petrobras's status remains untouchable, with expanding capital-intensive discoveries and the political weight of petroleum. Global economic circumstances (as of 2010) that increase the risk entailed in commodities exchange, uncertain capital markets and the political risks attached to non-renewable natural resources do not support the economic scenario under which privatizations would be attractive.

The debate about SOE has directed attention away from one of the earlier arguments that had supported structuralist advocacy of state intervention. Relying upon strong comparative advantage to thrive in globalized markets has meant that Brazilian prosperity has relied upon the vibrancy of markets for primary commodities. At the beginning of the twenty-first century, those commodities prominently feature iron ore as well as the output of large agro-industry, and prosperity requires strong price trends. This dynamic is the same vulnerability that structuralism strove to eliminate. The ability to channel prosperity in some sectors to the wider Brazilian economy – i.e., to distribute externalities – will determine the long-term success of the export-growth strategy of the early twenty-first century. Brazil is not alone at this crossroads; it is widely populated by the mining sectors throughout Latin America.[69]

Conclusion

The case study that is at the heart of this book is that of minerals, primarily iron ore, in Brazil. It claims that the iron ore experience set a precedent and was important by virtue of its effects for the economy and for economic governance. The book does not claim that the iron ore case was unique. The struggle to define and attain property rights over natural resources is ubiquitous. The controversies become public when conflicting claims to resources arise and when their value (indicative of their relative scarcity) increases. While iron ore motivated the redefinition of mineral rights in the 1930s, other examples of resource-rights conflicts with long histories that continued into the twentieth century include water and timber during the nineteenth century. The St John d'el Rey Company, which offered evidence about conflicting principles of property rights in Chapter 3, exhibited a continuing concern about securing water and timber as sources of energy.[70] After reopening its mine following a major accident in the 1890s, the company began construction of its own hydroelectric plant in 1903 to address this continuing problem.[71] The company's efforts were exceptional only by virtue of its success. The Water Code entered the corpus of legislative and regulatory control simultaneously with the Mining Code in 1934, when 'waterfalls and other sources of hydraulic energy in public waters and used in common [were] incorporated into the patrimony of the Union as inalienable property'.[72] The purpose of the Water Code was to establish a basis for state intervention in the supply and distribution of electricity. Jumping to the present, and the future, control over water continues to command significant resources and the ability to displace significant numbers of Brazilians in the effort to expand the use of hydropower. The struggle to control use of the Amazon River basin can be also be interpreted as an issue of public versus private property rights.[73] Even agricultural land has been thrown into the fray of resource-rights controversies, with some advocating its designation as a strategic resource that should disallow foreign ownership.[74]

Petroleum presents another strong example of the state stepping in to replace private industry while relying on state claims to resources. Escaping the anticipated exploitation of private foreign 'monopolies', notably Standard Oil of New Jersey and Royal Dutch-Shell, as had occurred in other Latin American countries (such as Colombia, Bolivia, Peru, Argentina and Venezuela) was one of the strong motivations for establishing a state-owned petroleum enterprise. Mexico and Iran offered international examples of nationalized oil monopolies.[75] Among the ironies emerging from petroleum nationalizations in recent years is the position that Petrobras found itself in, as the major producer of natural gas and petroleum in Bolivia, when Bolivia nationalized its hydrocarbon industry.[76] Petrobras transitioned from providing protection against foreign intervention for Brazilians to intervening in the resource extraction of its neighbours and others. As of year-end 2009, Petrobras has overseas sites for producing petroleum and natural gas in Angola, Argentina, Bolivia, Colombia, Ecuador, Nigeria, Peru and the US.[77] Equally, Vale has large international mining exploration, extraction and production operations, along with commercial offices in 38 nations.

Also in Bolivia, conflicts over water rights have led to violence in recent years, and access to rich lithium deposits looms. Whether petroleum in Ecuador, iron ore (mined by a Chinese company) in Peru, copper in Chile or innumerable other examples, fluctuating values of natural resources can alter the intensity with which economic actors seek access and control. Coordinating that access with existing economic and social interests is the job of institutions. The example of iron ore in Brazil has shown how complex that job can be.

CONCLUSION

During the second half of the twentieth century, the industrial base of the Brazilian economy both deepened and broadened. At the same time, the nation's presence in the global trade of commodities and manufactured goods took on new dimensions, and economic governance evolved to promote industrial growth. This book has demonstrated both the interrelationships of these three developments and the very long-term trajectory that culminated in these outcomes. Minerals, more specifically iron ore, have been an ever-present nexus throughout the history. Furthermore, the impact of iron ore development has extended into a wide venue of activities.

Understanding how Brazil initiated the path by which it emerged as one of the world's major producers of iron ore supports two fundamental conclusions. First, in the case of minerals – with high risk, long time-horizons, asymmetric information, capital intensity and large but subtle externalities – development efforts required the confluence of circumstances and the shifting weight of important interest groups. Successfully mediating these complications required centuries, important shifts of economic and political structure, and new arrangements with respect to the institutions of property, capital markets and economic governance. Secondly, a substantial expansion in the economic role of the state conciliated new with entrenched interests. The process of reaching these conclusions complicates the understanding of institutional change, emphasizing interactions among a variety of institutions and between resources and institutions.

In Brazil, the actual ownership of mineral veins mattered less than other important determinants of property rights such as indivisibility of fixed assets, mandated partibility of estates within families and business partnership practices. Gold discoveries of the late seventeenth century and abundant reserves of iron ore defined the resource endowment that motivated exploration and efforts to develop Brazilian minerals. The country's particular colonial history, with the transfer of the imperial government to the colony from 1808 to 1821, brought policy attention to the industrial needs of the colony, resulting in the first attempt to develop iron ore. However enlightened and well-intentioned (or even correct) it is difficult to see the efforts at the beginning of the nineteenth century to lay the foundation of an industrial policy based on iron ore as anything other than the endeavours of a small number of individuals.

From independence in 1822 until 1930, mining remained firmly a private sector activity, with private ownership and local regulation enacted in the first Constitution of republican Brazil. In the 1891 Constitution, the first meaningful change to the ownership and regulation of the subsoil occurred. The turn of the twentieth century also coincided with the slow emergence of iron ore's increasing importance as a tool for industrialization and as a source of revenues. Iron became the defining commodity for economic nationalism and a crucial ideological component of national security. A logic derived from Brazilian economic history can explain the sensitivity that iron ore acquired in policy circles. However, development also required that two increasingly strong interest groups, the military and industrial entrepreneurs, align their interests. The logistical, infrastructural and capital needs of the combined iron ore and steel project were beyond the scope of private Brazilian entrepreneurs. Simultaneously, foreign entrepreneurship became politically infeasible and these bottlenecks were increasingly seen as roadblocks to economic progress.

In Brazil, as in the US, mineral endowment was an important determinant in the trajectory of industrial growth.[1] In this sense, the concern of Brazilian entrepreneurs for linking the conditions for iron ore exploitation with industrialization was justified. By the middle of the twentieth century, industrialization was the generally accepted path to development.[2] Domestic industrial ambitions and ore requirements in the industrialized world combined to turn iron ore into a compelling political controversy within Brazil. The unique arrangements made possible by World War II culminated in the ability to finance both industrialized iron ore extraction and large-scale integrated-steel manufacturing. Technological and physical constraints did not require that the state become an industrial entrepreneur in order to resolve the infrastructure and capital bottlenecks of the twin ambitions of iron ore and steel. Rather, institutional constraints slowly moved the interested parties toward that solution. The political genius of the Vargas regime was to focus on the externalities of the two endeavours. Doing so transformed the projects of specific interest groups into national interest. Skilful use of the exogenous circumstances allowed for a resolution that maintained legal and institutional structures with respect to individuals, deriving from the colonial era, while building new institutional parameters for the state that transformed economic governance.

State-owned industrialized iron ore allowed the state to capture significant externalities, even if they were often different from the externalities anticipated. Iron ore provided export revenues and demonstrated a sophisticated policy of export growth for the purpose of supporting import-substituting industrialization. Large-scale physical infrastructure from these projects benefited all producers. Initially, both Campanhia Vale do Rio Doce and the National Steel Company also offered a demonstration effect in domestic capital markets, by maintaining active market-making quotations for their shares, and Vale contributed to monetary policies by virtue of their ability to operate within a multiple exchange rate regime without the pressure of shareholder profit expectations. Relieved of the profit-maximizing goals of a private enterprise, Vale met its initial ambitions. Whether another outcome that kept iron ore mining entirely within the private sector could have met those goals equally well is a counterfactual empirical question. Theory does not provide a clear expectation on this question. With respect to the ability of markets to routinely provide the information needed for natural resource investment and to capture and distribute externalities to those incurring their costs, theory leaves room for the argument that public sector investment was instrumental. In its early decades, the Companhia Vale do Rio Doce had a predominant, but relatively circumscribed, role in mining and other companies benefited from the externalities it generated, supporting the theoretical argument for public investment, even if not necessarily in the form of ownership.

With the state as entrepreneur, long-entrenched practices of capital accumulation among private individuals could be maintained while also developing new endeavours. This balancing mechanism reflected long-standing impediments to business organization, which manifested in many ways. The difficulty of reconciling indivisibility of physical assets with mandated partibility of personal estates impeded the formation of business partnerships. Subsequently, legislative practices accommodated individual over collective interests. The retrenchment and slow growth of participation in formal capital markets in the twentieth century demonstrated the long-term effects of these inhibitions to the formation of widely held, depersonalized enterprises, even with the financial tools available to potential investors. The history of mining development, where the effects of these dynamics were attenuated, brings important insight to the long-recognized difficulty of forming large private sector businesses.

State capitalism was an institution that arose out of the needs of newly influential interest groups while maintaining the practices of traditional groups. Although other forms of intervention may have been possible, circumstances and the willingness of the government resulted in this form, and it propelled the state into the position of being the owner of the largest industrial enterprises in Brazil. State-owned enterprise also vastly expanded the state's tools for implementing industrial policy. Once constructed, the edifice of state-owned enterprise found an ever-expanding range of applications. The case of petroleum was the most dramatic and important.

Theory of the new institutional economics posits that successful institutional change requires increasing returns to new arrangements, reconcilable path dependence (logical connections with, and departures from, previous arrangements) and declining transactions costs. Two additional factors emerge from this study: reconciliation with ancillary institutions and distribution of the gains to the actors incurring their costs. This history of iron ore also demonstrates the interaction between economic reality and ideology. The early efforts to develop mining and industry did not occur along a linear path, and the continuity of property regimes across time has been impressive.[3] The present and future of the mineral economy are also not necessarily linear. While privatization of enterprise, but not of un-mined minerals, had gained significant momentum in the 1990s, reasons have since arisen to question the durability of that trend. Many of the concerns that motivated the economic ideas and policies of state capitalism remain and re-emerge as public concerns.

Further, other institutional interests can arise to claim a position in the debates about the extraction of natural resources. Environmental regulation and degradation are topics falling within the rubric of state control and government regulation with respect to minerals (and non-renewable natural resources more broadly) that have not been addressed in this study. This silence matches the Brazilian silence on the topic generally, during the years of interest here.[4] While the 1988 Constitution was the first to address environmental issues, mandating environmental impact statements and fines for unanticipated negative impacts, commentary finds that avoiding environmental regulation is common and concludes that 'definitive reconciliation between mining and environmental protection' is a task for the twenty-first century.[5] The late emergence of environmental issues within the mining sector is not unusual for a resource-intensive, late-developing economy. It also reflects an attitude entrenched from a colonial history focused on providing natural resources.

Ever-present lofty economic ambitions and the abundance of iron ore combined to create a crucial, but unheralded, place in Brazilian economic history and political economy. The particular history of developing iron ore deposits into an economic commodity reflected Brazilian resource and institutional endowments as well as the confluence of specific historical events. Nevertheless, the issues impeding the economic use of this mineral were not unique. The special characteristics common to non-renewable natural resources and the complex requirements of their conversion from natural resource to economic commodity suggest that the issues predominant in this study – property rights, aligning institutional effects, the role of the state and historical trajectory – can be at least as important as the presence of resources in determining their use.

DATA APPENDIX

The newly accumulated empirical data for this book come from a wide variety of sources. The sources and treatment for these variables merit detailed explanation.

Laws and Decrees

In commemoration of its fiftieth anniversary (1992), the Companhia Vale do Rio Doce commissioned a five-volume history of mining in Brazil.[1] The *Coletânea da Legislação*, from this collection, offers identifying information and the *ementa* (brief abstract) of federal legislation affecting mining. This publication has served to identify national-level legislation from 1891 to 1946. When consulting the full text of legislation, I have relied on the official Brazilian government website.[2] Accumulating the appropriate legislation from the pre-Republican era and for the state of Minas Gerais required other sources. The comprehensive guide to the legislation of imperial Brazil[3] provided the finding aid to identify legislation by its subject. The official website provides identifying data, *ementa* and when necessary the text of the legislation. For the legislation from Minas Gerais (Chapter 4 and Appendix Table A.1B), I have relied on the indexation that the library of the state assembly is compiling (as of 2007, which they kindly shared with me). Laws passed but not enabled through subsequent legislation are not included. (However, Appendix Table A.1A, with the most important legislation that fundamentally shaped mining, identifies important laws that were passed, but did not take effect.) I have also excluded legislation that reauthorized, without change, existing provisions.

Until 1891, mining fell exclusively under federal jurisdiction. Both federal and state governments tinkered with mining rights from then until 1934. For this period, legislation and decrees from Minas Gerais and at the federal level capture the important trends in mineral rights.[4] After the Mining Code and a new Constitution became effective in 1934, governance emanated from the national level, with some input from the states; therefore I continue to consider both federal and *mineiro* (from Minas Gerais and few in number) law from 1880 until 1940 (Chapter 4). Despite the need to incorporate actions from varying jurisdictions, the laws and decrees define the Brazilian institutional environment.[5]

The legislation that determined access to mineral resources covered a wide range of topics, from the structural parameters of the sector to decrees allowing for individual actions, such as building trunk lines connecting to main rail-lines to transport ore. Categorizing each regulatory action that defined mineral rights from 1880 through 1940 by its intended purpose in Chapter 4 constructs a record of the legal environment of mineral property rights. As one caveat to this classification, the laws and decrees affecting railroad concessions are included only when initially granted or when changed to significantly affect mining capabilities. The multitude of intermediary decrees that approved specific feasibility studies, expenditures and minor routing changes (of lines that had previous approval) are not included.

For Chapter 4, I have consolidated the 108 laws and decrees from 1880 to 1940 that explicitly addressed subsoil rights and access to resources in the public domain, as well as provisions to support infrastructure that serviced mining (primarily railroads), tax or fiscal provisions and administrative procedures. Because of its central importance to Brazilian mining and frequent vertical integration, benefits and subsidies to steel companies are included in this group. I have separately considered regulatory actions put into effect from 1891 until 1934 that targeted their direct impact to specific individual beneficiaries. These beneficiaries achieved benefit by seeking legislative or executive decrees that offered tax relief, granted land that could be cleared for charcoal production, extended the time period for demonstrating beneficial use, and granted the ability the extend railway trunk lines.[6] Comparison with the extent of favours granted by the federal government for the same activities described here is not feasible, because of the scope of the data collection effort required. Because seeking individual benefit from the legislative and regulatory system, within Minas Gerais, did not begin until 1907 – seventeen years after the change in mining rights, I would argue that it was newly introduced behaviour, at least with respect to state-level regulation.

Appendix Table A.1A identifies the most important national legislative actions that structured mining rights; the important regulatory activity of Minas Gerais, 1889–1934 is in Table A.1B. Appendix Tables A.2A and A.2B summarize the number of all general legislative actions, by jurisdiction, annually.

Mining Concessions

The second body of empirical data for Chapter 4 is the tabulation of all of the concessions issued to prospect and mine in the state of Minas Gerais from 1880 to 1940. Concessions to prospect[7] did not always yield economically viable results. When they did, miners required a new concession allowing them to extract minerals.[8] The national government issued concessions to prospect and to mine in the form of executive decrees. From 1934, the Mining Code replaced 'concessions' to prospect with authorizations. They served essentially the same purpose. I have included them as concessions to prospect in order to avoid the unnecessary complication of introducing another term/variable.

The concessionary decrees offer ordinal, rather than nominal data. They identified the concessionaires and the location of the vein. The concessionary decree also stated any limitation on the mineral(s) that it covered; absent specific mention, prospectors and miners could prospect/extract any mineral. The decrees seldom specified normalized quantitative parameters that defined their limits, such as a measure of area, extent of vein or quantity of mineral. Mining concessions indicated the discovery of mineral deposits, but they did not necessarily result in mining. Other constraints were continually present, including limited infrastructure, technology and capital. Concessions were not transferable. Appendix Table A.3 reports the annual pattern of concessions from 1880 until 1940, as used in Chapter 4.

Concessions constitute a separate database from the laws and decrees (though an argument can support their inclusion in the regulatory data set as offering benefit to a specific agent). The *Coletânea da Legislação* also reports on the concessions and authorizations (initiated in the 1930s, and treated as concessions to prospect). I report newly issued concessions – gross new concessions to prospect and mine; those that were extended (in time), revoked, or transferred (only one) are not included. Usually, concessions were issued in the names of individuals, with the right of those individuals to subsequently form companies, without getting new concessions. When mining companies or already existing partnerships acquired additional concessions, that was noted.

Land-Transfer Registries

While privatized, the state of Minas Gerais issued few concessions.[9] Acquiring land in order to prospect and/or mine offered more secure access. Therefore, I also look at the sales of land in the municipalities of Sabará and Itabira (in Minas Gerais)[10] that the public notarial registries designated as mining-related. Sabará and Itabira were the areas of most intense iron ore development through the first half of the twentieth century, and Sabará was the regulatory seat of the longest-term and most successful gold mining in Brazilian history.[11] Land transfer registries are maintained by *município*, and the local chief justice controls outside access to the notarial registrations. The chief municipal judges of Sabará and Itabira, granted me access to categorize the transfers for this project.

Notarial registrations of sales are also ordinal data; they indicated the transfer of 'mining land' [*terra de mineração*];[12] they also identified the buyers and sellers and the value of the transaction, but not the size of land holding or estimated value of mineral deposits. These deeds noted whether the transfer was for *terra de mineração* (without indicating the extent or certainty of mineral deposits). Absent any other source, I have relied upon this categorization. The sale price is indicated in the registry entries; but natural features, rather than area measures, denote land boundaries. As a result, we cannot determine consistent market values. One of my original ambitions was to maintain a record of the share of all registrations that included mining land (this varied substantially). However, in the 1930s thousands of registrations for small parcels of residential housing were entered in Sabará for the newly burgeoning settlement of Belo Horizonte, and this measure became useless. Finally, I have removed outliers, as measured by the largest 1 per cent of transfers (five in number). These were specific corporate reorganizations that did not represent the accumulation of new properties. Appendix Table A.4 enumerates the 436 land transactions from 1880 to 1940 in these municipalities used in Chapter 4.

Counterfactual Estimates

1921 Itabira Iron Ore Company: Contribution to Brazilian Macroeconomy (Chapter 4 and Appendix Table A.6)

The first plan for the Itabira Iron Ore Company presented by Percival Farquhar to potential investors and to the Brazilian and Minas Gerais governments for approvals included projections of iron ore production and exports, as well as plans for a steel production plant.

In order to calculate the notional contribution that this project could have made to the Brazilian economy, I assume the most favourable conditions for the project: that it had started immediately, begun production on schedule and met original production targets immediately. With respect to iron ore, these assumptions are that exports would begin in 1923 at the level of 750,000 metric tons annually. Pig iron production is assumed to begin in 1925, with 125,000 metric tons per year. The pig iron production is assumed to be entirely for import-substituting purposes (i.e., reducing imports).

Notional iron ore exports =   actual iron ore exports + IIO plan   (750,000 metric tons/year)

Notional pig iron imports =   actual pig iron imports – IIO plan   (150,000 metric tons/year)

Total opportunity cost =   Notional exports + notional imports

For prices, I assume that the lower of international prices or domestic Brazilian prices would prevail for the production undertaken by IIO. Recognition of Brazil's position as a price-taker in international markets dictated the choice to use the lower-bound prices, and reliable international price indices for these commodities do not exist for the first half of the twentieth century. For iron ore, I assume an international price that was the lower of Brazilian or Swedish prices. (Sweden was Britain's traditional supplier of ore, and replacing this source justified the original international intervention for iron ore during World War II.) For pig iron, I assume prices to be the lower of Brazilian domestic prices (without the presence of Itabira production) or average US prices.

To translate the effects of trade into a result for the Brazilian economy, I use annual average exchange rates, from Global Financial Data (globalfinancialdata.com). Total actual Brazilian imports and exports are from IBGE *Estatísticas Históricas* (1990, Tables 4.3 and 11.2); GDP was calculated from Abreu (1989) Statistical Appendix. The calculation is shown in Appendix Table A.6 and the macro-level data are presented in Appendix Table A.10.

Capital Costs of the Itabira Iron Ore Project (Chapter 4)

Although quantifying the capital cost of a large-scale mining sector is rife with problems and extends beyond the scope of this project, an idea of its magnitude appears in Chapter 4 and the data are embedded in Table 4.3. This section explains that analysis. The available evidence derives from plans to develop the Itabira iron ore deposits between 1911 and 1942. The plans differed with respect to scale of operation, strategy for infrastructure development and market expectations. The anticipated level of investment was subject to a wide range of variables, with an unspecified allocation between equity and debt. The macro-level data are inconsistent for these years; therefore, the terms of comparison are similarly problematic. Further, accessing international debt markets for much of the period was infeasible for Brazilian enterprise since the Brazilian Treasury was in default on its international debt obligations from 1932 until 1945.[13] Despite these constraints, we know that entrepreneurs actively pursued the Itabira project, and that any feasible project for industrial development of iron ore mines required three capital-intensive efforts: development of mines, railroads and ports, and the construction of a refining and concentration plant.

Taken independently, without relying on the anticipated externalities of widely dispersed industrial development, wealth creation or predictions of future investment, the plans for this one project[14] would have required financial resources on a scale that Brazilians could not expect to mobilize (see Table 4.1). Alternatively, if financed entirely by external debt at the time each plan was under consideration, the Itabira project would have accounted for about

3 per cent to 11 per cent of total international debt. Projected debt service can serve as a proxy for the opportunity cost of the project. The servicing obligations in the first year of each of the Itabira project proposals, under the overly optimistic assumption that the Itabira project could assume debt at the rate of sovereign borrowing, would have been the equivalent 6 per cent to 10 per cent of the existing public debt service.[15] As a private sector project, exploiting the Itabira deposits could have equalled an amount that ranged from about 40 per cent to more than the full amount of private and public capital inflows in the year the project variations were proposed.[16] At the other end of the continuum of financing options, capitalized entirely as a private Brazilian enterprise at any time between 1911 and 1940, the Itabira project would have registered statutory capital three to ten times larger than the largest company listed on the Rio de Janeiro exchange.

Explicit projections for the Itabira investment plan of 1928 and the actual initial distribution of capital and long-term debt in 1942 both allocated about 40 per cent of the initial investment to equity; long-term debt provided the remainder of the resources. The domestic equity assumed in the 1928 projection, which did not anticipate public sector investment, would have resulted in an enterprise with statutory capital ten times larger than any private Brazilian company at the time, and almost twice as large as any firm (with public, private or mixed ownership) that was not a bank or railroad. When the Companhia Vale de Rio Doce opened on the Bolsa de Valores in 1942 as a mixed state-owned/private enterprise, its statutory capital was 200,000 *contos*, one-third larger than the next largest enterprise, and its long-term debt (US $14 million, extended by the US Export-Import Bank) more than doubled the par value of the firm's long-term liabilities.[17]

Capital Markets

No overall data compilations for capital market activities exist for Brazilian exchanges prior to 1964. The data used in Chapter 5 cover the mining and metallurgy companies listed on the Rio de Janeiro Stock Exchange, and they come from two sources. The annual reports of the professional association of stockbrokers[18] listed the actual trades that the brokers transacted, with their price; they also listed all of the companies eligible to trade, with the par (or book) value of the equity shares. The annual reports offer data on the basis of full-year results (maximum and minimum trading prices and, for some years, the volume of trading). Book value of equity and corporate listings are reported at year-end. These reports are organized by sector, categorizing mining and metallurgy as a distinct sector. Because trading in equity shares remained quite thin during the period that I have considered (1890–1960) I also accumulated the price quotations from market-making brokers that had been manually recorded in the 'Movimento da Bolsa', currently housed at the Arquivo Nacional.[19] These data are available for selected years from 1940 to 1960, and daily quotes were aggregated into annual un-weighted averages. From these data, I calculate both actual and notional market to book price ratios (for selected years) in Chapter 5 and Appendix Tables A.8A–A.8C.

Companhia Vale Do Rio Doce Financial Data

The financial and production data from Vale come from the company's publicly available annual reports. Because of complicated accounting practices, the financial statements are difficult to understand. Rather than attempting to restate the financial reports to ensure consistency, I have used them in their unadjusted form (Appendix Tables A.7A and A.7B. I also report the financial results in *cruzeiros*, rather than US dollars; any distortions created by multiple exchange rates result from the company's reporting, rather than my (clumsy) attempts to restate them.[20]

Production and Export Data

To the extent possible, production and export data come from United Nations Publications (the *Statistical Yearbook* and *International Trade Statistics*, respectively). These data offer the benefits of consistency and global comparability. Both features are important in Chapter 5. An alternative data source, the International Iron and Steel Institute *Yearbook* does not agree with the United Nations data, either by country or in the aggregate. Private communication with the IISI indicated that the discrepancy probably arises from reporting methodology. The United Nations relies on government-provided aggregate data; IISI aggregates data reported from producing companies. The IISI recommendation to users is to use one source or the other, without indicating an opinion about the accuracy of either.[21] Historical data (for the period prior to 1934, in Chapter 4) come from Gonsalves, 'O Ferro na Economia' (1937). These data do not include explanatory or methodological clarification; but they concord with the sources form the United Nations statistical publications, used in Chapter 5. The availability of data is:

		First year available
Iron ore	Production	1932
	Exports	Sporadically before 1944
Pig iron	Production	1911
	Exports	1930 (sporadically from 1910)

Note: Iron ore production data are unavailable after 1990 (for unknown reasons).

Data were not collected consistently until the 1940s. The occasional collection prior to these years left the definitions of categories unclear. For example, the data on the production of iron ore are reported differently in the Brazilian *Anuário Estatístico* and the United Nations *Statistical Yearbook* (and the degree of ore refinement does not appear to explain the difference); the data reported in these sources on pig iron agree. As a result, macro-level analysis is severely limited, and the quantitative results can only be interpreted with great caution and within the context wider historical evidence.

In considering the volume of exports, I have chosen to report on quantities (thousands of metric tons). However, when considering Brazil's share of world exports, comparable data are only available in value (US dollars) terms, and global aggregates are only available from 1967. Export data for iron ore and pig iron (SITC codes 281 and 671, respectively) are available. 'Crude steel' is a composite of SITC 3-digit codes that cannot be aggregated reliably, and was not the focus of Brazilian trade development efforts; therefore, I have not included that category in Figures 5.3 and 5.4.

Interest Rates

For international bond prices, to determine their yields (interest rate), I have used *The Economist* (London) for 1911 and the *Chronicle of Finance and Commerce* (New York) for post-World War I (in Chapters 4 and 5). These prices represent the location of the most vibrant markets for Brazilian bonds placed internationally. Brazilian international debt was in default from 1932 to 1945, therefore no interest rate can be applied to these years.

APPENDIX TABLES

Table A.1A: Mining legislation through Brazilian history, national level.

D-M-Year	Type	No.	Purpose or impact on mining
Colonial Period			
11-2-1601	A	NA	Establish the *Quinto* on gold
15-8-1603	A		Regulate mineral lands (*Código Filipino*)
8-8-1618	A		Reaffirm Regulation of 1603
7-6-1644			Divide mines in south
0-0-1694	CR		Promise honors and riches to discoverers of gold mines
0-0-1700			Tentative regulate gold mining
19-5-1702			Establish the *Guarda-mór* (regional superintendency), with responsibility for regulating gold mines
9-5-1703	CR		Open *Casa de Registro de Ouro*
0-0-1713	CR		Prohibit clergy from mining
24-2-1720			Regulate water
17-10-1733	A		Construct roads in mining areas and expand regulatory authority for *Gurada-mór* to include deep-shaft mines
24-12-1734	A		Establish diamond mines as royal patrimony
11-8-1735	A		Establish monopoly for trading mines
19-5-1736			Define (for first time) public domain resources (*terras devolutas*) to include mineral veins
19-2-1752	L		Exempt miners with more than thirty slaves exempt from bankruptcy penalties (*Lei da Trinteina*)
29-10-1756	A		Prohibit Portuguese emigration to the mines of Brazil
22-12-1761	L		Abolish the office of *Contador-mór*
28-2-1765	CR		Grant exclusive ten-year concession to Domingos Ferreira to mine iron, lead and tin and to establish a factory
5-1-1785	A		Regularize *sesmarias*, by requiring registration and demarcation of boundaries

D-M-Year	Type	No.	Purpose or impact on mining
27-5-1795	A		Abolish tax on iron ore and conceded freedom to open iron foundries
9-8-1795	CR		Approve first iron foundry; limit price to cost of production + 10%
12-7-1799	CR		Permit to metallurgist João Manco Pereira to open a iron forge in SP (first to access Sorocaba-Ipanema)
24-4-1801	A		Permit to create (another) foundry in Sorocaba
13-5-1803	A		Designate royal signia to establish legal concession and the royal mint in Minas Gerais (*Real Junta Administrativa de Mineração e Monedagem*)
1-4-1808	A		Establish freely of any type of manufacturing factory in Brazil
Portuguese Court in Brazil			
1-9-1808	A		Regulate flow of coinage, and prohibit circulation of gold in powdered form
1-9-1808	CR		Determine the size of the army to go to Minas Gerais
5-9-1808	D		Establish, within Royal Treasury, a director and administration for diamond mining
10-10-1808	D	41	Specify administration of diamond industry and establish foundry in Minas Gerais (with Royal subsidy)
5-11-1808	D		Govern the exchange of powdered gold and Spanish *patacas* in Minas Gerais
24-11-1808	CR		Grant ten-year tax exemption for production of iron
18-1-1809	D	3	Allow recruitment of overseers for ranching, farms and miners
27-10-1809	CR		Regulate *sesmaria* and mineral *datas* of the Rio Doce in Minas Gerais
3-11-1809	D		Nominate the first and second directors for the exploration of gold lands in São Pedro do Rio Grande do Sul on behalf of Royal Treasury
13-11-1809	CR		Create council to collect diamond taxes in Cuyabá, Mato Gross
7-2-1810	D	6	Issue instructions on gold exploration in São Paulo do Rio Grande do Sul
12-2-1810	A		Provide instruction to control trade in powdered gold
13-5-1810	D		Advance royal loan (100,000 *contos*) for the establishment of arms factory at Ipanema, provisioned by factory at Sorocaba
4-12-1810	CR		Fund an iron ore mining enterprise in Sorocaba, São Paulo
12-1-1811	A		Recommend the establishment of companies to regularly work with machines appropriated to gold mines
12-7-1811	CR		Establish further provisions for iron ore mining in Sorocaba, São Paulo
28-8-1811	CR		Establish further provisions for iron forge in Sorocaba, São Paul
30-8-1811	CR		Approve subscription for partnership to establish a foundry in Congonhas, Minas Gerais

D-M-Year	Type	No.	Purpose or impact on mining
25-9-1811	CR		Instruct on tax collection of the *quinto* to provide for collection on gold powder in Minas Gerais
12-11-1811	A		Require each army regiment to maintain their arms, and delay replacement
12-5-1812	D	16	Halt gold exploration on behalf of the Royal Treasury in São Pedro do Rio Grande do Sul
8-6-1812	D		Allow establishment of a diamond polishing factory
17-11-1813	A		Extend to all miners the privileges conceded by *Lei da Trinteina* to those possessing more than 30 slaves
16-1-1817	CR		Approve statutes of the new Cuyabá Mining Company.
12-8-1817	CR		Approve the establishment of mining companies in Minas Gerais, and established the statutes
7-4-1818	D		Create, within Banco do Brasil, an office for buying and selling gold
29-3-1819	CR		Concede the exclusive privilege of extracting and forging iron \to the Cuyabá Mining Company in Mato Grosso
8-7-1819	A		Clarify wording of the *alvará* of 17 November 1813 (extending the *Lei da Treitena*)
7-9-1820	D		Provide support to mining in Minas Gerais
28-9-1820	A		Set framework for granting concessions to miners
21-2-1821	CR		Recharter the Anicuns Mining Company of Goyaz
17-7-1822			Suspend new grants of *sesmarias*

Brazilian Empire

D-M-Year	Type	No.	Purpose or impact on mining
20-10-1823	Const. Assembly		Continue Portuguese law, after independence, unless specifically changed
25-3-1824	LC		Limit rights of 'public power' over private property, separate surface & subsoil (Article 179), implicitly include mines in *Patrimónío da Coroa* (Section 21)
16-9-1824	D		Allow formation of mining companies with Brazilian and foreign partners
17-9-1824	D		Send notification to legally working mines that they continue under the same laws and orders as colonial rule
12-8-1825	D		Protect against abuses that the formation of mining companies in London can introduce
10-5-1827			Exempt all mining companies from the deposits that they had been required
26-10-1827			Finalize customs rules
13-11-1827	L		Regulate the mode of payments for public contracts or alienable property sales, and abolish the privileges raised in Minas Gerais for the payment of public debt

D-M-Year	Type	No.	Purpose or impact on mining
27-1-1829	D		Declare that subjects of the Empire do not need authorization to undertake mining, with Brazilian or foreign partners, on lands that they own.
20-3-1829			Provisionally recognize all known deposits by the Council of the Province of Minas Gerais
26-3-1829			Provisionally approve the financing for the resolution of the Council of the Province of Minas Gerais to register known mineral deposits
27-8-1829	D		Reaffirm the right, independent of authorization or license, to mine on privately owned land by Brazilian owners, either by themselves or through companies
25-7-1831			Allow nationals [Brazilian citizens] to form mining companies
6-7-1832			Authorize the government to receive gold at the *Casa da Moeda* [mint] until the end of June 1833, independently of other rules and regulations
25-10-1832	L		Confirm that all current and future diamond mines are property of the nation
30-8-1833			Subject the mining and sugar factories and cane fields to the general laws
8-10-1833			Establish a new monetary standard and a deposit bank, and authorize the government to enter into contracts with individuals or companies to mine land in the public domain
27-5-1834			Authorize the formation of a company to mine *candonga* in the province of Minas Gerais
23-3-1839			Require the General Assembly to authorize diamond mining
24-9-1845	L	374	Reconfirm public domain of diamond mines
14-5-1849			Specify that the license to mine does not automatically extend to foreigners
12-5-1850		25	Commercial Code
18-9-1850	L	601	Land Law (Article 16, §4 on ownership and subsoil)
26-8-1853		1222	Alter the table of rates for coinage, forging and refining of gold
31-7-1854	CCE		Declare that the coal mines belong in the domain of the state
22-10-1858	L	982	Authorize third-party mining on private land through expropriation, with authorization
22-8-1860			Establish regulations for issuing banks, currency and mining companies
6-10-1863	A		Require approval of legislative power for mining concessions
21-3-1864	D	3236	Define size of gold *data* (in Article 1; reaffirmed in 1876)
24-9-1864	L	1237	Prohibit mortgages on land with mining access (general mortgage law)

D-M-Year	Type	No.	Purpose or impact on mining
29-11-1864			Establish time period for mining concessionaires to begin mining, and to re-begin interrupted work
19-8-1866	CCE		Declare that landowners need license from government to mine on their land
6-10-1866	A		Declare that the quality of the soil does not impinge a mining authorization
24-9-1868	A		Declare that mines and diamond territories belong to the domain of the State
19-8-1870	CCE		Declare that the discovery of minerals does not confer *ipso facto* to the discoverer the right to extract, neither does it provide the same right to the landowner, but requires a license of the Government
7-2-1871	A		Affirm principles about the discovery of mines and their property [first right of extraction belongs to veins' discoverer], and declare that coal, bituminous schist and other substances are equipped as [legally treated equally with] precious metals

Provisional Government

29-3-1890	D	288	Regulate the transfer of mineral veins and vacate explorations, reconfirm that concessions are not transferable
31-5-1890	D	451-B	*Registro Torrens* (land registry)
22-7-1890	D	510	Establish private property, state that the mines belong to the owner of the land (pre-Constitutional decree)
5-11-1890	DL	955-A	Enabling legislation for *Registro Torrens*

First Republic

24-2-1891	LC		Constitution (Article 72, §17, Article 73, §16 Article 64; [devolve public domain to states; Brazilians & foreigners allowed to mine and subsoil attached to surface])
7-6-1891	L	47	Regulate mining (first attempt during First Republic)
4-7-1895	D	275	Exempt from import duties the material and machinery intended for coal mining
9-10-1899	D	3432	Cancel all mining and prospecting concessions that had not met the requirements to demonstrate beneficial use
29-12-1906	L	1601	Establish a Ministry of Agriculture, Industry and Commerce that includes jurisdiction over mining
10-1-1907	D	6323	Create the Geology and Mineralogy Service within Ministry of Agriculture
11-1-1911	D	2406	Authorize government to concede favours to steel companies
4-1-1912	L	2544	Close Fábrica de Ferro de São João de Ipanema (Army's arms plant)

D-M-Year	Type	No.	Purpose or impact on mining
5-3-1913	D	10105	Re-regulate public-domain land to allow the federal government some claims
6-1-1915	D	2933	*Lei Calógeras*; first attempt to move subsoil rights back to federal government
10-2-1915	D	11485	Revoke public domain law (No. 10105) of 1913
1-1-1916	L	3071	Civil Code; reaffirm subsoil as accessory to land (Section VI, Article 590, sub-section 2) and define conditions for expropriating if land owner resists
16-8-1917	D	3316	Authorize subsidies for steel companies
3-10-1917	D	3347	Authorize subsidies for coal companies
30-3-1918	D	12943	Establish national favours for supplying coal
30-3-1918	D	12944	Specify terms of national government's first participation within steel
23-3-1919	L	750	Increase export tax on iron ore, but establishes an exemption if exporter establishes domestic iron and steel plants
5-1-1921	D	14605	Prohibit export of gold, silver, nickel, bronze and other metals used as coinage or in bars
6-1-1921	D	4246	Establish further steel and coal subsidies
15-1-1921	D	4265	*Lei Simões Lopes* (enabling *Lei Calógeras*) establish mines as real property, accessory to the surface, but distinct from it (Article 6); landowner can separate mine from surface and mine can be mortgaged (Article 8). Lessee cannot sublease mine or transfer lease (if a business unwinds). First discoverer has preferential access; foreigners can mine; size of concessions defined.
28-12-1922	D	15211	Regulate mines (under *Lei Simões Lopes*); possible heirs to a mine, limited to necessary heirs & surviving spouse
10-8-1922	L	4555	Revoke previous government contracts for steel and set up incentives to start steel companies; also create new incentives for gold mining
10-1-1925	D	4910	Provide tax relief on coal- and gold- mining related equipment
7-9-1926	LC		Amend Constitution; reaffirmed Article 72, Section 17 joining subsoil to surface, but allow for right of expropriation for national security; prevent foreign ownership of mining land that might be subject to expropriation for reasons of national security

Provisional Government

D-M-Year	Type	No.	Purpose or impact on mining
17-7-1931	D	20223	Suspend alienation of all *jazidas* (with further amendments: 16 December '31, 23 August '32, 24 October '33)
16-11-1932	D	22096	Establish mining works as 'public good' – specifically in context of supporting industrialization
11-1-1933	D	22338	Organize the Institute of Geology and Mineralogy
28-7-1933	D	23016	Create General Directorship of Mineral Production within Agriculture Ministry (antecedent to DNPM)

D-M-Year	Type	No.	Purpose or impact on mining
7-12-1933	D	23566	Prohibit export of Brazilian iron, steel, copper, tin, lead, zinc, aluminum and antimony
21-2-1934	D	23900	Set transport prices for minerals (including iron ore)
27-2-1934	D	23936	Regulate exploration on private lands
Vargas Regime			
10-7-1934	D	24642	Mining Code
11-7-1934	D	24673	Water Code
16-7-1934	LC		Constitution
10-9-1935	L	94	Extend time period for registering mines
14-1-1936	D	585	Regulate areas for exploring and mining concessions, as specified in Mining Code
10-11-1937	LC		Constitution; Articles 16, 122, 143, 144: mines in public domain; only Brazilians can explore
14-12-1937	DL	66	Modify Mining Code: only Brazilians or Brazilian companies can mine (brings into conformity with Constitution)
11-4-1938	D	366	Govern oil pipelines (which are specified to be mineral)
8-12-1938	D	938	Require federal authorization for mining companies
8-4-1938	D	1202	Set the conditions for devolving administration of federal mining regulation to the states
29-1-1940	DL	1985	Amend Mining Code to exclude petroleum and natural gas from its purview
12-11-1940	DL	2778	Allow Brazilians married to foreigners to be shareholders in mining companies
7-5-1941	DL	3236	Establish petroleum and natural gas legislation
21-6-1941	DL	3365	Reaffirm that mineral veins are public goods, subject to expropriation
25-8-1941	DL	3553	Establish that President of the Republic can mandate corporate reorganization of foreign-owned mining companies
13-5-1942	LC		Amend Constitution (Article 11) restate and clarify nationality constraints to access of mines and water
25-8-1942	DL	4613	Nationalize coal
18-1-1943	DL	5201	Suspend mining temporarily
Post-Vargas Regimes			
1-1-1946	LC		Constitution
1-1-1967	LC		Constitution
27-2-1967	DL	227	Restatement of Mining Code (allows foreign participation)
1-1-1988	LC		Constitution (transfer ownership of mines to the state, abandoning *res nullius* status) and exclude foreign participation

Table A.1B: Mining legislation, Minas Gerais, 1890–1940.

D-M-Yr	Type	No.	Purpose or impact on mining
24-5-1890	L	82	Establish state export taxes
25-6-1892	L	27	Regulate demarcation of public domain land
9-11-1892	D	597	Approve regulatory instructions for the commission of geographic and geological exploration in the state of Minas Gerais
4-9-1896	L	173	Explicate the legitimization for concession of public lands
8-10-1896	D	967	Approve the regulation of diamond land
27-8-1899	L	269	Concede to all Brazilian citizens who request in a free lot of 20, 30, or 50 hectares of land
18-9-1899	L	285	Regulate the exploration of mines
18-9-1905	L	320	Regulate concession of railroads for metallurgical and mining industries
3-5-1906	D	1516	Regulate the concession of land to industries and associations [partnerships] and the sale to private parties
16-9-1906	L	344	Authorize state government to concede prospecting privileges for minerals on riverbanks within Minas Gerais
25-9-1910	L	437	Create Geology Service, attached to the General Directorate of Agriculture, Industry and Infrastructure, an information section for mining and other natural resources of the state, with affiliated offices overseas
12-9-1911	L	455	Authorize state government to freely concede, to foreigners with family within the state, lots of public domain land
20-9-1915	L	574	Authorize state government to make concessions for mineral exploration
23-11-1917	D	4050	Approve the regulation of diamond land
13-9-1920	L	675	Grant two years to occupants of public domain land to legitimate holding
22-11-1922	D	5121	Set taxes on goods destined for export
24-9-1923	L	750	Raise the export tax for iron ore
17-9-1924	L	777	Establish the tax for exported manganese for exporters who install electric furnaces for the manufacture of ferro-manganese
19-9-1924	L	789	Re-establish the *Comissão Geográfica e Geológica*
29-9-1925	L	823	Authorize the concession to each of the first five businesses that propose to establish steel companies with annual production of 60,000 tonnes of iron and steel in the state
1-11-1927	L	857	Issue dispositions regarding the use of existing mineral veins in the state and the regulation and incentives to mining and metallurgy industries
2-12-1927	D	6413	Grant tax exemption for the export of plant-based coal

D-M-Yr	Type	No.	Purpose or impact on mining
5-2-1931	D	7478	Re-validate concessions on diamond lands on the banks of the Jequitinhonha River
26-2-1931	D	7535	Nominate members of the Council of Mines
24-5-1931	D	7647	Approve the regulation of manganese exports from the state
30-8-1931	L	947	Authorize the to commission studies of the state's subsoil to verify the existence of petroleum and euxenite
20-10-1933	L	1129	Modify manganese export tax
13-9-1934	L	1155	Prolong the term for title holders of concessions of public domain land to register
28-12-1939	L	54	Approve the agreement between the federal government and the state of Minas Gerais for the execution of the Mining Code
28-6-1944	L	708	Fix state and municipal tax on minerals

Note: Table A.1 only includes important structural legislation – provisions that do not confer concession (except during colonial era), corporate statutes or privileges to specific individuals or companies. Inevitably, some decisions on inclusion are subjective.
The following abbreviations have been used throughout Table A.1:*

A	*Alvará*
CR	*Carta Régia* (Royal Letter)
D	Decree
DL	Decree-law (*Decreto-lei*)
L	Law
Const	Constitution
ConstA	Constitutional Amendment
LC	*Lei Constitucional*
CCE	Council of State Opinion (*Consulta do Conselho do Estado*)

* Especially in the earlier political regimes, I have not always been able to find the type or number of each action.
Source: see Data Appendix.

Table A.2A: Regulation for mining and mining access 1880–1940, by jurisdiction, all generally applicable regulation.

	Empire	Federal	Minas Gerais	Total		Empire	Federal	Minas Gerais	Total
1880				0	1911		1	1	2
1881				0	1912		1	0	1
1882				0	1913		1	1	2
1883				0	1914		0	1	1
1884				0	1915		2	1	3
1885				0	1916		1	0	1
1886				0	1917		2	1	3
1887				0	1918		2	0	2
1888				0	1919		1	2	3
1889				0	1920		0	1	1
1890	4	0	1	5	1921		5	0	5
1891		2	1	3	1922		1	1	2
1892		0	2	2	1923		0	2	2
1893		0	0	0	1924		1	3	4
1894		0	0	0	1925		1	2	3
1895		1	1	2	1926		1	0	1
1896		0	4	4	1927		0	2	2
1897		0	0	0	1928		0	0	0
1898		0	1	1	1929		0	1	1
1899		1	2	3	1930		0	1	1
1900		0	0	0	1931		2	6	8
1901		0	0	0	1932		2	1	3
1902		0	0	0	1933		5	2	7
1903		0	0	0	1934		5	3	8
1904		0	0	0	1935		1	0	1
1905		0	1	1	1936		1	0	1
1906		1	2	3	1937		2	0	2
1907		1	2	3	1938		2	0	2
1908		0	0	0	1939		2	1	3
1909		0	0	0	1940		3	1	4
1910		0	2	2					
					Total	4	51	53	108

Source: see Data Appendix.

Table A.2B: Regulation for mining and mining access; Minas Gerais, individual beneficiaries, 1891–1934.

		Incentive:		
	Total	Positive	Negative	Neutral
1891	0			
1892	0			
1893	0			
1894	0			
1895	0			
1896	0			
1897	0			
1898	0			
1899	0			
1900	0			
1901	0			
1902	0			
1903	0			
1904	0			
1905	0			
1906	0			
1907	1	1		
1908	1	1		
1909	1	1		
1910	1	1		
1911	2	2		
1912	1		1	
1913	0			
1914	0			
1915	2	2		
1916	4	3		1
1917	0			
1918	0			
1919	2			2
1920	0			
1921	0			
1922	0			
1923	1		1	
1924	2	2		
1925	1	1		

Table A.2B: Regulation for mining and mining access; Minas Gerais, individual beneficiaries, 1891–1934 (continued).

	Total	Positive	Incentive: Negative	Neutral
1926	2	2		
1927	2	2		
1928	1	1		
1929	0			
1930	2	2		
1931	1	1		
1932	2	1		1
1933	2			2
1934	4	3		1
Total	35	26	2	7

Source: see Data Appendix.

Table A.3: Number of concessions issued, 1880–1940.

	Mining	Prospect		Mining	Prospect
1880	0	5	1911	0	0
1881	1	6	1912	0	0
1882	6	7	1913	0	0
1883	2	7	1914	0	0
1884	0	2	1915	0	0
1885	0	4	1916	0	0
1886	0	1	1917	0	0
1887	0	5	1918	0	0
1888	2	27	1919	0	0
1889	2	4	1920	0	1
1890	2	15	1921	0	1
1891	0	5	1922	0	1
1892	0	0	1923	0	1
1893	0	0	1924	0	3
1894	0	0	1925	0	5
1895	0	0	1926	0	3
1896	0	0	1927	0	3
1897	0	0	1928	0	2
1898	0	0	1929	0	2
1899	0	0	1930	0	1
1900	0	0	1931	0	0
1901	0	0	1932	1	1
1902	1	2	1933	10	7
1903	0	3	1934	19	0
1904	0	1	1935	1	0
1905	0	0	1936	2	0
1906	0	0	1937	4	0
1907	0	0	1938	3	1
1908	0	0	1939	4	0
1909	0	0	1940	0	0
1910	0	1			

Source: see Data Appendix.

Table A.4: Land transfer registrations, Sabará and Itabira: 1880–1940.

	Sabará		Itabira			Sabará		Itabira	
Year	Number	Avg value	Number	Avg value	Year	Number	Avg value	Number	Avg v
1880	2	62,150	0						
1881	0		0		1911	15	23,935	15	24,02
1882	1	12,043	0		1912	5	844	42	12,25
1883	1	15,000	0		1913	17	35,464	12	4,97
1884	4	13,883	0		1914	12	13,381	9	82
1885	0		0		1915	0		3	1,93
1886	1	60,000	0		1916	2	1,750	11	4,46
1887	2	32,250	0		1917	11	17,271	3	34
1888	1	13,000	0		1918	1	500	0	
1889	1	5,414	0		1919	1	30	2	18
1890	0		2	688	1920	3	1,407	2	3,10
1891	5	9,259	0		1921	7	1,871	1	6,00
1892	1	63,000	0		1922	3	267	7	4,17
1893	3	7,200	0		1923	12	7,396	2	10,45
1894	1	15,000	0		1924	2	2,000	0	
1895	3	17,167	0		1925	6	598	2	3,00
1896	2	2,850	2	2,400	1926	4	6,313	0	
1897	2	4,200	2	5,000	1927	5	2,960	7	2,23
1898	6	25,700	2	20,125	1928	1	1,500	1	40,00
1899	10	14,910	0		1929	4	1,467	2	10,00
1900	13	316	0		1930	4	7,620	0	
1901	18	2,950	0		1931	1	230	0	
1902	6	1,298	0		1932	1	10,000	2	1,85
1903	10	3,311	0		1933	2	4,500	2	2,17
1904	10	6,983	1	100	1934	2	201,500	1	11,36
1905	7	2,545	0		1935	8	14,163	1	93
1906	2	240	1	166	1936	5	4,318	3	16,38
1907	8	1,446	0		1937	0		0	
1908	11	8,419	0		1938	3	13,583	2	1,60
1909	5	37,457	0		1939	0		0	
1910	11	1,672	7	66,186	1940	3	21,000	0	

Source: Sabará and Itabira (Minas Gerais) notarial registrations of real estate transactions
(See Data Appendix).
Note: Average value in *mil-réis*.

Table A.5: Size of metallurgy companies, total and Minas Gerais, 1907 and 1919.

Total Metallurgy	1907	1919	Factor of increase, 1919/1907
Total Brazil			
Number of companies	107	509	4.8
Statutory capital (*contos*)		67,157	
Value of production	45,696	103,646	2.3
Average: statutory capital (*contos*)		132	
production (*contos*)	427	204	0.5
Expenses: total		76,165	
transport expenses		2,167	
transportation, percentage total		2.8	
Minas Gerais			
Number of companies	6	76	12.7
Statutory capital (*contos*)		3,217	
Value of production	890	3,874	4.4
Average: statutory capital (*contos*)		42	
production (*contos*)	148	51	0.3
Expenses: total		3,008	
transport expenses		271	
transportation, percentage total		9.0	
Minas Gerais, percentage total Brazil			
Average statutory capital		32.1	
production		25.0	
Transportation percentage total expenses		316.7	
Forging and lamination of iron ore			
Total Brazil			
Number of companies	169	116	0.7
Statutory capital (*contos*)	22,964	23,870	1.0
Value of production		33,051	
Average: statutory capital (*contos*)	136	206	1.5
production (*contos*)		285	
Expenses: total		23,442	
transport expenses		536	
transportation, percentage total		2.3	

Table A.5: Size of metallurgy companies, total and Minas Gerais, 1907 and 1919 (continued).

Total Metallurgy	1907	1919	Factor of increase, 1919/1907
Minas Gerais			
Number of companies		32	
Statutory capital (*contos*)		1,317	
Value of production		1,536	
Average: statutory capital (*contos*)		41	
production (*contos*)		48	
Expenses: total		na	
transport expenses		na	
Minas Gerais, percentage total Brazil			
avg statutory capital		20.0	
production		16.8	

Sources: Industrial Census 1907 (as cited in Correa de Lago), Recenseamento 1920 (1927), table 4, on pp. 24–5; table 5, on pp. 38-9, table 16, on p. 186, table 24, on p. 394 and table 28, on p. 457.

Table A.6: Notional effect of Itabira Iron Ore Company project, 1921.

	Iron ore exports (750,000 mT/yr)		Import-substitution effect, pig iron (150,000 mT/yr)		National production	Actual production (mT,000)		
	International price (US$/mT)	Notional value of increment (*contos*)	International price (US$/mT)	Notional value of increment (*contos*)	Notional value of increment (*contos*)	Exports Iron ore	Imports Pig iron	Production Pig iron
1923	3.68	7,761		0	7,761	0.4	5.3	25.2
1924	3.72	50,658		0	50,658		16.5	25.0
1925	3.72	45,988	20.50	34,792	80,780		11.7	30.0
1926	3.76	39,713	20.28	39,026	78,739		16.2	21.3
1927	3.84	48,727	18.49	40,994	89,721		10.5	15.3
1928	3.74	47,048	17.36	39,220	86,268		2.9	25.8
1929	3.72	47,431	17.95	37,430	84,861		4.7	33.7
1930	3.71		17.47	37,162		0.0	2.0	35.3
1931	1.44	15,988	15.74	39,336	55,324	0.4	0.6	28.1
1932	2.07	17,372	14.11	33,767	51,139	1.5	0.7	28.8
1933	2.32	22,031	15.34	37,407	59,438	12.8	1.2	46.8
1934	3.13	-24,170	17.52	37,097	12,926	7.1	0.7	58.6
1935	2.48	22,704	17.99	35,001	57,705	47.2	0.5	64.1
1936	3.30	21,853	18.91	45,085	66,938	111.0	1.3	78.4
1937			22.76	51,150				98.1
1938	3.15	40,299	21.46	58,823	99,122	368.5		122.4
1939	2.52	35,714	19.63	55,720	91,434	396.9		160.0
1940	3.18	47,554	18.88	56,420	103,974	255.5		185.6
1941	3.71	54,895	21.67	64,204	119,099	420.8		208.8
1942	3.78	55,115	27.58	80,411	135,525	308.9		213.8

Sources: Gonsalves (1937), pp. 78–80; *Mineração e Metalúrgia*, 10:57 (July 1945), p. 122; Ribeiro (2001), p. 118; Appendix Tables A.10 and A.11.

Table A.7A: Companhia Vale do Rio Doce, balance sheet, 1943–64; assets.

| | Real property | | Depreciation | Railroad | | Mines | | |
	Prop-erty	Monetary correction		Prop-erty	Monetary correction	Prop-erty	Monetary correction	Total assets
1943	154							1,071
1944								
1945	352		0					2,248
1946	411							2,217
1947	559							2,288
1948	703		0					2,785
1949	808		8					2,745
1950	954		20					2,536
1951	1,337		75					2,565
1952	1,551		200					2,609
1953	1,636		323					2,651
1954	1,742		448					2,712
1955	1,897		636	1,634		256		2,443
1956	2,233	1,950	810	1,874		347		4,932
1957	2,528	1,950	982	2,070		442		5,449
1958	2,996	1,950	1,176	2,442		536		6,359
1959	3,765	1,950	1,388	3,115		609		11,283
1960	6,436	4,739	1,714	5,100		989		21,030
1961	9,611	7,291	2,170	7,541		1,438		29,784
1962	15,156	7,291	2,697	8,068		1,798		50,508
1963	24,482	17,969	4,634	13,403		4,540		88,001
1964	75,881	37,908		23,373	2,569	5,786	7,819	166,929

Source: Vale, Annual Report, various years.
Notes: Columns will not sum to the Total.
Cells with 0 indicate that the reporting item and its level were identified; left blank indicates that the category was not reported.

Table A.7B: Companhia Vale do Rio Doce, balance sheet, 1943–64
(*Cruzeiros*, millions); liabilities.

	Statutory capital	Reserves	Provision for: General	Provision for: Exchange adjustment	Dividend payable	Gains and losses Current period	Gains and losses Previous period	Total	Gross revenue	Dividend paid
3	200	12	1			−10		−10	40	
4								0		
5	300	16	6			−9	12	3	68	
6	300	20	10			−3	21	19	57	
7	300	26	11			−7	24	17	88	
8	650	32	14			−4	31	27	140	
9	650	41	6			−22	27	5	173	
0	650	52	10			23	5	23	218	
1	650	67	11		11	71	7	78	399	11
2	650	113	27		19	182			615	11
3	650	247	44		28	265			730	11
4	650	395	29		67	288	108	397	929	43
5	650	461	218	148	125	294	27	320	1,561	65
6	2,600	671	104	311	190	497			2,224	78
7	2,600	1,140	112	367	263	737			3,311	156
8	2,600	1,671	209	673	392	1,093			3,535	156
9	2,600	2,772	1,271	720	594	1,399	2	1,401	5,199	228
0	7,800	3,554	2,232	631	892	4,152			10,336	384
1	10,400	5,839	3,431	1,799	313	2,623			15,315	0
2	15,600	7,956	2,146		447	5,024			23,023	0
3	23,400	10,875	3,083		974	5,215			33,789	
4	39,000	22,708	582		1,799	33,502			90,562	

Source: Vale, Annual Report, various years.
Note: Cells with 0 indicate that the reporting item and its level were identified; left blank
indicates that the category was not reported.

Table A.8A: Mining and metallurgy companies traded on Rio de Janeiro Bolsa de Valores, 1893–1952 (selected years, 1945–52); average market-to-book value.

	Vale	CSN	Belgo-Mineira	Other mining	Steel and metallurgy	Petroleum	Coal
1893–8: No trading in mining and metallurgy							
1899			1.00				
1900							
1901							
1902			1.03				
1903			1.08				
1904							
1905			0.88				
1906							
1907			0.53				
1908			0.74				
1909			0.05				
1910							
1911							
1912			0.16				
1913							1.00
1914							1.00
1915							
1916			1.00				1.05
1917			1.58				1.50
1918							
1919			0.25				0.57
1920			0.10				0.58
1921			0.13				0.24
1922			0.07				0.49
1923			0.10				0.25
1924							
1925			0.04				1.25
1926			0.03				0.15
1927			0.03	0.75	0.96		
1928			0.06				
1929			0.04				1.90
1930							0.10
1931			0.90		1.00		
1932			1.00		1.05		
1933			0.68				
1934							
1935							
1936			0.04		1.00		
1937			0.28				0.14
1938		2.18	0.35				
1939		1.79	0.41				
1940		1.73	0.42				

Table A.8A: Mining and metallurgy companies traded on Rio de Janeiro Bolsa de Valores, 1893–1952 (continued).

	Vale	CSN	Belgo-Mineira	Other mining	Steel and metallurgy	Petroleum	Coal
1941			2.19	0.33	1.81		1.10
1942			2.94	0.82	2.90	3.53	1.36
1943		1.81	4.29	0.30	3.91	3.51	1.60
1944	0.95	1.12	1.96	0.32	2.79	2.88	1.50
1945	0.58	0.87	2.27	0.10	1.74	2.73	1.54
1950	0.45	0.90	1.98	0.10	1.05	1.32	0.39
1952	0.58	0.95	1.76	0.67	1.48	0.94	0.36

Notes: Subsector averages are weighted by number of shares traded. Blank cells indicate that no trading occurred for any companies in the relevant category for the given year.
Source: Câmara Syndical, Relátorios, various years.

Table A.8B: Mining and metallurgy companies traded on Rio de Janeiro Bolsa de Valores, 1893–1952 (selected years, 1945–52); number of shares traded.

	Vale	CSN	Belgo-Mineira	Other mining	Steel and metallurgy	Petroleum	Coal	Total
1893–8								0
1899				10				10
1900								0
1901								0
1902				500				500
1903				275				275
1904								0
1905				100				100
1906								0
1907				250				250
1908				125				125
1909				200				200
1910								0
1911								0
1912				100				100
1913							100	100
1914							275	275
1915								0
1916				320			205	525
1917				310			25	335
1918								0
1919				1,125			3,742	4,867
1920				4,110			492	4,602
1921				11,375			281	11,656
1922				3,475			407	3,882
1923				6,401			247	6,648
1924								0
1925				1,300			75	1,375
1926				6,156			241	6,397
1927				550	100	2,150		2,800
1928				1,250				1,250
1929				250			20	270
1930							702	702
1931				40		60		100
1932				570		50		620
1933				200		25		225
1934								0
1935								0
1936				2,250		6		2,256
1937				70			220	290
1938			300	105				405
1939			9,616	200				9,816
1940			20,767	1,112				21,879

Table A.8B: Mining and metallurgy companies traded on Rio de Janeiro Bolsa de Valores, 1893–1952 (continued).

	Vale	CSN	Belgo-Mineira	Other mining	Steel and metallurgy	Petroleum	Coal	Total
1941			24,866	4,109	1,300		97,560	127,835
1942			47,865	1,885	2,265	9,285	172,959	234,259
1943		13,533	87,094	100	15,568	10,736	147,113	274,144
1944	1,268	11,819	106,347	100	2,863	6,285	51,183	179,865
1945	2,613	6,902	195,707	200	11,566	2,224	36,100	255,312
1950	473	27,187	26,827	4,423	25,379	2,755	51,287	138,331
1952	2,647	27,986	34,967	1,632	29,622	2,028	55,276	154,158

Note: Blank cells indicate that no trading occurred for any companies in the relevant category for the given year.

Source: Câmara Sindical, Relatório, various years.

Table A.8C: Mining and metallurgy companies traded on Rio de Janeiro Bolsa de Valores, 1893–1952 (selected years, 1945–52); number of companies traded.

	Other Mining	Steel and metallurgy	Petroleum	Coal	Total*
1893–8					0
1899	1				1
1900					0
1901					0
1902	1				1
1903	1				1
1904					0
1905	1				1
1906					0
1907	1				1
1908	1				1
1909	1				1
1910					0
1911					0
1912	1				1
1913				1	1
1914				1	1
1915					0
1916	1			1	2
1917	2			1	3
1918					0
1919	2			2	4
1920	1			1	2
1921	1			1	2
1922	1			2	3
1923	1			1	2
1924					0
1925	1			1	2
1926	1			1	2
1927	1	1	1		3
1928	1				1
1929	1			1	2
1930				1	1
1931	1		1		2
1932	2		1		3
1933	2		1		3
1934					0
1935					0
1936	1		1		2
1937	1			1	2
1938	1				2
1939	1				2
1940	1				2

Table A.8C: Mining and metallurgy companies traded on Rio de Janeiro Bolsa de Valores, 1893–1952 (continued).

	Other Mining	Steel and metallurgy	Petroleum	Coal	Total*
1941	3	1		2	7
1942	2	1	1	2	7
1943	1	2	1	4	10
1944	1	1	1	3	9
1945	1	3	1	1	9
1950	2	10	3	1	19
1952	3	10	4	1	21

* Includes Vale, CSN and Belgo-Mineira, when they traded. Therefore from 1938, total will not represent the sum of the individual columns.

Note: Blank cells indicate that no trading occurred for any companies in the relevant category for the given year.

Source: Câmara Sindical, *Relatório*, various years.

Table A.9: Mining and metallurgy companies quoted on Rio de Janeiro Bolsa de Valores, 1894–1945.

Company	Year founded	First quoted on RJBolsa	Last quoted on RJBolsa	#shares (most recent year)
Aurifera de Minas Gerais	1892	1898	1905	1,000
Benficiamento de Minaerais	1941	1941		2,500
Branía de Petróleo		1936		6,000
Brasileira Carbonífera de Ararangúa	1917	1918		30,000
Brasileira Carbonífera de Cálcio	1912	1926		9,000
Brasileira Carbonífera de Cálcio		1943		6,000
Brasileira de Minas de Santa Matilde	1916	1916	1937	6,000
Brasileira de Usinas Metalurgicas	1941	1941		35,000
Brasileira Diamantifera		1894		30,000
Brasileira Minerais	1925	1926	1929	5,000
Carbonífera Minas de Butiá	1941	1941		360,000
Carbonífera Prospera		1944		24,000
Carbonífera Prospera	1924	1928	1924	9,600
Carbonífera Rio Grandense	1917	1936		50,000
Carbonífera Urussana	1918	1936		25,000
Combustéveis Nacional	1911	1912	1921	12,000
Extractiva e Pastoril Brasileira	1907	1907	1921	9,000
Extractiva Mineral Brasileira	1902	1902	1921	6,000
Federal de Fundição	1943	1943		10,000
Federal de Fundição		1904	1940	2,000
Ferro Brasileiro	1941	1941		175,000
Ferro Manganese	1930	1932	1930	6,000
Geral de Mineração	1917	1917	1921	6,000
Hime Comércial e Industria-ord		1944		20,000
Hime Comércial e Industria-pref		1944		15,000
Industria de Mineração e Obras-ord		1944		75,000
Industria de Mineração e Obras-pref		1944		50,000
Industria Martins Ferreira		1944		150,000
Itatig Petróleo, Asfalto e Mineração		1944		20,000
Laminação Brasileira de Ferro		1944		15,000
Manganese Queluz	1903	1904	1929	5,000
Marvin		1925		4,000
Mina de Rio de Carvão		1936		20,000
Minas de Carvão de Jacuí	1917	1917		15,000
Minas Sul RioGrandense	1911	1912	1921	1,000
Mineira Siderurgia		1945		3,000
Mineração do Brasil	1901	1903	1921	2,000
Mineração do Penedo	1918	1918	1929	1,000
Mineração e Metalurgia	1917	1918	1931	10,000
Morro da Mina	1901	1907	1921	8,000
Nacional Combustéveis	1922	1926	1929	55,000
Nacional de Petróleo	1921	1924		4,000
Nacional Mineira	1905	1908	1921	5,000

Table A.9: Mining and metallurgy companies quoted on Rio de Janeiro Bolsa de Valores, 1894–1945 (continued).

Company	Year founded	First quoted on RJBolsa	Last quoted on RJBolsa	#shares (most recent year)
Nacional Mineira	1905	1908	1921	10,000
Niquel do Brasil	1932	1932		60,000
Parafusos e Metalurgia Santa Rosa		1944		150,000
Paulista de Combustévies	1917	1925	1930	20,000
Refineria Mangalhães	1927	1927	1932	2,000
Siderurgia Belgo-Mineira – ord	1938	1938		600,000
Siderurgia Belgo-Mineira – pref				250,000
Siderurgia Nacional		1943		3,750000
Siderurgia Nacional		1943		2,500000
Sindicato de Mineração	1925	1925	1928	10,000
Sociedade Geral as Minas de Manganez	1911	1905	1911	17,500
Vale Rio Doce – ord	1943	1943		110,000
Vale Rio Doce – pref	1943	1943		90,000

Source: Câmara Sindical, *Relatório*, various years; includes all mining, metallurgy, coal, petroleum (including refining) companies actively traded on the Rio de Janeiro *Bolsa de Valores*.

Mining and the State in Brazilian Development

Table A.10: Exports of iron ore, pig iron and crude steel (metric tons, 000; 1931–97).

	Iron ore, concentrates	Iron and Steel	Pig iron	Iron and steel ingots	Iron and non-alloyed steel, flat	Iron and non-alloyed steel flat, clad	Iron and steel wire
1931	0						
1932	0						
1933	2						
1934	13						
1935	7						
1936	47						
1937	111						
1938	369						
1939	397						
1940	256						
1941	421						
1942	309						
1943	na						
1944	na						
1945	na						
1946	na						
1947	197						
1948	599						
1949	676						
1950	890						
1951	1,320						
1952	1,561						
1953	1,547						
1954	1,678						
1955	2,565						
1956	2,745	101					
1957	3,550	41					
1958	2,831	2					
1959	3,988	1					
1960	5,240	33					
1961	6,282	47					
1962	7,650	11	5				0
1963	8,268	54	47	0			0
1964	9,730	250	151	49			35
1965	12,731	482	112	201			156
1966	12,910		4	30	10		96
1967	14,279		267	76	19		242
1968	15,050		69	131	27		144
1969	21,478		55	118	44		160
1970	28,061		184	212	221		138
1971	31,020		134	89	99		69
1972	30,512		299	80	152		171
1973	44,963		472	191	124		104
1974	59,439		304	80	108		33
1975	72,522		572	33	65		38

Table A.10: Exports of iron ore, pig iron and crude steel (metric tons, 000; 1931–97) (continued).

	Iron ore, concentrates	Iron and Steel	Pig iron	Iron and steel ingots	Iron and non-alloyed steel, flat	Iron and non-alloyed steel flat, clad	Iron and steel wire
1976	67,086		870	92	101	37	32
1977	58,541		965	113	217	15	30
1978	66,370		1,175	333	382	149	53
1979	75,588		1,160	480	384	444	150
1980	78,958		1,012	285	215	744	258
1981	85,798		975	137	637	769	283
1982	80,927		902	224	627	1,302	172
1983	74,200		2,159	465	1,430	2,956	229
1984	90,294		2,782	1,445	1,850	2,489	492
1985	94,218		2,804	2,943	2,003	2,215	336
1986	90,942		2,662	2,505	1,231	2,029	355
1987	95,309		2,380	3,518	1,122	1,669	
1988	112,725		2,949	5,063	1,912	3,463	349
1989	118,431		3,382	7,032	1,584		334
1990	113,469		3,923	5,188	1,846	1,553	
1991	113,301		2,930	6,757	1,654	2,023	395
1992	108,183		2,937	6,955	2,103	2,363	348
1993	115,131		2,389	7,467	2,245	2,172	282
1994	122,801		3,046	6,416	1,977	2,293	320
1995	130,178		3,012	6,103	1,041	2,132	313
1996	128,990		2,983	6,907	762	2,206	323
1997	134,093		2,973	6,669	657	1,406	3,532

Sources: Prior to 1932: *Mineração e Metalurgia*, 10:57 (July 1945), p. 122; 1932–97: United Nations *Statistical Yearbook*, various years.

Note:

SITC Code	Product
281	Iron order, concentrates
67	Iron and steel
671	Pig iron
672	Iron and steel ingots
673	Iron and non-alloyed steel, flat
674	
678	Iron and steel wire

Table A.11: Production of iron ore, pig iron and crude steel; Brazil and world (metric tons, 000, 1911–97).

	Brazil			World		
	Iron ore	Pig iron	Crude steel	Iron ore	Pig iron	Crude steel
1911		3				
1912		4				
1913		8				
1914		12				
1915		3				
1916		4				
1917		8				
1918		12				
1919		11				
1920		14				
1921		18				
1922		18				
1923		25				
1924		25	5			
1925		30	8			
1926		21	10			
1927		15	8			
1928		26	21	73,200	83,350	
1929		36	27	83,000	94,250	
1930		35	21	72,100	74,600	89,100
1931		28	23	44,200	50,000	63,200
1932	1	29	34	24,300	32,800	44,800
1933	9	47	34	29,900	41,700	61,200
1934	5	59	62	40,300	51,900	72,700
1935	32	64	64	47,600	60,900	87,000
1936	75	78	74	62,500	76,400	107,700
1937	126	98	76	81,400	88,700	117,600
1938	251	122	92	59,200	66,900	91,600
1939	363	160	114	72,700	84,800	117,500
1940	404	186	141	76,600	87,600	124,000
1941	563	209	155	84,000	97,400	138,600
1942	479	214	160	88,200	102,600	142,500
1943	551	248	186	86,900	106,100	147,900
1944	523	292	221	na	96,700	138,200
1945	442	260	206	na	78,810	113,300
1946	396	371	343	72,500	78,500	111,500
1947	415	481	387	90,100	98,200	136,000
1948	1,069	552	483	104,100	112,500	155,300
1949	1,284	512	615	104,600	115,200	159,700
1950	1,351	729	769	115,900	133,700	189,300
1951	1,637	775	843	138,100	149,900	210,800
1952	2,510	812	893	140,200	152,600	211,500
1953	2,460	894	1,016	159,200	168,300	234,700
1954	2,088	1,109	1,148	142,800	158,800	223,500
1955	2,300	1,087	1,162	174,500	192,900	269,300
1956	2,771	1,188	1,375	186,700	196,700	278,900
1957	3,384	1,289	1,299	202,500	206,300	287,000

Table A.11: Production of iron ore, pig iron and crude steel (continued).

	Brazil			World		
	Iron ore	Pig iron	Crude steel	Iron ore	Pig iron	Crude steel
1958	3,526	1,407	1,362	182,100	187,270	263,000
1959	6,057	1,588	1,608	193,300	203,900	301,600
1960	6,355	1,783	2,260	232,100	231,300	346,600
1961	6,950	1,976	2,443	246,100	256,700	351,200
1962	7,301	2,009	2,565	252,300	265,500	360,200
1963	7,629	2,375	2,824	266,700	281,200	386,800
1964	11,534	2,449	3,016	301,100	317,200	438,000
1965	13,725	2,390	2,983	325,800	334,900	459,900
1966	15,763	2,950	3,782	339,000	347,000	475,700
1967	14,772	3,016	3,724	337,800	358,000	493,200
1968	16,682	3,173	4,453	371,000	386,900	528,700
1969	18,748	3,792	4,925	387,000	419,500	572,300
1970	24,739	4,296	5,300	421,300	439,800	582,900
1971	25,490	4,812	6,011	427,200	434,800	575,700
1972	31,600	5,511	6,318	427,300	460,700	634,400
1973	37,413	5,781	7,140	467,800	509,400	643,200
1974	62,212	6,140	7,309	513,800	522,300	704,200
1975	73,550	7,383	7,829	522,500	485,070	642,545
1976	73,530	8,561	9,168	521,500	507,500	673,400
1977	68,336	9,879	11,164	512,143	493,200	644,800
1978	70,649	10,520	12,120	522,560	520,200	704,200
1979	79,901	12,647	11,176	551,460	525,828	699,828.5
1980	94,993	14,774	10,232	555,019	531,456	695,457
1981	83,442	12,859	8,410	534,919	519,992	684,132
1982	81,559	12,916	7,660	481,116	465,324	616,869
1983	77,649	13,407	8,166	461,183	465,630	636,839
1984	97,813	17,628	10,797	532,863	499,284	677,091
1985	113,718	18,961	20,563	541,407	494,286	724,310
1986	119,493	20,163	21,343	568,038	490,489	719,347
1987	91,458	20,944	22,228	547,585	497,863	740,625
1988	99,285	23,454	24,747	565,585	525,091	781,913
1989	104,516	24,363	25,084	569,968	533,446	786,265
1990	na	21,141	20,631	587,027	518,909	773,287
1991	na	22,695	22,617		490,795	728,509
1992	na	23,057	23,934		489,963	715,192
1993	na	23,900	25,207		491,967	712,005
1994	na	25,092	25,747		512,226	714,050
1995	na	25,021	25,093			
1996	na	23,978	25,237			
1997	na	25,013	26,153			

Sources: Prior to 1932: *Mineração e Metalúrgia,* 10:57 (July 1945), p.122; 1932–97; United Nations; *Statistical Yearbook,* various years.

Notes: World: prior to 1946, excludes the Soviet Union. Data from the UN *Statistical Yearbook* and the International Iron and Steel Association *Yearbook* do not agree. Communication with the IIS reveals that they are aware of the difference, and the counsel data-users to accept either source, consistently. I have used the UN data because they agree with the data from the Brazilian *Anuário Estatístico*.

NOTES

The following abbreviations have been used throughout the notes:

AANC	Assembléia Nacional Constituinte, *Anais da Assembléa Nacional Constituinte (1933–4)*
AC	Câmara dos Deputados, *Anais da Câmara dos Deputados*
ACC	Congresso Nacional, *Anais do Congresso Constituinte de 1890/91*
CPDOC	Centro de Pesquisa e Documentação de História Contempôraneo do Brasil
CPDOC: AGM	Agamenom Magalhães
CPDOC: CMA	Clemente Mariani
CPDOC: EMS	Eduardo Macedo Soares
CPDOC: GC	Gustavo Capenema
CPDOC: HB	Júlio Caetano Horta Barbosa
CPDOC: HS	Herbert de Souza
CPDOC: JT	Juarez Távora
CPDOC: OA	Oswaldo Aranha
DAN	Congresso Nacional, *Diários da Assembléia Nacional Constituinte de 1933/34*
DCN	Congresso Nacional, *Diário do Congresso Nacional*
IBGE	Instituto Brasileiro de Geografia e Estatística
Leis	'Coleção das Leis e Decretos'
MAR	Ministério da Agricultura
MRE	Ministério das Relações Exteriores
MV Imobiliário	Morro Velho Imobiliário
MV *Registro*	*Registro de Documentos*, Morro Velho Imobiliário
PF	Percival Farquhar Papers Beinecke Manuscript Room, Yale University
Reptrospecto Comercial	*Retrospecto Comercial de Jornal do Commércio*
SJdR Annual Report	*Annual Report to Shareholders*
SOE	State-owned enterprise
Vale, Annual Report	Companhia Vale do Rio Doce, *Relatório da Diretoria ... apresentado α Assembléia Geral Ordinária*

Introduction

1. For example, Libecap has used the perspective of property rights to conclude that increasing levels of rulemaking among Comstock Lode prospectors helped to remove the uncertainty of their claims (G. D. Libecap, *The Evolution of Private Mineral Rights: Nevada's Comstock Lode* (New York: Arno Press, 1978)). From a different approach, Clay and Wright mitigate the expectation that strong mineral rights uniformly resulted in increasing efficiency by identifying that effective rule-making helped to secure the claims of existing claim-holders in California, but could establish a barrier to new entrants. They also find a high rate of legal appeal for initial settlement disputes, implying that self-regulation may have been less effective and efficient than initially portrayed (K. Clay and G. Wright, 'Order Without Law? Property Rights During the California Gold Rush', *Explorations in Economic History*, 42:2 (2005), pp. 155–83). Building on these findings, McDowell concludes that explicit and applied rules were the source of regulation and stable order among miners in California during the middle of the nineteenth century (A. G. McDowell, 'From Commons to Claims: Property in the California Gold Rush', *Yale Journal of Law and the Humanities*, 14:1 (2002), pp. 1–72). See also J. Umbeck, 'The California Gold Rush: A Study of Emerging Property Rights', *Explorations in Economic History*, 14 (1977), pp. 197–226. Outside of the United States of America and Canada the subject seems to be quite neglected.

2. For perspectives on economic aspects of this issue see W. Fritsch, *External Constraints on Economic Policy in Brazil, 1889–1930* (Pittsburgh, PA: University of Pittsburgh Press, 1988); S. Topik, *The Political Economy of the Brazilian State, 1889–1930* (Austin, TX: University of Texas Press, 1987); G. D. Triner, *Banking and Economic Development: Brazil, 1889–1930* (New York: Palgrave Press, 2000).

3. The seminal theoretical works in the field include D. C. North, *Structure and Change in Economic History* (New York: Norton, 1981); D. C. North, *Institutions, Institutional Change, and Economic Performance* (Cambridge: Cambridge University Press, 1990); C. Ménard, *Institutions, Contracts and Organizations: Perspectives from New Institutional Economics* (Cheltenham and Northampton, MA: Edward Elgar Publishing, 2000); Y. Barzel, *A Theory of the State: Economic Rights, Legal Rights, and the Scope of the State*, Political Economy of Institutions and Decisions Series (Cambridge and New York: Cambridge University Press, 2002); G. D. Libecap, 'Property Rights in Economic History: Implications for Research', *Explorations in Economic History*, 23:3 (1986), pp. 227–52; T. J. Yeager, *Institutions, Transition Economies, and Economic Development* (Boulder, CO: Westview Press, 1999).

4. The best overall surveys on the topic are J. H. Coatsworth, 'Structures, Endowments, and Institutions in the Economic History of Latin America', *Latin American Research Review*, 40:3 (2005), pp. 14–53; J. H. Coatsworth, 'Inequality, Institutions and Economic Growth in Latin America', *Journal of Latin American Studies*, 40 (2008), pp. 145–69. One notable exception to the US-centric scholarship is J. L. Carvalho, 'Private Sector Development and Property Rights in Latin America', *Revista Brasileira de Economia*, 50:3 (1996), pp. 351–77. Unfortunately, this work lacks theoretical depth.

5. The seminal work on this topic includes D. C. North and R. P. Thomas, *The Rise of the Western World: A New Economic History* (Cambridge: University Press, 1973). Its implications in modern Brazil have been most prominently applied to modern land disputes (L. J. Alston, G. D. Libecap and B. Mueller, *Titles, Conflict, and Land Use: The Develop-*

ment of Property Rights and Land Reform on the Brazilian Amazon Frontier (Ann Arbor, MI: University of Michigan Press, 1999)).

6. O. E. Williamson, *The Economic Institutions of Capitalism: Firms, Markets, Relational Contracting* (New York and London: Free Press Collier Macmillan, 1985).

7. Ibid., p. 178.

8. Ibid., p. 166.

9. On finance, see J. J. Ryan, 'Credit Where Credit is Due: The Evolution of the Rio de Janeiro Credit Market, 1820–1900' (PhD disseratation, University of California, 2007); A. Musacchio, *Experiments in Financial Democracy: Corporate Governance and Financial Development in Brazil, 1882–1950* (New York: Cambridge University Press, 2009). On land, see Alston et al., *Titles, Conflict, and Land Use*; L. M. O. Silva, *Terras devolutas e latifúndio: Efeitos da lei de 1850* (Campinas, SP, Brasil: Editora da Unicamp, 1996). Z. L. Frank, *Dutra's World: Wealth and Family in Nineteenth-Century Rio de Janeiro* (Albuquerque, NM: University of New Mexico Press, 2004) offers an interesting perspective the use of slaves as tangible property.

10. Neo-institutional economic history focuses on the interaction between private sector actors, using the state as a tool, and recent trends in general historiography treat the state ambiguously. In 'late developing' and 'post-colonial' states of the second half of the twentieth and the twenty-first centuries, the state serves a significant role in mediating economy, society and culture. The historical roots of these incursions are not sufficiently understood.

11. A. A. Alchian and H. Demsetz, 'The Property Rights Paradigm', *Journal of Economic History*, 33:1 (1973), pp. 16–27; H. Demsetz, 'Toward a Theory of Property Rights', *American Economic Review*, 56:2 (1967), pp. 347–59.

12. A. C. Metcalf, *Family and Frontier in Colonial Brazil: Santana de Parnaíba, 1580–1822* (Berkeley, CA: University of California Press, 1992); Lewin, *Surprise Heirs*, 2 vols (Stanford, CA: Stanford University Press, 2003).

13. See P. Pierson, *Politics in Time: History, Institutions, and Social Analysis* (Princeton, NJ: Princeton University Press, 2004); A. Hira and R. Hira, 'The New Institutionalism: Contradictory Notions of Change', *American Journal of Economics and Sociology*, 59:2 (2000), pp. 268–82; A. J. Field, 'The Problem with Neoclassical Institutional Economics: A Critique with Special Reference to the North/Thomas Model of Pre-1500 Europe', *Explorations in Economic History* 18:3 (1981), pp. 174–98. An alternative research strategy of specifying a highly detailed model with few opportunities for wider generalization and not operational because of the empirical specification problems is unsatisfactory as a research framework, though it is often invoked among economists. Hira and Hira, 'The New Institutionalism' note that institutional change is usually specified as originating with exogenous circumstance.

14. An important example of the large overly-generalized debates is that positing colonialism as the determining variable in the quest for economic development against those arguing for the primary importance of resource endowment. The major representations of these debates are: D. Acemoglu, S. Johnson and J. Robinson, 'The Colonial Origins of Comparative Development: An Empirical Investigation', *American Economic Review*, 91:5 (2002), pp. 1369–401; also available in *Revista de Economia Institucional*, 7 (2005); W. F. Maloney, 'Missed Opportunities: Innovation and Resource-Based Growth in Latin America', *Economia*, 3:1 (2002), pp. 111–67; S. L. Engerman and K. L. Sokoloff, 'Factor Endowments, Inequality, and Paths of Development Among New World Economies', *Economia*, 3:1 (2002), pp. 41–109, including comments. For an example of a narrowly

defined question with limited application, see S. Haber, N. Maurer, and A. Razo, 'When the Law Does Not Matter: The Rise and Decline of the Mexican Oil Industry', *Journal of Economic History*, 63:1 (2003), pp. 1–32.

15. The issues under consideration in this paper have received attention from a developmentalist perspective, leaving the important institutional concerns unaddressed. See, for example M. Zorzal e Silva, 'A Companhia Vale do Rio Doce no contexto do estado desenvolvimentista' (PhD disseration, Universidade de São Paulo, 2001).

16. Social scientists refer to the problem of 'the small *n*'.

17. For a discussion of the characteristics of a model of the 'optimum' rate of resource extraction, see J. A. Krautkraemer, 'Nonrenewable Resource Scarcity', *Journal of Economic Literature*, 36:4 (1998), pp. 2065–107.

18. M. Olson, *The Logic of Collective Action: Public Goods and the Theory of Groups* (Cambridge, MA: Harvard University Press, 1971). Olson focuses on the special difficulty for a private entrepreneur to provide collective goods. See also M. Olson and R. Zeckhauser, 'The Efficient Production of External Economies', *American Economic Review*, 60:3 (1970), pp. 512–17.

19. Other forms of state-provided goods could be seen as part of the public bureaucracy (e.g., child-welfare services), through a public operating 'authority' (e.g., operating commission for toll roads), by subsidy to private enterprise in exchange for regulatory control (often, railway construction).

1 Historical Setting

1. G. Wright, 'The Origins of American Industrial Success', *American Economic Review*, 80:4 (1990), pp. 651–68.

2. Mining and further production (whether forging or steel production) remained conflated in the actions of producers and the perspectives of policy makers for most of the time period under consideration. See for example: Ministério da Agricultura (Departamento Nacional de Producção Mineral, Serviço de Fomento e Producção Mineral) *Relatório da Directoria* (Rio de Janeiro: Impresa Natcional, 1934–5), p. 157.

3. C. V. Moog, *Bandeirantes e pioneiros; paralelo entre duas culturas* (Rio de Janeiro: Editôra Globo, 1954); Metcalf, *Family and Frontier*.

4. M. de Oliveira Lima, *Dom João VI no Brasil* (1908; Rio de Janeiro: Topbooks, 2006).

5. The political historiography of the nineteenth century focuses on issues of political process, patronage and representation. The best-known sources in English on nineteenth-century political history are J. D. Needell, *The Party of Order: The Conservatives, the State, and Slavery in the Brazilian Monarchy, 1831–1871* (Stanford, CA: Stanford University Press, 2006); R. J. Barman, *Brazil: The Forging of a Nation, 1798–1852* (Stanford, CA: Stanford University Press, 1988); R. Graham, 'Government Expenditures and Political Change in Brazil, 1880–1899: Who Got What', *Journal of Interamerican Studies and World Affairs*, 19:3 (1977), pp. 339–68; J. Murilo de Carvalho, *Teatro de sombras: A política imperial*, Formação do Brasil, 4 (Rio de Janeiro: IUPERJ; Vertice, 1988).

6. W. R. Summerhill III, *Order against Progress: Government, Foreign Investment, and Railroads in Brazil, 1854–1913* (Stanford, CA: Stanford University Press, 2003).

7. W. R. Summerhill III, *Inglorious Revolution: Political Institutions, Public Debt and Financial Development in Imperial Brazil* (New Haven, CT: Yale Uniebvrsity Press, forthcoming).

8. M. B. Levy, *História da bolsa de valores do Rio de Janeiro* (Rio de Janeiro: IBMEC, 1977).

9. Within the mineral regions, mining engineering, geology and the implications of government policy retained their importance, even if they were not prominent on the national political and economic agenda.

10. J. Murilo de Carvalho, *A Escola de Minas de Ouro Preto: O peso da glória* (Belo Horizonte: Editora UFMG, 2002). The school has since been converted to the Universidade Federal de Ouro Preto.

11. K. M. de Queiros Mattoso, *To Be a Slave in Brazil, 1550–1888* (New Brunswick, NJ: Rutgers University Press, 1986); A. K. Manchester, *British Preeminence in Brazil, its Rise and Decline: A Study in European Expansion* (Chapel Hill, NC: University of North Carolina Press, 1933).

12. J. B. Nugent and V. Saddi, 'Abolition and the Evolution of Property Rights in Land: The Role of Immigrant Labor and its Recruitment in Brazil' (unpublished paper, University of Southern California, 2007).

13. J. Nabuco, *Abolitionism: The Brazilian Antislavery Struggle (O abolicionismo)* (1880; Urbana, IL: University of Illinois Press, 1977).

14. See for example B. Fausto, *História geral da civilização brasileira (III) O Brasil republicano (1) Estrutura de poder e economia (1889–1930)* (Rio de Janeiro: Ed. Bertrand Brasil, 1989).

15. W. Dean, *The Industrialization of São Paulo* (Austin, TX: University of Texas Press, 1969); A. G. Hanley, *Native Capital: Financial Institutions and Economic Development in São Paulo, Brazil, 1850–1920* (Stanford, CA: Stanford University Press, 2005).

16. P. C. Dutra Fonseca, *Vargas: O capitalismo em construção* (São Paulo: Brasiliense, 1987); J. Murilo de Carvalho, *Forças armadas e política no Brasil* (Rio de Janeiro RJ: Jorge Zahar Editor, 2005); S. Draibe, *Rumos e metamorfoses: Um estudo sobre a constituição do Estado e as alternativas da industrialização no Brasil, 1930–1960* (Rio de Janeiro, RJ: Paz e Terra, 1985); E. Diniz, *Estado e capitalismo no Brasil: 1930–1945* (Rio de Janeiro: Editora Paz e Terra, 1978); E. Diniz, 'A progressiva subordinação das oligarquias regionais ao governo central', in T. Szmrescsányi and R. G. Granziera (eds), *Getúlio Vargas e a economia contemporânea* (Campinas SP: Editora da Unicamp, 2004), pp. 38–46; J. A. Ribeiro, *A era Vargas*, 3 vols (Rio de Janeiro, RJ: Casa Jorge, 2001); M. C. Soares d'Araújo, 'A volta de Vargas ao poder e a polarização das forças políticas e sociais', in T. Szmrescsányi and R. G. Granziera (eds) *Getúlio Vargas e a economia contemporânea* (Campinas SP: Editora da Unicamp, 2004), pp. 112–24; R. M. Levine, *The Vargas Regime: The Critical Years, 1934–1938* (New York: Columbia University Press, 1970); J. W. F. Dulles, *Vargas of Brazil: A Political Biography* (Austin, TX: University of Texas Press, 1967).

17. B. Weinstein, *For Social Peace in Brazil: Industrialists and the Remaking of the Working Class in São Paulo, 1920–1964* (Chapel Hill, NC: University of North Carolina Press, 1996).

18. G. Vargas, *A nova política do Brasil* (Rio de Janeiro: J. Olympio Editora, 1938).

19. E. Diniz and R. R. Boschi, *Empresários, interesses e mercado: Dilemas do desenvolvimento no Brasil* (Belo Horizonte and Rio de Janeiro: Editora UFMG; IUPERJ, 2004), p. 158.

20. J. M. Mizael de Souza, 'Será que o Brasil acordará para a importância da mineração?', in A. D. Leite and J. P. d. Reis (eds), *O novo Governo e os desafios do desenvolvimento* (Rio de Janeiro: Ed José Olympio, 2002), pp. 528–48, p. 536; M. L. Amarante de Andrade, L. M. da Silva Cunha and M. do Carmo Silva, 'Balança comercial do setor mínero-metalúrgico: Desafios para o crescimento', *Mineração e Metalurgia*, 16 (2002), pp. 105–22, on p. 107; Brasil, Instituto Brasileiro de Mineração, *Mineração e constituinte: histórico e*

sugestões a nova constituião brasileira (Belo Horizonte: Instituto Brasileiro de Mineração, 1986), p. 7.

21. Amarante de Andrade et al., 'Balança comercial do setor mínero-metalúrgico', p. 108. Petroleum and other hydrocarbons are treated separately from minerals. Although knowledge is currently in great flux, Brazil and its offshore deposits may account for as much as one-quarter of global petroleum reserves.

22. Mizael de Souza, 'Será que o Brasil acordará para a importância da mineração?', p. 537.

23. Further, one particularly rich gold vein intermittently provided strong returns to one mining company in the nineteenth century. On iron ore, see J. C. da Costa Sena, 'Viagem e estudos metallurgicos no centro da provincia de Minas Gerais', *Annaes da Escola de Minas de Ouro Preto*, 1 (1881), pp. 106–43, on p. 106. Authors continually noted the high quality and low cost of iron ore extraction. See, for example A. Vivacqua, *A nova política do sub-solo e o regime legal das minas* (Rio de Janeiro: Editora Panamericana, 1942), p. 306; J. P. Calógeras, *As minas do Brasil e sua legislação geológica econômica do Brasil*, expanded by Djalma Guimarães, 2nd edn, 3 vols (São Paulo: Companhia Editora Nacional, 1938 (1904/05)), vol. 3, ch. 5. On gold, see M. C. Eakin, *British Enterprise in Brazil: The St. John d'el Rey Mining Company and the Morro Velho Gold Mine, 1830–1960* (Durham, NC: Duke University Press, 1989).

24. O. Derby, 'The Iron Ores of Brazil', in *The Iron Ore Resources of the World: An Inquiry Made upon the Initiative of the Executive Committee of the XI International Geological Congress*, 2 (Stockholm, 1910), pp. 813–22. This report was part of an extensive survey undertaken for a 1910 conference on the extent of global iron ore reserves (1910 Stockholm Conference of the International Geological Society), and it found that 23 per cent of known global reserves of iron ore were located in Brazil, and most of the known Brazilian reserves were in Minas Gerais. In 1942, the Itabira mines were estimated to have 700 million tons of iron ore, about 54 per cent of Brazilian reserves. D. J. Pimenta, '*Companhia Vale do Rio Doce*' (Rio de Janeiro: Imprensa Oficial, 1947), p. 24.

25. The most prominent study, in English, is W. Baer, *The Brazilian Economy: Growth and Development*, 4th edn (Westport, CT: Praeger, 1995). See also L. A. Corrêa do Lago, F. Lopes de Almeida and B. M. F. de Lima, *A indústria brasileira de bens de capital: Origens, situação recente, perspectivas* (Rio de Janeiro: Fundação Getúlio Vargas, 1979).

26. State-level governments also participated in local commercial activity (M. C. Eakin, *Tropical Capitalism: The Industrialization of Belo Horizonte, Brazil* (New York Houndmills: Palgrave, 2001)).

27. The general histories of both companies are widely published. In English, see D. E. Rady, *Volta Redonda: A Steel Mill comes to a Brazilian Coffee Plantation; Industrial Entrepreneurship in a Developing Economy* (Albuquerque, NM: Rio Grande Publishing Co., 1973); Levine, *The Vargas Regime*. On the political debates they engendered, see J. D. Wirth, 'Brazilian Economic Nationalism: Trade and Steel under Vargas', DAI-A 27/04 (PhD disseration, Stanford University, 1966) ; J. D. Wirth, *The Politics of Brazilian Development 1930–1954* (Stanford, CA: Stanford University Press, 1970).

2 Minerals, the Subsoil and Property Law

1. A recent debate on the efficacy of Roman (or Napoleonic) legal systems, for economic development has not yet reached firm conclusions. R. LaPorta, F. Lopez-de-Salinas, A. Shleifer and R. Vishny, 'Law and Finance', *Journal of Political Economy*, 106:6 (1998), pp. 1113–55, on p. 1142; A. Musacchio, 'Laws versus Contracts: Legal Origins, Shareholder

Protections and Ownership Concentration in Brazil, 1890–1950', *Business History Review*, 82:3 (2008), pp. 445–73; N. R. Lamoreaux and J.-L. Rosenthal, 'Legal Regime and Business's Organizational Choice: A Comparison of France and the United States during the Nineteenth Century', in *NBER Working Paper No. 10288* (Cambridge, MA: National Bureau of Economic Research, 2004).

2. J. O. de Lima Pereira, *Da propriedade no Brasil* (São Paulo: Casa Duprat, 1932), pp. 5–9. Lima Pereira also emphasizes the Emperor's right to require compensation from the use of resources in his domain.

3. B. Mueller, 'A evolução histórica dos direitos de propriedade sobre as terras no Brasil e nos EUA', *História Econômica e História de Empresas*, 9:2 (2006), pp. 23–54; Alston et al., *Titles, Conflict, and Land Use*; A. P. Canabrava, 'A repartição da terra na capitania de São Paulo, 1818', *Estudos Econômicos*, 2:6 (1972), pp. 77–129; W. Dean, 'Latifundia and Land Policy in Nineteenth-Century Brazil', *Hispanic American Historical Review*, 51:44 (1971), pp. 606–25. After the early system of granting *doações*, arguments were not put forward that prohibited private ownership of land, even if the sovereign (crown or state) laid claim to large portions of land. Even though very large, *sesmarias* were a fraction of the size of *doações*, which had divided all of Portuguese America into fifteen tranches. Squatters could stake a claim (*posse*) to public or private (*sesmaria*) land that was not otherwise in use. This practice always represented a threat to the largest, partially settled, holdings.

4. The Land Law of 1850 offered the opportunity to recognize and legalize existing land occupations, seemingly without changing constraints on the limitations of ownership. In Minas Gerais the registration period lasted until 1856. The Land Code provided a process for squatters to gain title to land they had occupied and it tried to prevent subsequent squatting. Under the Land Code, all existing land titles required re-registration and new claims on land (*posses*) could be formalized. For examples of some of the St John d'el Rey's re-registrations under these provisions, see St John d'el Rey Co., MV Imobiliário (real estate transactions), file 13.10.15.22. For more on the Land Law, see M. D. Dantas, *Fronteiras movediças: Relações sociais na Bahia do século XI (a comarca Itapicaru e a formação do arraial de Canudos)* (São Paulo: Aderaldo & Rothschild Editores: FAPESP, 2007); Dean, 'Latifundia and Land Policy', E. Viotti da Costa, *The Brazilian Empire: Myths and Histories* (Chicago, IL: University of Chicago Press, 1985); A. M. C. Maia, *O instituto das terras devolutas e a legislação fundiária do Estado de Minas Gerais* (Belo Horizonte: Fundação Rural Mineira de Colonização e Desenvolvimento Agrária, 1994).

5. M. Junqueira, *Inconstitucionalidade do Código de Minas: Impugnação da Fazenda do Estado de São Paulo á applicabilidade do Decreto Federal No. 24642* (São Paulo: Procuradoria de Terras do Estado de São Paulo, 1936), p. 36.

6. Leis, *Alvará*, 15 August 1608. The rights to specific natural resources on the surface (timber, water, etc.) could also be subject to transfer separately from other resources (especially the right to cultivate). These transactions were left to the market, and their contractual enforcement was no different from other types of transactions. The historical basis for distinguishing between surface and subsoil rights was based on the power of the sovereign. These laws were known as the *Ordenações Filipinas*.

7. By 1750, the first cycle of gold mining had largely run its course. However, exploration remained active (R. C. Simonsen, *História econômica do Brasil, 1500–1820* (São Paulo: Editora Nacional, 1962)). The first laws targeted iron ore mining, although they also were developed with a hope of applying them to more precious substances. Within Por-

tugal, sovereign rights to the subsoil had been codified in the *Ordenações Afonsinas* in 1446, as a means to efficiently regulate and conserve natural resources (A. L. de Seabra, *A propriedade: Philosophia do direito* (Coimbra: Imprensa da Universidade, 1850), pp. 150–2).

8. Prominent among these scholars are A. J. R. Russell-Wood, 'Technology and Society: The Impact of Gold Mining on the Institution of Slavery in Portuguese America', *Journal of Economic History*, 37:1 (1977), pp. 59–83; T. J. Trebat, *Brazil's State-Owned Enterprises: A Case Study of the State as Entrepreneur* (Cambridge and New York: Cambridge University Press, 1983). Trebat identifies the discovery of gold as the trigger for state participation in the economy.

9. M. S. Cardozo, 'The Collection of the Fifths in Brazil, 1695–1708', *Hispanic American Historical Review*, 20:3 (1940), pp. 359–79.

10. Leis, *Alvará*, 15 August 1603; Vivacqua, *A nova política do sub-solo*, p. 499; Companhia Vale do Rio Doce, *A mineração no Brasil e a Companhia Vale do Rio Doce* (Rio de Janeiro: CVRD, 1992), p. 29.

11. This survey of early colonial mining regulation comes from Simonsen, *História econômica*, pp. 276–9; Russell-Wood, 'Technology and Society'.

12. This law has not been studied. Simonsen states, logically enough, that it limited credit to miners (*História econômica*, p. 280). While such a prohibition would limit short-term credit, mining enterprises in the early eighteenth century were hardly good candidates for long-term debenture issuance. In *História da bolsa de valores do Rio de Janeiro* Levy states, without citation, that the *Lei da Trintena* 'could only be prosecuted for one-third part of their mining profits' (p. 25).

13. Simonsen, *História econômica*, p. 182. The Commercial Code of 1850 included a provision for joint-stock companies with legislative charter and unlimited liability. Standardized rules for chartering joint-stock companies and for limited liability were not enacted until the Commercial Code of 1890.

14. Brasil, Ministério da Fazenda. Museu da Fazenda, *Ciclo da mineração* (Rio de Janeiro: Ministério da Fazenda, 1984), pp. 87–94; F. I. Ferreira, *Legislação das minas, repertório jurídico do mineiro, consolidação alphabética e chronológica* (Rio de Janeiro: Typographia Nacional, 1884).

15. This principle was a generalized version of the indivisibility provisions of the 1603 *alvará*. 'Indivisibility' applied to real assets in a general sense. Sugar plantations and mills were equally protected, and these provisions made it impossible, into the twentieth century, to establish credit markets to finance real estate (mortgages) because of the inability to offer the property as collateral. See S. B. Schwartz, *Sugar Plantations in the Formation of Brazilian Society: Bahia 1550–1835*, Cambridge Latin American Studies Series, 52 (Cambridge: Cambridge University Press, 1985), pp. 202–4; Triner, *Banking and Economic Development*, pp. 135–8.

16. Metcalf, *Family and Frontier*, pp. 95–6. Metcalf offers the most thorough discussion in English of the concept of family property and inheritance in early colonial Brazil. She distinguishes between inheritance possibilities for nobility and commoner, and goes so far as to say that, among noble families, the concept of property was familial rather than individual.

17. Some of the most explicit examples from this strand of historiography in English are Lewin, *Surprise Heirs*; S. Lauderdale Graham, *Caetana Says No: Women's Stories from a Brazilian Slave Society* (Cambridge and New York: Cambridge University Press, 2002); Frank, *Dutra's World*.

18. Metcalf, *Family and Frontier*, ch. 4. Constraints on distribution for non-noble, but propertied, families were strong. Among all propertied families, patriarchal control governed efforts to keep estates whole, even while preserving a legal structure that protected the ownership of assets for women. M. Nazzari considers some of the implications of family inheritance patterns for British-Brazilian mercantile partnerships in the nineteenth century ('Widows as Obstacles to Business: British Objections to Brazilian Marriage and Inheritance Laws', *Comparative Studies in Society and History*, 37:4 (1995), pp. 781–802).

19. Calógeras, *As minas do*, vol. 1, p. 137.

20. MV Imobiliário, file 13.4.1.1 ('Informações', p. 4). See also file 13.4.4.4, 'Histórico', letter dated February 1908 to G. Chalmers (superintendent)).

21. A *braça* was the equivalent of 2.2 meters (S. W. Miller, *Fruitless Trees: Portuguese Conservation and Brazil's Colonial Timber* (Stanford, CA: Stanford University Press, 2000)).

22. In theory, this arrangement would direct mining towards land in the public domain, in order to avoid the additional cost of landowner compensation.

23. The legal concept of *terras devolutas* originated in heavily-populated early-modern Portugal to free up unused land for agriculture. In colonial Brazil, the Portuguese applied the laws for opposite reasons. In attempts to force land settlement, land grants were tied to putting territory into productive use. According to complicated laws and formulae, unimproved territory would revert to the Crown. In the 1850 Land Code, the right to expropriate resources rested with the national government (Maia, *O instituto das terras*, pp. 24–5). This concept has continued in use throughout Brazilian history. The Constitution of 1934 provided for the concept; the 1949 Land Law invoked the 1850 Land Code, as its authority for declaring resources *devolutas*; and a law of 1964 reinforced the ideas (O. M. Alvarenga, *Teoria e prática do direito agrário* (Rio de Janeiro: CONSAGR-Comunicações Sociais Agrárias, 1983), pp. 29–37; Leis, *Lei 4504/64*). The concept of *terras e minas devolutas* continues as the basis for land dispossessions and claims by the Movimento de Sem Terra in late twentieth- and early twenty-first-century Brazil. With many changes in the specific terms, the principles of requiring beneficial use for privately owned property remains in effect. See Alston et al., *Titles, Conflict, and Land Use* for some of the implications in the late twentieth century.

24. These provisions did not distinguish between private ownership or concessions for use (as with mining veins). In theory, returning privately owned (land) resources to the public domain required compensation (de Lima Pereira, *Da propriedade no Brasil*, pp. 6–9).

25. Given the difficulty of policing colonial, nineteenth-century Brazil, almost all claims of unproductive use came from private actors trying to gain assets.

26. A. R. Barbosa, 'Breve panorama da legislação minerária', *Revista de Direito Administrativo*, 197 (1994), pp. 64–73; Junqueira, *Inconstitucionalidade*, pp. 24–6. This point was subtle, and not always recognized in public debate.

27. AC, 11 November 1902, vol. 9, pp. 259–84. As late as 1884, a legal analyst stated that the law 'considers minerals as the property of the State' (Ferreira, *Legislação das minas*). Some based this conclusion on the constitutional provision (of 1824) that, unless specifically changed, pre-existing colonial law remained in effect (A. H. de Souza Bandeira, *A propriedade das minas: estudo de direito administrativo* (Rio de Janeiro: Imprensa Nacional, 1885), pp. 15–28).

28. For example, at various times the St John d'el Rey Company paid taxes at rates between 0 and 10 per cent. MV Historical Notes; St John d'el Rey Co., Board of Directors Letters, 2 August 1878 (hereafter 'MV Board Letter').

29. Vivacqua, *A nova política do sub-solo*, pp. 517–18.
30. Constituição dos Estados Unidos do Brasil (Rio de Janeiro: Impresa nacional, 1891), also available at: http://pdba.georgetown.edu/Constitutions/Brazil/brazil1891.html (1891), Article 72, §12.
31. Brazil was not unique among Latin American countries in making substantial changes to subsoil rights at this time. For example, the Mexican government asserted its ownership of subsoil resources in the Constitution of 1917 and went further by nationalizing the petroleum industry in 1938 (L. B. Hall, *Oil, Banks, and Politics: The United States and Postrevolutionary Mexico, 1917–1924* (Austin, TX: University of Texas Press, 1995)). Despite efforts to institute specific mining laws during the Republic (most notably with the *Leis Calógeras* and *Simões Lopes* in 1915 and 1921, respectively) the only significant change was in 1926 when a constitutional amendment prohibited the transfer to foreigners of mines or mineral veins deemed necessary for national security (Leis, *Decreto* 2933, 6 January 1915, enabled by *Decreto* 4265, 15 January 1921; Constitution amended 7 September 1926, §17). See also Barbosa, 'Breve panorama', p. 69).
32. The St John d'el Rey Mining Company was still mining; by 1930, the Ouro Preto Mining Company still owned, but was not mining, the Passagem Mine. A third company had recently closed (Minas Gerais, Presidente del Estado, *Mensagem dirigida pelo Presidente do Estado ao Congresso Mineiro em sua xx sessão ordinária da xx legislatura, no anno* (Imprensa Nacional, 1889, 1926), pp. 61–4, 7, 77,), online at http://www.crl.edu/content/brazil/mina.htm (1889) [accessed 3 March 2011].
33. W. Suzigan, *Indústria brasileira: origem e desenvolvimento* (São Paulo: Brasiliense, 1986); F. R. Versiani, 'Industrialização e economia de exportação antes de 1914', *Revista Brasileira de Economia*, 34:1 (1980), pp. 3–40.
34. The first explicit attention to industrial metals, in policy circles at the end of the nineteenth century, seems to have occurred in 1886, when Antônio Prado brought the topic to the attention of the government, without much effect (R. Martins and O. E. A. Brito, *História da mineração no Brasil* (São Paulo: Empresas das Artes, 1989), p. 79).
35. AANC (Rio de Janeiro Imprensa Nacional, 1933–4), 26 March 1934, vol. 13, pp. 379–80 (remarks by José Alkmin) and 12 April 1934, vol. 14, p. 207 (remarks by Djalma Guimarães), also available at http://www2.camara.gov.br/publicacoes. The most prominent views supporting the idea that reaction against imperial law motivated support for the change belonged to Calógeras, *As minas do Brasil*, vol. 1, p. 227); see also Vivacqua, *A nova política do sub-solo*, p. 446. As late as 1986, this institutional change remained 'inexplicable' to Brazilian legislative analysts (Brasil, Instituto Brasileiro de Mineração, *Mineração e constituinte*, p. 10).
36. A. Werneck, *Relatório apresentado ao Dr. Presidente do estado de Minas pelo Secretário de Estado dos Negócios da Agricultura, Commércio e Obras Públicas* (Cidade de Minas: Imprensa Official de Minas Gerais, 1899), p. 33; Calógeras, *As minas do Brasil*, vol. 2, p. 601, and vol. 3, p. 60.
37. W. Freire, *Comentários ao Código de Mineração* (Rio de Janeiro: Aide Editora e Comércio de Livros, 1995), pp. 14–5.
38. Common examples of the application of *res nullius* in the twenty-first century include activities that take place outside of landed boundaries, such as deep-sea mining and space exploration, and intellectual property rights that attach to general characteristics, such as patent rights to the genome of any species or to specific genes.
39. Vivacqua, *A nova política do sub-solo*, pp. 407–10.

40. ACC (Rio de Janeiro: Imprensa Nacional 1890/91), also available at http://www2. camara.gov.br/publicacoes, 8 November 1902, vol. 9, p. 180 (speech by Estevão Lobo)). See also AC, 14 November 1914, vol. 10, pp. 59–60 (speech by João Pandiá Calógeras).
41. This was the position of Prof. Furtado de Menses of the Escola de Minas de Ouro Preto (AANC, 19 March 1934, vol. 11, p. 581).
42. AC, 8 November 1909, vol. 9, p. 181; G. Paiva, 'O código de minas e o incremento da mineração no Brasil em 1940', in Ministério da Agricultura, DNPM, Serviço de Fomento da Producção Mineral, *Avulso No. 47* (Rio de Janeiro: Imprensa Nacional, 1942), p. 67.
43. Brazilian debate questionably identified English and US legal mining regulation as systems of acessão (Vivacqua, *A nova política do sub-solo*, p. 467; AANC, 26 March 1934, p. 377 (comments by José Alkmin)).
44. Ferreira, *Legislação das minas*; de Souza Bandeira, *A propriedade das minas*.
45. Ferreira, *Legislação das minas*, pp. xv–xiii. See also P. Xisto, 'Limitação do direito de propriedade' (PhD dissertation, Recife: Escolas Profissionaes do Colegio Salesiano, 1923); C. da Matta, *O direito de propriedade e a utilidade publica: Das expropriações* (Coimbra: Imprensa da Universidade, 1906).
46. ACC, 22 November 1890; MMG (1891), p. 62. The assets then in the public domain were allocated to the states; the right to expropriate assets became a conflicted issue. Mining remained in the federal domain in the specific instances of mineral resources in the Federal District, lands on which the federal government was the property owner, and to meet the needs of national defense (A. Milton, *A constituição do Brasil: Notícia, histórica, texto e commentário* (Rio de Janeiro: Imprensa Nacional, 1898), pp. 178, 335).
47. Vivacqua, *A nova política do sub-solo*, p. 582. Serzedelo Correia was the first to introduce wording to dispute the original draft, in favour of applying a strictly 'liberal' interpretation of property to land and mines. The most prominent advocates of the former position included Rui Barbosa, José Bocayuva and José Hygino; Theodureto Souto and Americo Lobo led the campaign for unrestricted federal sovereignty.
48. 'Mining interests' determined by indication of profession as miner or mining engineer, or educational background from the Escola de Minas de Ouro Preto (the only mining engineering school in Brazil at the time). Sources: Brasil, Câmara dos Deputados; Anais e Diários das Assembléias Constituintes, 1890–1; Minas Gerais, *Annaes do Congresso Constituinte de Estado de Minas Gerais, 1891*; I. Beloch and A. Alves de Abreu (eds), *Dicionário Histórico-Biográfico Brasileiro, 1930–1983*; N. de Góis Monteiro (ed.), *Dicionário Biográfico de Minas Gerais: Periodo Republicano, 1889–1930*.
49. Barbosa, 'Breve panorama', pp. 68–9.
50. A. Sarmento, 'A exploração de minas: defesa da lei de 6 de Janeiro de 1915', Discurso pronunciado na Camara dos Deputados na sessão de 7 de novembro de 1916 (Rio de Janeiro: Imprensa Nacional, 1916), pp. 9–10.
51. For recognition of this asymmetry, see Calógeras, *As minas do Brasil*, vol. 2, ch. 11, p. 576).
52. R. Jacob, *Minas Geraes no século XX* (Rio de Janeiro: Gomes Irmão & Cia., 1911), p. 230. In 1899, a Federal decree (*Decreto* 3432, 9 October 1899) cancelled all prospecting and mining concessions that had not met starting-time requirements.
53. Cited in Vivacqua, *A nova política do sub-solo*, p. 528. Complaints about the impediments caused by the lack of regulation arose as early as 1893 (*Revista Industrial de Minas Gerais*, 4:7 (1893), p. 151).
54. MV *Registro*, document 10/1; MV Historical Notes, p. 4.

55. Calógeras found that 'Until then [Constitution of 1891] litigation could arise between two badly defined concessions, between miners and land owners linked by their works, causes in the end, that were simple and promptly resolved. Now there are interminable questions over the regularity of titles, over partnerships [*condomínio*] and the complaints that they initiate.' Calógeras also complained that land in mining regions was overvalued as a result of the joining of surface and subsoil rights (Calógeras, *As minas do Brasil*, vol. 1, p. 233 and vol. 2, p. 602; Werneck, *Relatório apresentado*, p. 33).

56. Companhia Vale do Rio Doce, *A mineração no Brasil*, pp. 150–1; Junqueira, finds that the incompatible concepts of devolving mining regulation to the states while also joining subsoil rights to the surface were not resolved in the Constitution of 1891 (*Inconstitucionalidade*, pp. 45–9).

57. Bahia, *Lei* no. 436, 6 August 1901. The constitutionality of this law remained in doubt for the remainder of the First Republic.

58. MMG (1902), p. 351.

59. Jacob, *Minas Geraes no século XX*, pp. 229–30. Jacob argued that the state's body of mining law remained badly articulated and administered.

60. MAR (Rio de Janeiro: Imprensa Nacional,1892), p. 37.

61. AC, 24 September 1897, vol. 5, pp. 452–3.

62. AC, 28 August 1899, vol. 4, p. 319; see also MMG (1897), p. 14.

63. MAR (1900), p. 8; (1901), p. 16; (1902), p. 7.

64. Calógeras, *As minas do Brasil*. This classic study, with its origins as a legislative background report, has provided the basis for many subsequent legal and engineering arguments. Much of the statistical work presented in the volumes has also gone uncontested.

65. 'Pandiá Calógeras na opinião de seus contemporâneos' (Belo Horizonte, 1934).

66. Calógeras, *As minas do Brasil*, vol. 2, p. 602.

67. The security of the collateral was significantly diminished by the prior claims of landowners.

68. Leis, *Decreto* 2933, 6 January 1915.

69. AC, 30 June 1916, vol. 3, pp. 73–7. See also *Retrospecto Comercial* (1914), p. 184.

70. Leis, *Decreto* 4265, 15 January 1921, article 5. See also Companhia Vale do Rio Doce, *A mineração no Brasil*, pp. 151–2.

71. S. H. Serra, *Direitos minerários: Formação, condicionamentos e extinção* (São Paulo: Ed. Signus, 2000), p. 35.

72. A. A. de Barros Penteado, *A legislação mineira do Brasil* (Rio de Janeiro: Cruzeiro do Sul, 1941), p. 25.

73. Calógeras, *As minas do Brasil*, vol. 1, pp. 227–33 and vol. 2, p. 602.

74. Through the 1920s, limits on all types of property gained attention and sharper articulation (P. Calmon, *Direito de propriedade: A margem dos seus problemas juridicos, sociologicos, historicos e politicos* (Rio de Janeiro: Imprensa Nacional, 1925); Xisto, *Limitação do direito de propriedade*; R. Octavio, *Do domínio da União e dos Estados, Segunda a Constituição Federal* (São Paulo: Saraiva & Co., 1924)).

75. MMG (1920), p. 91–3.

76. See for example MMG (1923), pp. 69–73.

77. AC, 3 November 1916, vol. 12, p. 76.

78. J. Távora, 'O Código de Minas e desenvolvimento', *Geologia e metallurgia*, 14 (1956), pp. 152–94.

79. Companhia Vale do Rio Doce, *A mineração no Brasil*, p. 171; Wirth, *The Politics of Brazilian Development*, introduction.
80. For a fuller discussion of the concept of 'economic nationalism' as invoked by Brazilians of this era, see Wirth, 'Brazilian Economic Nationalism', pp. 26–66.
81. Its framers intended the Constitution of 1934 to specify the transition from federal principles to structuring a 'representative republic' governed by collective social goals, despite referring to Brazil as a federal unit (Brasil, *Constituição*, 16 July 1934, Articles 113, 114 §17 and 116); J. A. Mendonça de Azevedo, *Elaborando a constituição nacional: Atas da subcomissão elaboradora do anteprojeto 1932/33*, Edição Fac-Similar (Brasília: Imprensa Nacional, 1993), see especially Sessão 26, 2 February 1932, p. 512; Sessão 37, pp. 707, 711–14; and Sessão 39, 23 March 1933, p. 770); AANC, vol. 9, p. 341). During the constitutional debates, even such prominent private sector industrialists as Alexandre Siciliano supported this increasingly activist role for the national government (AANC, 6 March 1934, vol. 9, pp. 344–55,).
82. Vargas, *A nova política do Brasil*; and the 1931 speech in Belo Horizonte.
83. Brasil, Instituto Brasileiro de Mineração, *Mineração e constituinte*; DAN (Rio de Janeiro: Imprensa Nacional), 1933/4, 11 April 1934, vol. 2, number 77, pp. 2376–7 (Vargas statement on his constitutional proposal), also available at http://imagem.camara.gov.br/diarios.asp [accessed 22 October 2010]; A. Pinheiro, *Direito das minas: Comentários e legislação* (Rio de Janeiro: Imprensa do 'Jornal do Commercio', 1939), pp. 109–42).
84. Companhia Vale do Rio Doce, *A mineração no Brasil*, p. 171.
85. This was the argument put forward by Minister of Agriculture Júarez Tavora during the Constituent Assembly debates (AANC, 2 May 1934, pp. 186–200).
86. Leis, *Decreto* 20799, 16 December 1931.
87. Leis, *Decreto* 22096, 16 November 1932; Vivacqua, *A nova política do sub-solo*, p. 571. The term 'public good' was used in much the same way as economists use the term today.
88. AANC, 16 November 1933, vol. 10, pp. 248–50. The commission was headed by Cincinnato Braga, a former finance minister. Nevertheless, state sovereignty over the subsoil had become an actively debated issue during the latter years of the First Republic when Nelson da Senna first articulated the link between developing the steel industry and national defense (AC, 26 September 1923, vol. 8, pp. 609–22).
89. AANC, 19 March 1934, vol. 11, pp. 577–81. Legislators continued to phrase the rights as proportionate shares of an enterprise, rather than as physical property.
90. AANC, 6 March 1934, vol. 9, p. 356. The restriction was also to have applied to hydroelectricity plants. Alexandre Siciliano, a leading industrialist who came to advocate the state assuming a large role in steel production, was the author of these comments.
91. Código de Minas; Leis, *Decreto* 24642 (Rio de Janiero: Imprensa Nacional). See also MV Historical Notes, p. 4; Eakin, *British Enterprise in Brazil*. The Mining Code was one prong of a strategy for the state to reclaim control of natural resources. A water code was implemented the day after the Mining Code, with the prospect of developing hydroelectric facilities in mind (Código de Aguas; Leis, *Decreto* 24673, 11 July 1934). The Constitution specified that the responsibility of the national government to regulate the subsoil and mining and to legitimize the re-separation of the subsoil from the surface, while the Mining Code determined the specifics of mining regulation (Brasil, *Constituição 1934*, Articles 118 and 119 §3–6; Brasil, 1934: Leis, *Decreto* 24642, Código de Minas).
92. Leis, 'Constituição 1934', Article 118.

93. Freire, *Comentários*, p. 16. Others did not interpret the legal provisions in this manner. L. Lacerda Rocha, *Das minas e jazidas no direito brasileiro (Comentários ao Código de Minas atualizado e legislação subseqüente)* (Rio de Janeiro: Ed. Livraria Agir, 1947), p. 17.

94. Mizael de Souza, 'Será que o Brasil acordará para a importância da mineração?', p. 532.

95. Mendonça de Azevedo, *Elaborando a Constituição*, Sessão 39, 23 March 1933, p. 773. One of the useful provisions of the Mining Code was to accept the explicit demarcation of geographic area as the means of specifying mining rights, even while continuing administrative contention (Pinheiro, *Direito das minas*, pp. 109–10).

96. PF, box 7, folder 94, Carl Kincaid, 'Outline of Brazilian Mining Legislation' (30 November 1934). According to this memo: 'the nation is not the proprietor of the mines (except those under land belonging to the Nation, which is negligible), although it makes their industrial use dependent on an authorization of the Federal Government'. Existing concessions were subject to the constraint that they had been appropriately registered and had been in 'productive use' or in 'temporary suspension' at the time the Mining Code was put into effect.

97. See, for example, AANC, 19 March 1934, vol. 11, p. 578 and 2 May 1934, vol. 14, p. 186 (speech by Minister of Agriculture Juarez Távora). Some have suggested that the Mining Code was a response to miners' complaints (de Figueiredo Murta, Comicio, 'Código de Minas, notável conquista da revolução' *Mineração e Metalurgia*, 7:40 (September–October 1943), pp. 199–200.

98. J. L. J. De Moraes, 'O direito de propriedade no Código de Minas'; *Mineração e Metalurgia*, 1:3 (May–June 1936); da Silva Emygdio Ferreira, 'A propriedade mineral e a Constituição e as Leis', *Mineração e Metalurgia*, 7:37 (1943), pp. 21–3.

99. The National Department of Mining Production (DNPM) issued 6,766 individual authorizations from the time of the 1934 Mining Code until individual authorizations were discontinued. This total included both existing mining sites and new explorations (Companhia Vale do Rio Doce, *Coletânea da legislação sobre mineração no Brasil* (Rio de Janeiro: Companhia Vale do Rio Doce, 1993)).

100. Authorization was a separate process from concession; although a complicating factor, it is not crucial to the issues of this chapter (S. Fróes Abreu, *A riqueza mineral do Brasil* (São Paulo: Companhia Editora Nacional, 1937), p. 21).

101. Beneficial-use provisions are discussed below.

102. MV Historical Notes, p. 6; Vivacqua, *A nova política do sub-solo*, pp. 603–5.

103. MV Historical Notes, p. 6.

104. Vivacqua, *A nova política do sub-solo*, pp. 552–6. Vivacqua also pointed out that 'the Constitution of 1934 adopted as a fundamental principle the separation of the two properties – the territory and the mineral' (p. 545) and 'the Constitution of 1934 as well as the current Constitution [1937] follows Napoleonic Code (Law of 1810) and separated the property of the soil from the mineral for purposes of mining or industrial uses' (p. 575). On the debate about surface industrial minerals (and specifically iron ore) see CPDOC: CMA, pi Penteado, 'A quem pertenence as jazidas?', pp. 3–6.

105. The language of debate, discussion and legislation uses the term 'subsoil' in this extended manner, despite the seeming contradiction. I have not found any reference to interpretation of the term 'subsoil' prior to the 1934 changes that would indicate inclusion of minerals found on the surface (such as iron ore).

106. Exploration for coal deposits was a secondary goal of the transfer of sovereignty. However, as late as 1968 industrial scale coal production still was not feasible (A. Venâncio

Filho, *Intervenção do Estado no domínio econômico: o direito público econômico no Brasil* (Rio de Janeiro: Fundação Getúlio Vargas, 1968), p. 188).

107. DAN, 11 April 1934, vol. 2, number 77, p. 2377 (Vargas's statement on his constitutional proposal).

108. *Constituição* 1934: Article 119, §4. The reformation of the Mining Code in 1937 (*Lei* 65, 14 December 1937) strengthened this provision.

109. The 1934 Mining Code revoked the first attempts (in 1926) to limit foreign participation in mining (Barbosa, 'Breve panorama', p. 69).

110. The confusion about 'authorizations' and 'concessions' resulted from both wording imprecision and incomplete delineation of state and national domain (Junqueira, *Inconstitucionalidade*; PF, box 6, folder 83, 'Notas sobre o Código de Minas'). Vivacqua, *A nova política do sub-solo*, p. 570, distinguishes an 'authorisation', as a license to explore, from a concession, which attributed a property right to extracted minerals.

111. Procedurally, the Mining Code had been passed (but not announced) prior to the Constitution, rendering it questionable whether the Constitution governed the Code. The major inconsistency between the two documents was that the Constitution did not specifically identify minerals as items of public property.

112. Leis, *Decreto* 24642 (1934), Article 5 §1 and Article 10. This was a departure from previous applications of the beneficial-use provisions, which relied upon private parties to petition for a concession to be declared *devoluta* when they wished to gain access to the vein.

113. Junqueira, *Inconstitucionalidade*, p. 81.

114. *Constituição* (1934), Article 119 §4. Issues of military and national security had arisen during the First Republic. In 1901, a proposed bill tried to define mining as an activity crucial to national defense and 'public utility'. These continued sporadically through the regime (AC, 7 August 1901, vol. 4, pp. 101–2; 26 September 1923, vol. 8, pp. 609–10; 19 October 1926, vol. 12, pp. 21–35).

115. *Constituição* (1937), with enabling legislation, Leis, *Decreto-Lei* 66, 14 December 1937. On the role of generals drafting the Constitution, see F. D. McCann, *Soldiers of the Pátria: A History of the Brazilian Army, 1889–1937* (Stanford, CA: Stanford University Press, 2004), ch. 6.

116. See Junqueira, *Inconstitucionalidade*, p. 104; see PF, box 6, folder 83, for arguments against the constitutionality of the 1934 Mining Code.

117. Barbosa, 'Breve panorama', p. 69; Companhia Vale do Rio Doce, *A mineração no Brasil*, p. 176; P. Rache, *A grande siderúrgia e a exportação de minério de ferro brasileiro em larga escala* (Rio de Janeiro: Imprensa Oficial, 1939), pp. 32–5; PF, box 7, folder 88, 'Preliminary Memo Regarding the Legal Aspects of Proposed Acquisition of Itabira Mines ...' (1939).

118. CPDOC: JT, 'Código de Minas e Aguas', 21 May 1947. To accommodate this regulation, many foreign companies transferred their assets to Brazilian-domiciled subsidiaries. Equity shares in Brazilian mining companies could be issued in 'bearer' form, obscuring the nationality of equity owners. One option, adopted by the St. John d'el Rey Mining Co., was to form a Brazilian subsidiary that was the holder of record of their mining concession (G. D. Triner, 'Property Rights, Family and Business Partnerships in Nineteenth- and Twentieth-Century Brazil', *Enterprise and Society*, 8:1 (2007), pp. 35–67). One of the continuing ambiguities of mining regulation was the question: Did 'nationalization' mean public sector ownership, or ownership by Brazilian citizens (Vivacqua, *A nova política do sub-solo*, p. 595)? Vivacqua suggests that 'nacionalização' referred to

reserving ownership rights for Brazilian nationals; though, he also concedes that the Constitution (of both 1934 and 1940) conflated the concepts.

119. *Constituição* (1937), Articles 122 and 144; Barbosa, 'Breve panorama'; Rache, *A grande siderúrgia e a exportação de minério*, pp. 151–66. Rache makes clear that strong opposition arose in the *Câmara dos Deputados* (the lower legislative chamber) against state-ownership of mining and metal manufacturing industries.

120. Wirth, 'Brazilian Economic Nationalism', p. 122; Lacerda Rocha, *Das minas e jazidas*. Even so, important ambiguities remained. For example, mining land previously in private ownership remained with the owner, but all newly discovered veins were in the national public domain. Newly discovered veins under privately owned land were in limbo (CPDOC: JT, 'Código de Minas e Aguas', October 1943).

121. This summary is based on Barbosa, 'Breve panorama'; E. Bedran, *A mineração à luz do direito brasileiro: Comentário, doutrina e jursiprudência* (Rio de Janeiro: Editora Alba, Limitada, 1957).

122. *Mineração e Metalurgia*, 12:69 (July–September 1947), pp. 93–102.

123. Companhia Vale do Rio Doce, *A mineração no Brasil*, pp. 281–4. Landowners, however, remained protected with an indemnisation.

124. M. J. Villela Souto, 'O programa brasileiro de privatização de empresas estatais', *Revista de Direito Mercantil*, 29:80 (1990), pp. 54–65, on p. 55; Freire, *Comentários*, p. 16. The first attempt to codify these conditions appeared in the Constitution of 1934.

125. Leis, *Decreto-Lei* 227, 28 February 1967. The decree-law offered a new delineation of the means to gain access to mineral rights (Serra, *Direitos minerários*, p. 43).

126. Legislators looked for ways to allow foreign mining investment while formulating the 1967 Constitution (F. M. d. Vasconcellos, 'O novo Código de Mineração: Palestra proferida no Centro Moraes Rêgo' (São Paulo, 1967), p. 2).

127. F. S. S. Earp, *A questão mineral na Constituição de 1988* (Rio de Janeiro: CETEM/ CNPq, 1988).

128. *Constituição* (1988), Article 176.

129. Freire, *Comentários*, p. 195.

130. Villela Souto, 'O programa brasileiro de privatização de empresas estatais'.

3 Iron and Gold in Pre-Industrial Brazil

1. The classic depiction of gold exploration motivating heroic expansion of the Brazilian frontier is Moog, *Bandeirantes e pioneiros; paralelo entre duas culturas*. See, more recently, Metcalf, *Family and Frontier*. By 1751, gold output had declined to the levels of the beginning of the eighteenth century (see Figure 3.1).

2. The reforms of the Marquis de Pombal (1750–77) represented an orchestrated attempt to restore the Portuguese Crown to its earlier position of European political and economic strength. The tools that these reforms invoked included widening the perimeter of the mercantile unit to introduce direct inter-colonial trade, the construction of stronger fiscal bureaucracy, and tightening the primacy of the Crown's claims to local control, especially relative to the Church (K. Maxwell, *Pombal, Paradox of the Enlightenment* (Cambridge: Cambridge University Press, 1995)). Traditional and highly generalized sources that discuss the period include C. Furtado, *Formação econômica do Brasil*, 40th edn (1959; São Paulo: Ed. Brasiliense, 1993); C. Prado Jr, *História econômica do Brasil* (1942; São Paulo: Editora Brasilense, 1993); F. A. Novais, *Portugal e Brasil na crise do antigo sistema colonial (1777–1808)* (São Paulo: Editora HUCITEC, 1979).

3. P. R. de Almeida, 'A formação econômica brasileira a caminho do autonomia política: Uma análise estrutural e conjuntural do período pré-Independência', in L. V. de Oliveira, R. Ricupero and A. Domingues (eds), *A abertura dos portos* (São Paulo, SP: Editora Senac São Paulo, 2007), pp. 256–83; C. G. Mota, 'Da ordem imperial pombalina à fundação do Império brasileiro (1750–1831): O significado da Abertura dos Portos (1808)', in L. V. d. Oliveira, R. Ricupero and A. Domingues (eds), *A abertura dos portos* (São Paulo, SP: Editora Senac São Paulo, 2007), pp. 60–99. In 1796–7, 84 per cent of all goods exported from Portuguese colonies originated in Brazil; therefore, the perception of this colony's importance in overall Portuguese wealth was a reasonable one (though it may have not been as accurate as it was obvious). This datapoint is cited in J. Caldeira, *A nação mercantilista: Ensaio sobre o Brasil*, 1st edn (São Paulo: Editora 34, 1999).

4. D. J. Pimenta attributes the beginning of state interest in iron ore deposits to the transfer of the Court to Brazil in 1808 ('O minério de ferro na economia nacional: Evolução do minério de ferro; Part 1', *Revista do Serviço Público*, 4:1 (1949), pp. 101–12, on p. 101); evidence suggests however, at least a burgeoning awareness of the issue prior to the Court's arrival.

5. Dom João's regency effectively began in 1792, although he did not ascend to the office formally until 1799. A notable dearth of research on the economic history of this period remains in Brazilian historiography. The end-date of João's rule is also somewhat ambiguous; his son, Pedro, ruled in his stead after João's return to Lisbon in 1821, and then in his own name from the time of political independence in 1824. In English, the standard general survey sources do not even cover the 'interregnum' of João's regime; the few sources on mining also do not cover this period (D. M. Davidson, 'How the Brazilian West Was Won: Freelance and State on the Mato Grosso Frontier, 1737–1752', in D. Alden (ed.), *Colonial Roots of Modern Brazil* (Berkeley and Los Angeles, CA: University of California Press, 1973); L. Bethell (ed.), *The Cambridge History of Latin America*, 11 vols (New York: Cambridge University Press, 1984), vols 4 and 5; Russell-Wood, 'Technology and Society'; E. J. Rogers, 'The Iron and Steel Industry in Colonial and Imperial Brazil', *Americas*, 19:2 (1962), pp. 172–85). Neither do the major works in Brazil consider the issue. De Oliveira Lima, *Dom João VI no Brasil*.

6. R. Ricupero, 'O problema da abertura dos portos', in L. V. Oliveira, R. Ricupero, and A. Domingues (eds), *A abertura dos portos* (São Paulo SP: Editora Senac São Paulo, 2007), pp. 16–59. On the transfer of the Court see P. Wilcken, *Empire Adrift: The Portuguese Court in Rio de Janeiro, 1808–1821* (London: Bloomsbury, 2004); J. J. de Andrade Arruda, *Uma colônia entre dois impérios: A abertura dos portos brasileiros, 1800–1808* (Rio de Janeiro: Edusc, 2006). The transfer of the seat of government also occasioned widespread local improvements within the colony. The physical and cultural infrastructure introduced into Rio de Janeiro offered important externalities of Portuguese imperial government that accrued to Brazil (K. Schultz, *Tropical Versailles: Empire, Monarchy, and the Portuguese Royal Court in Rio de Janeiro, 1808–1821* (New York: Routledge, 2001)).

7. S. F. Figueirôa, *As ciências geológicas no Brasil: Uma história social e institucional, 1875–1934* (São Paulo: Editora Hucitec, 1997).

8. The earlier Pombaline reforms, with regard to these issues, are more accurately characterized as trade policies; they expanded trade opportunities among Portuguese colonies, but retained significant production constraints within Brazil (Bethell (ed.), *The Cambridge History of Latin America*). See also R. de Freitas e Souza, 'Trabalho e cotidiano

na mineração inglesa em Minas Gerais: A mina da Passagem de Mariana (1863–1927)' (PhD dissertation, Universidade de São Paulo, 2009), p. 56.

9. Calógeras later judged the approximately 4,000 slaves brought to Minas Gerais annually to be insufficient (Calógeras, *As minas do Brasil*, vol. 1, pp. 111–35).

10. E. P. de Oliveira, 'A política do ouro (October 1934)', *Mineração e Metalurgia Avulso*, 29 (1937), pp. 10–11. Oliveira cites these estimates as coming from Calógeras and Eschwege. We do not have sufficient information on the construction of these data sets to be able to resolve their differences. Both sets of data refer to Minas Gerais only; Calógeras estimated, another 270,000 kilograms of gold produced elsewhere in Brazil throughout the colonial era (1500–1822).

11. Leis, 'Alvará com força de lei relativa à nova administração das minas de ouro e diamantes do Brasil', 13 May 1803.

12. J. Vieira Couto, *Memória sobre a Capitania das Minas Gerais; seu território, clima e produções metálicas: sobre a necessidade de restabelecer e animar a mineração decadente do Brasil; sobre o commércio e exportação dos metaes e interesses regiões* (Belo Horizonte: Sistema Estadual de Planejamento, Fundação João Pinheiro, Centro de Estudos Históricos e Culturais, 1994); Murilo de Carvalho, *A Escola de Minas de Ouro Preto*, p. 33. Anecdotal evidence reports that in Minas Gerais, imported iron tools fetched prices six times higher than in Portugal. Taxes and transport costs doubled the price of imported tools between their arrival in Brazilian ports and their destination in Minas Gerais (Companhia Vale do Rio Doce, *A mineração no Brasil*, p. 86).

13. Source: E. P. de Oliveira, 'A política do ouro (October 1934)', *Mineração e Metalurgia Avulso*, 29 (1937), pp. 10–11.

14. Traditional tools of fiscal, labour and tax regulation were not neglected, as will be discussed.

15. Antonil trumpeted rich deposits of iron ore in 1711 (cited by Calógeras in *As minas do Brasil*, vol. 2, p. 10, invoking the 1837 Brazilian edition of *Cultura e Opulencia do Brasil suas Drogas e Minas*).

16. F. de Assis Barbosa, *Dom João VI e a siderúrgia no Brasil* (Rio de Janeiro: Biblioteca do Exército; Coleção Tauney, 1958); Calógeras, *As minas do Brasil*, vol. 2, ch. 5. In English, brief summaries of Calógeras's research are in Rogers, 'The Iron and Steel Industry in Colonial and Imperial Brazil'; W. Baer, *The Development of the Brazilian Steel Industry* (Nashville, TN: Vanderbilt University Press, 1969).

17. The first two foundries documented in the colony opened in 1609 in Biraçoiba and Santo Amaro, both in São Paulo (F. L. T. Vinhosa, *Brasil sede da monarquia: Brasil reino (2a parte)*, História Administrativa do Brasil, 8 (Brasília, DF: Editora Universidade de Brasília: Fundação Centro de Formação do Servidor Público, 1984), p. 41).

18. Companhia Vale do Rio Doce, *A mineração no Brasil*, p. 59; G. M. Barros, *História da siderurgia no Brasil, século XIX* (Belo Horizonte: Imprensa Oficial de Minas Gerais, 1989). As discussed below, Eschwege later adapted this technology to initiate the first hydraulic energy used in Brazilian mining.

19. Calógeras, *As minas do Brasil*, vol. 1, p. 33. Calógeras goes so far as to blame failed economic development throughout the seventeenth century to the failure to develop iron foundries.

20. I thank Teresa Marques for a copy of this legislation.

21. The *alvará* also prohibited the distribution of gold powder as currency within Brazil. This was, apparently, a continuing means of avoiding the controls on minting – and, by

extension, taxation. At least four additional legal efforts (in the form of *cartas régias*) also prohibited the practice.

22. D. R. S. Coutinho, *Textos políticos, econômicos e financeiros (1783–1811)* in A. M. D. Silva (ed.), *Colecção de Obras Clássicas do Pensamento Económico Português* (Lisboa: Banco do Portugal, 1993), pp. 277–303. See also Companhia Vale do Rio Doce, *A mineração no Brasil*, pp. 89–91; Junqueira, *Inconstitucionalidade*, p. 21. Junqueira attributes this law to the influence of José Bonifácio de Andrada e Silva, whose participation in formulating mining policy, as well as the early structure of the state was formidable.

23. Authorities anticipated that registration of land and concession transfers would allow them to monitor for speculative transfers (*Lei* of 1808, Article 6, number 5).

24. *Minas devolutas* (mines returned to the public domain) had the same legal status as *terras devolutas*, and they were subject to the same possibilities for misuse. In practice, through the nineteenth century, private parties invoked beneficial-use requirements when they wanted to gain access to either an idle concession, or other resources. The interpretation of 'idle' was often difficult (Triner, 'Kinship Groups, Firm Structure and Property Rights').

25. Leis, *Alvará*, 13 May 1803, Article 7.

26. Limited liability of partners was not introduced at this time.

27. As a result, mining companies were to own between 252 and 1,008 slaves. The intent of the specification of a 'slave-equivalent' was to ensure adequate labour to work a mine.

28. Again, the inconsistency of measuring concessions by specific land units with both the separation of subsoil from surface and the indivisibility of physical assets prevailed.

29. Property rights to water and timber often were of greater concern to miners than those attached to minerals.

30. It is not clear if the reference to selling concessions suggests that authorities were willing to accommodate the formation of a market for concessions beyond the event of declining slave labour force. If so, it is not clear when this change was initiated. This *alvará* also increased the time period for demonstrating beneficial use of a concession, and it increased the area allocated per slave.

31. In the event that the debt exceeded the value of the mine (including the concession, all working slaves, equipment and buildings) and the creditor kept the mine whole and productive, a mine could be repossessed. I have found no evidence that this occurred. The provisions of the law also gave creditors the right to one-third of the earnings of debtor-miners in arrears. An *alvará* of 19 July 1819 further clarified the specific property exempt from creditor claims.

32. A bank for small-scale miners was, in fact, first proposed by Menezes in 1780; it never came into operation (Calógeras, *As minas do Brasil*, vol. 1, p. 146).

33. Leis, *Carta Régia*, 12 August 1817; preamble. The language about the state of decline in gold mining had become boilerplate wording by 1817.

34. Although mining rights to foreigners (individual or partnership) were not explicitly offered until the 1824 Constitution, nothing in previous regulations prevented foreign participation.

35. From 25 to 128 shares, with book value of 400 mil-réis, or three male working slaves, would capitalize the mining partnerships. The discoverer of new veins and surface landowners were guaranteed participation by receiving one share each (Leis, *Carta Régia*, 12 August 1817).

36. Vinhosa, *Brasil sede da monarquia*, pp. 44–6; Simonsen, *História* econômica, p. 442. Within Brazilian historiography the lack of interest in iron ore and iron production is

notable. The major survey references do not mention iron ore at all. For example, no reference to iron ore or smelting appear in A. J. R. Russell-Wood's essay on 'The Gold Cycle' in Bethell, *Colonial Brazil* or in Bethell's *Brazil: Empire and Republic, 1822–1930*. Mining iron ore and processing it into useful products were treated as one industry. Conflating mining and processing into a combined activity prevailed in Brazil until the middle of the twentieth century. Barros's *História da siderurgia* is a rare exception.

37.   A. R. C. da Silva, *Construção da nação e escravidão no pensamento de José Bonifácio, 1783–1823* (São Paulo: Editora da Unicamp, 1999).

38.   Menezes, in fact, began his official efforts to increase iron ore smelting as early as 1780, when he assumed the governorship of Minas Gerais. His first efforts backfired and resulted in the prohibition of further smelting plants; this prohibition remained in place from 1785 until 1795 (see J. R. de Menezes's 'Exposição sobre o estado da decadência da Capitania de Minas Geraes e meios de remedial-a', originally published in 1780 and reprinted in *Revista do Arquivo Público Mineiro*, 2:18 (1897), p. 320). See also M. Carneiro de Mendonça, *O Intendente Câmara: Manuel Ferreira da Câmara Bethencourt e Sá, Intendente Geral das Minas e Diamantes: 1764–1835* (São Paulo: Companhia Editora Nacional, 1958), vol. 301; A. Antunes, *Do diamante ao aço: A trajectória do Intendente Câmara* (Belo Horizonte: UNA, 1999).

39.   Vieira Couto, *Memória*. Calógeras identifies the Vieira Couto report as the basis for Dom João's iron policies; it was the first to propose state participation in the construction of large, industrially-oriented factories.

40.   Calógeras, *As minas do Brasil*, vol. 2, pp. 20, 99–116, 75–80.

41.   Eschwege, 'Pluto Brasiliensis', cited in D. J. Pimenta, 'O minério de ferro na economia nacional: Evolução do minério de ferro; Part 2', *Revista do Serviço Público*, 4:3 (1949), pp. 107–17. To emphasize his point, Eschwege estimated that the value of imported tools in Minas Gerais was sixteen times the value of their metal content.

42.   Leis, *Alvará*, 27 May 1795; Calógeras, *As minas do Brasil*, vol. 2, p. 60.

43.   River transport was not a viable option, given Brazil's geography.

44.   Manuel Ferreira da Câmara Bethencourt e Sá initially began exploring for iron ore in the area in the 1780s (Carneiro de Mendonça, *O Intendente Câmara*; Antunes, *Do diamante ao aço*).

45.   *Decisão número* 41 of 10 October 1808, preamble. In 1809–11, 18 *contos* would have been worth £650–700 (valued at the average month-end rate for the Portuguese real/ British pound sterling (Global Financial Data)). Given the vagaries of exchange valuation in the uncertain period, this estimate must be taken with a pinch of salt.

46.   See below for Eschwege's endeavours (A. D. Gonsalves, *O ferro na economia nacional* (Rio de Janeiro: Ministério da Agricultura, Directoria de Estatística da Produção, Secão de Estatística da Producção Extrativa, 1937), p. 19). I have been unsuccessful in finding biographical information on Schonewolf.

47.   Calógeras, *As minas do Brasil*, vol. 2, p. 88. The technological competence of the effort has not been studied by modern scholars.

48.   Production converted to metric tons at: 1 *arroba* = 1.47 kilograms. 1 *conto* = 1000 *mil-réis*. Sources: production: F. L. T. Vinhosa, *Brasil sede da monarquia*, pp. 43–74; operating income: Calógeras, *As minas do Brasil*, vol. 2, pp. 90–9 (Pilar not available).

49.   This plant was located near to the first ore discoveries of the mid-sixteenth century. Varnhagen was another German metallurgist who came to Brazil with the transfer of the Portuguese Court (Gonsalves, *O ferro na economia*, pp. 17–9). He settled permanently in Brazil and his son was one of the first professional historians of Brazil. The transfer

of responsibility from Karl Hedberg (the Swede) to Varnhagen has been portrayed as a response against Hedberg's shysterism (Calógeras, *As minas do Brasil*, vol. 2, p. 7982; Carneiro de Mendonça, *O Intendente Câmara*, 197; Pimenta, 'O minério de ferro', part 1, p. 103).

50. Leis, *Cartas Régias*, 13 May 1810, 4 December 1810, 12 July 1811, and 28 August 1811.
51. Without additional study, it can only be assumed that other local consumers complained about Ipanema's use of available fuel. In August 1811, a *carta régia* also specified that land be given to the expatriate Swedes in order to 'make their ties to the country permanent' (Calógeras, *As minas do Brasil*, vol. 2, p. 88).
52. Ibid., vol. 2, p. 66.
53. Production dwindled until the factory was closed in 1832. The Brazilian Empire later re-opened the Ipanema foundry in an effort to provision the army during the Paraguayan War (1864–70).
54. This company worked the Passagem mine near the town of Vila Rica (Ouro Preto); it was one of the longest operating gold mines in Brazil (Companhia Vale do Rio Doce, *A mineração no Brasil*, p. 100; Calógeras, *As minas do Brasil*). In the middle of the nineteenth century, a British consortium bought the mine and revived its operations.
55. This method was also used in the local small forges that Eschwege had studied. He mentioned that the province of Minas Gerais had at least sixteen of these forges (Calógeras, *As minas do Brasil*, vol. 3, pp. 91–9; Simonsen, *História econômica*, p. 448).
56. de Freitas e Souza, 'Trabalho e cotidiano na mineração'.
57. Leis, *Carta Régia*, 30 August 1811.
58. The Crown's hope in chartering this company was to 'have the result of convincing and motivating locals [*os povos*] to agree with greater satisfaction in the establishment of additional factories of a similar nature in other districts' (Leis, *Carta Régia*, 30 August 1811).
59. Gonsalves, *O ferro na economia*, p. 19.
60. A fourth attempt to produce iron in Cuyabá Matto Grosso (another region rich in hopes for gold deposits) was chartered in January 1817, with a twenty-year monopoly concession for iron ore in Matto Grosso, but apparently without financial subsidy from Dom João. The statutes for this company were approved in March 1819. Nothing seems to have come of the company.
61. Gonsalves, *O ferro na economia*, p. 21. This volume of output includes the efforts sponsored by Dom João.
62. One further attempt to establish a large-scale iron smelting plant began during João's regime. Undertaken by Jean Antoine de Monlevade, a French engineer, this was the only totally private endeavour during João's regime. This plant began production in 1825, after Brazilian independence.
63. The major exception to this characterization was the re-opening and expansion of the Ipanema plant to provision the Brazilian Army during the Paraguayan War (1864–70) (Calógeras, *As minas do Brasil*, vol. 2, p. 105).
64. Murilo de Carvalho, *A Escola de Minas*; Figueirôa, *As ciências geológicas*.
65. MV Historical Notes, p. 1. This provision was one of many that opened the new Empire to business with non-Portuguese Europeans in the early nineteenth century.
66. In practice, at least for most of the nineteenth century, companies negotiated tax rates with the national government. The St John d'el Rey was taxed at rates between zero and 10 per cent (MV Historical Notes, p. 3; MV Board Letter, 2 August 1878).
67. W. Dean, *With Broadax and Firebrand: The Destruction of the Brazilian Atlantic Forest* (Berkeley, CA: University of California Press, 1995), pp. 170–1; D. C. Libby, *Trabalho*

escravo e capital estrangeiro no Brasil: o caso de Morro Velho (Belo Horizonte: Editora Itatiaia, 1984), pp. 29–30; Eakin, *British Enterprise in Brazil*, pp. 15–20 and table 1.

68. D. C. Libby, *Transformação e trabalho em uma economia escravista: Minas Gerais no século XIX* (São Paulo: Editora Brasiliense, 1988), pp. 266–7. Libby finds that the company was the fourth foreign gold mining company to enter. See also Eakin, *British Enterprise in Brazil*, table 1. Eakin identifies Morro Velho as the second British company. For more on the history of the company also see Triner, 'Kinship Groups, Firm Structure and Property Rights'; B. Carsalade Villela, *Nova Lima: Formação histórica* (Belo Horizonte: Editora Cultura, 1998).

69. The St John d'el Rey Mining Company is a useful prism for studying property issues, not because it was unique, British or successful. Rather, its struggling longevity, well-defined corporate structure and interests in a wide variety of property offer a unique opportunity to view concisely the institutional constraints of property rights.

70. The average life of British gold mining companies in Minas Gerais during the nineteenth century was twenty-six-and-a-half years (Eakin, *British Enterprise in Brazil*, table 1). These include the fourteen companies for which Eakin has known dates of operation. (Four companies are of unknown opening or closing dates. Excluding the St John d'el Rey and these four, the average life of gold mining companies was eighteen-and-a-half years. The Ouro Preto Gold Mines Co., Ltd, the second most recent British mining company, closed in 1927.)

71. Of course, following veins below the subsurface rendered the company's extension of subsurface mining area questionable.

72. The company's long-term and prolific property manager, R. H. Wharrier, compiled a master list documenting the history of the company's property and the supporting legal documentation of deed, registry titles, etc (MV Imobiliário, file 13.10.66.4). He also oversaw the compilation of a *Registro* that summarized the acquisitions and all subsequent legal challenges. These compilations map the property history; other sources (letters, court documents, annual reports etc) provide the stories behind the legal documents. Wharrier must have been an ongoing nuisance to the mining staff of the company; but his administrative efforts offer an archival trove to the historian. I thank Marshall Eakin for pointing me to this source.

73. The St John d'el Rey Company both owned and hired slave labour until the abolition of slavery. In this regard the company had a stake in the laws governing humans as property (Libby, *Trabalho escravo e capital estrangeiro*).

74. The company first acquired land for the purpose of gaining timber rights in 1839. Recurrent concerns about the deforestation of local lands arose as a problem from the first years of operation. By 1845, as a result of the shortage of timber, the company purchased more than one-half of its supply, and in 1892 the company considered importing lumber from the United States of America (SJdR Annual Report, 1839, p. 26 and 1845; MV Board Letter, 1 January 1892).

75. While the company tried to acquire land that included water and timber rights, it sometimes also purchased water rights. I have not seen cases of the company acquiring timber rights on land they did not own. However, at least one important court case (discussed below) was concerned with a party claiming timber from the company.

76. SJdR Annual Report, 1905, pp. 48–9. The annual reports to shareholders in 1909 and 1912 again refer to efforts to consolidate holdings, enter into exchanges and judicial divisions in order to ensure their sole ownership of property. These efforts antedate those of the 1930s and 1940s (see below).

77. This practice predated the company. They note that 'The Mine and Fazenda do Morro Velho along with the adjoining Fazenda da Ana da Cruz belonged to José Correa da Silva and Wife Ana Joaquina da Silva' (MV Historical Notes, appendix B). The same practice seems to continue currently, if in less rigid form.

78. MV *Registro*, documents 12, 33, 31 and 32, 'Esboços históricos' and associated document lists. Figure 3.2 displays other examples of contiguous holdings. As another example (not identified on Figure 3.2), Fazendas das Feixas and Varginha de Ouro Podre, acquired in 1832 and 1903, were considered separate properties (MV *Registro*, documents 21/1 and 21/2). The company's records trace the original registration of this estate to the registration of land, water and mineral rights from 1769 to 1783.

79. For example, during the late 1940s and early 1950s, the company donated land to accommodate the route of the highway between Belo Horizonte and Rio de Janeiro. On 16 May 1950, they registered two distinct donations of contiguous land that came from estates they had previously acquired separately (MV *Registro*, documents 23/1 and 24/1).

80. Source: St John d'el Rey Archive, Nettie Lee Benson Library, University of Texas, Austin Texas.

81. The St John d'el Rey's first land purchase in the 'Morro Velho Mine and Estate' (after its failures in São João region) were in two transactions with three of the original British partners (or the heirs of one of the partners), who seemed to function at least as much as real estate scouts as miners. Both transactions were dated 3 December 1834. The third piece from the fourth partner was dated 8 December 1834. Additional small purchases of small plots retained by one previous resident were completed in 1834, 1839 and 1845 (MV *Registro*, documents 1/1–1/5).

82. Chronologically, the Mingú acquisition began two months prior to the Morro Velho purchase; its deed was dated 9 October 1834. The company's History does not indicate why this purchase is recorded as the second estate. The value of the initial transaction was insignificant (about 0.5 per cent of the value of the Morro Velho land (MV *Registro*, document 2.1; MV Imobiliário, file 13.10.66.4, MV Historical Notes)).

83. MV *Registro*, document 2 (Esboço Histórico). The term 'a companhia tem posse absoluta, mansa e pacífica que lhe assegura o direita sobre todo o imóvel agora denominada 'Morro do Bonfim ou Mingú' denoted that no known outstanding claims challenged the company's holding.

84. MV *Registro*, documents 2/1–2/16.

85. MV *Registro*, documents 39/1–39/27.

86. Through its history, the St John d'el Rey had to resolve many property disputes arising from ambiguous demarcation of geographic boundaries.

87. MV *Registro*, documents 19/1–19/3 (Fazenda dos Gorduras [*sic*] 'Esboço Histórico' and supporting documents).

88. MV *Registro*, document 19/3.

89. These documents do not record a settlement payment to the disputants. Such payments were recorded in the *Registro de documentos*, suggesting that none took place in this case.

90. A portion of the holding was on the same mountain (Morro Velho) as the original land purchases. Pedro Paulo was located at the western side of the company's holdings (see Figure 3.2).

91. The documents in the company's possession do not address the slaves' legal status. Emancipation and land rights were completely independent of each other.

92. MV *Registro*, document 54/2.

93. MV *Registro*, document 54/2, 13 June 1911. This wording indicates that the parties had established *de facto* geographic boundaries to their uses of the property.
94. MV Historical Notes, appendix D.
95. This time period, however, was still prior to the passing of ten generations of descendants. It is not clear how the Church became the recognized owner of the land that it would have received after ten generations (beginning in 1839); neither is it consistent with later wording.
96. MV *Registro*, document 54 'Esboço Histórico'. The practice of *de facto* geographic division of land use among common properties seems to have been usual.
97. MV *Registro*, document 54/1. Another 'descendant of the Negro Slaves' tried again to assert a claim against the St John d'el Rey in 1955, but withdrew it a year later (MV Imobiliário, file 13.10.66.4, 56).
98. MV Imobiliário, files 13.10.66.4, 'List of Documents'; and 13.4.4.4, 'Histórico de Cuiabá'. The first indication that the St John d'el Rey was considering the acquisition came in a Board letter of 8 September 1873, raising the issue of negotiation with the British partner's estate (MV Board Letter, 8 September 1873). The original 1827 partnership in this holding, the National Brazilian Mining Association organized as a British company, provided for the indivisibility of the estate. At the partnership's expiration in 1876, the property reverted to the heirs of one of the British partners. John Pennycock Brown's heirs (95 per cent of the partnership) sold to the St John d'el Rey. The remaining 5 per cent transferred in to the National Brazilian Mining Co., which subsequently failed (MV Imobiliário, file 13.4.4.4, 'Histórico de Cuiabá', pp. 3, 10–11; MV Board Letter, 8 December 1877). In 1897, the National Brazilian tried to claim the mining lodes based on their prior ownership, despite having left the lodes unexplored. In 1918 the company settled with the successor of the failed National Brazilian in order to drop all subsequent claims (MV Imobiliário, file 13.10.37.1, 'Decreto Guarda-mór').
99. MV Imobiliário, file 13.10.37.1, 'Concession of the Guarda-mór'.
100. MV Imobiliário, file 13.4.4.4 and MV *Registro*, document 60/1.
101. MV Imobiliário, file 13.4.4.4, 'Histórico de Cuiabá' and annexed 'Brief description of right of Company at Cuiabá, extracted from Dr Fonseca's reports of 7 January 1888 and 29 January 1889', p. 2. When purchasing this estate, the company believed that 'the National Brazilian Company or their creditors – the Brazilian Land and Mining Company have no freehold rights, the Board understand, on any part of the property purchased from the Executors of the late Mr. Brown will exclude them from any mining or water rights they may have fancied, or been informed by their attorney in Brazil, they were entitled to' (MV Board Letter, 8 April 1878). See also Calógeras, *As minas do Brasil*, vol. 1, ch. 227.
102. MV Imobiliário, files 13.4.1.2, 'Asuntos diversos da Região de Cuiabá', letter dated 31 May 1947, from Wharrier, Estate Agent; and 13.4.4.4, 'Histórico de Cuiabá'. The leading Brazilian jurist, Rui Barbosa, argued the final appeals before the Brazilian Supreme Court on behalf of the St John d'el Rey's ownership claims in 1901 (MV Imobiliário, file 13.4.4.5). The legal requirement that land and natural resource concessions be 'in productive use' was a continuing challenge for all property owners (MV *Registro: passim*). The concept remains a underlying principle of Brazilian land claims.
103. MV Imobiliário, file 13.10.66.4 and MV *Registro*, document 60/1.
104. Between 1900 and 1911 (the settlement with Rotulo) the St John d'el Rey entered into seven agreements to settle claims. Another eighteen settlements were contracted between 1917 and 1928 (MV Imobiliário, file 13.10.66.4, 'List of Documents').

105. See, for example, MV Imobiliário, file 13.4.1.22. A deed from 1838 represented that Brigadier Texeira and his wife were one-quarter partners of the mines of Cuiabá. As individuals settled into dwellings and resource use, *de facto* assertions to specific resources emerged, and these holdings acquired separate names. However, they did not achieve legal status (MV Imobiliário, file 13.4.1.1, 'Informações Histórico', pp. 21–36).

106. MV Imobiliário, file 13.4.1.1, 'Informações sobre a Região de Cuiabá', pp. 9–13; and 'Histórico do Imóvel', pp. 21–3. The original Brazilian owner had ten children.

107. MV Imobiliário, file 13.4.1.2, 'Asuntos diversos' memo dated November 1932, entitled 'Cuiabá Properties-Observations, extracts from report'. Between 1879 and 1933, the St John d'el Rey entered into forty-two transactions to preclude this set of potential claimants.

108. MV Imobiliário, file 13.4.4.4 'Histórico de Cuiabá', letter of 1 December 1957 to H.G. Watson [General Manager], pp. 1–3; this text refers to the 1940s).

109. MV Imobiliário, file 13.4.1.2, 'Cuiabá land question'. The company always saw Abdo as an opportunist, who persistently pressed a frivolous suit. They referred to him as 'a well known meddler in property disputes' and variously as an 'Arab', 'Syrian' or 'Turco'. The company probably was correct that he was an opportunist; but, he was able to keep the company in court and to exert a serious claim for a substantial portion of their resources for more than twenty-five years.

110. MV Imobiliário, file 13.4.1.1, 'Informações', p. 4.

111. MV Imobiliário, file 13.4.1.1, 'Informações', p. 4. See also file 13.4.4.4, 'Histórico de Cuiabá', letter dated February 1908 to G. Chalmers (superintendent)).

112. MV Imobiliário, file 13.4.4.4, 'Histórico de Cuiabá', pp. 26–7.

113. MV Imobiliário, files 13.4.1.2, 'Cuiabá land question', 14 August 1951; and 13.4.1.1, 'Informações', letter dated 1 December 1957 from Wharrier to H. G. Watson (general manager)), p. 4.

114. MV Imobiliário, file 13.4.1.1, 'Histórico do Imóvel', p. 36 and file 13.4.1.2, judicial proceedings of 8 June 1960. I do not know the disposition of this final suit, or if it was frivolous in nature.

115. MV *Registro, passim.*

116. The St John d'el Rey Company, Ltd continued to mine gold, despite two serious accidents during the nineteenth century. Its major mine, Morro Velho, continues to produce gold for its current owner, the Anglo-American-Ashanti Corporation. The Passagem Mine produced gold intermittently until 1974.

117. Constitution (1824); MV Historical Notes, p. 1.

118. Dean, 'Latifundia and Land Policy in Nineteenth-Century Brazil'; Viotti da Costa, *The Brazilian Empire*, ch. 5.

119. Calógeras comes to similar conclusions in his broad historical survey of Brazilian mining law (*As minas do Brasil*, vol. 3, p. 476).

120. The depictions, prevailing through the early twentieth century, of propertied families sending their sons to settle new frontier lands and open new fazendas, while leaving behind diminishing estates, supports this interpretation. Selling off depleted land, to transform to new uses, was common (Metcalf, *Family and Frontier* and Dr Geraldo Arruda, interview with author, 10 June 2004).

121. P. L. Eisenberg, *The Sugar Industry in Pernambuco: Modernization without Change, 1840–1910* (Berkeley, CA: University of California Press, 1974); Metcalf, *Family and Frontier.*

122. Dean, *The Industrialization of São Paulo*; S. J. Stein, *Vassouras, a Brazilian Coffee County, 1850–1900* (Cambridge, MA: Harvard University Press, 1957); W. Dean, *Rio Claro: a Brazilian Plantation System, 1820–1920* (Stanford, CA: Stanford University Press, 1976).

4 The Subsoil as Private Property

1. Pimenta, 'O minério de ferro na economia nacional', part 1.
2. A. de Roure, *A constituinte republicana* (Rio de Janeiro: Imprensa Nacional, 1918), pp. 176–9.
3. T. Priest, *Global Gambits: Big Steel and the U.S. Quest for Manganese*, International History Series (Westport, CT: Praeger, 2003); J. D. Wirth, *Minas Gerais in the Brazilian Federation, 1889–1937* (Stanford, CA: Stanford University Press, 1977).
4. This conflation has a basis in logic; ore processed (refined) into pig iron is the first step to its further transformation to steel. The elimination of impurities resulted in a relatively homogeneous mineral composition: about 3½ per cent to 4½ per cent carbon, 3 per cent to 4 per cent other minerals and the remainder is iron. I thank Carter Kaneen for this technological consultation. The measurement of both pig iron and ore that remained unconverted into pig iron did not begin until 1933. The Data Appendix contains a summary of the available data.
5. This observation does not include artisanal production or production within vertically integrated firms (which, until the late 1920s, usually remained small).
6. As this chapter will demonstrate, the difficulty of studying 'failure' lies as much with identifying what did *not* happen as with understanding what *did* happen.
7. Olson, *The Logic of Collective Action*; D. Rodrik, *One Economics, Many Recipes: Globalization, Institutions, and Economic Growth* (Princeton, NJ: Princeton University Press, 2007).
8. Concessions are also identified in Companhia Vale do Rio Doce, *Coletânea da legislação*.
9. These were accumulated from the public notarial registries, land transfer registrations (1872–1940) Itabira and Sabará (both in Minas Gerais), with the permission of the Chief Justices of both *municípios*.
10. The data on concessions covers all concessions in the state of Minas Gerais; land transfers are limited to the *municípios* of Sabará and Itabira.
11. In contrast to much Brazilian historiography, which ignores or dismisses the role of legal change, my research indicates that the laws were important. I find in previous work that, under many circumstances, laws worked as they had been intended. I consider the circumstances under which the law 'worked' and when it did not. Conveniently, Brazil strongly follows Roman legal tradition, in which detailed codification of practices define institutions and permissible activity (Triner, *Banking and Economic Development*; Triner, 'Property Rights, Family and Business Partnerships').
12. Brasil, Leis, *Decreto* 4265, 15 January 1921 (commonly referred to as the *Lei Simões Lopes*) clearly resolved the right of the national government to enforce beneficial-use requirements.
13. As discussed in Chapter 2, beneficial-use laws require that natural resource assets controlled by private parties were not actively exploited (or in 'beneficial use'), be returned to the public domain.
14. Vivacqua, *A nova política do sub-solo*, pp. 552–3, 556. Vivacqua also pointed out that 'the Constitution of 1934 adopted as a fundamental principle the separation of the two

properties – the territory and the mineral' (p. 545) and 'the Constitution of 1934 as well as the current Constitution (1937) follows Napoleonic Code (Law of 1810) and separated the property of the soil from the mineral for purposes of mining or industrial uses' (p. 575).

15. These regulatory actions applied to all actors in the mining sector. They do not include the actions targeted to individual beneficiaries. Source: Appendix Table A.2A.

16. Source: Derived from data underlying Appendix Tables A.2A and A.2B.

17. Minas Gerais, Presidente do Estado, *Mensagem dirigida pelo Presidente do Estado ao Congresso Mineiro em sua 2 sessão ordinária da 4 legislatura, no anno 1904'* (Imprensa Nacional, online at http://www.crl.edu/content/brazil/mina.htm).

18. Minas Gerais; *Leis* Nos 597, 9 November 1892; 285, 18 September 1899; 574, 20 September 1915, respectively.

19. N. C. de Senna, 'A função social do Estado e a desapropriação de minas para fins públicos', *Anais da Câmara dos Deputados do Congresso Mineiro* (Rio de Janeiro: Belo Horizonte, Imprensa Ofical, 1907), pp. 247–60. I thank Paulo Coelho Mesquito Santos for bringing this source to my attention.

20. If the period under consideration is lengthened to the entire period for which I have data (1880–1940) the proportion of *mineiro* regulation with neutral effect remained as 58 per cent; the proportion of neutral federal regulatory actions declined to 38 per cent.

21. Comparison with the extent of favours granted by the federal government for the same activities described here is not feasible, because of the scope of the data collection effort required. Because seeking individual benefit from the legislative and regulatory system, within Minas Gerais, did not begin until 1907 – seventeen years after the change in mining rights, I would argue that it was newly introduced behaviour, at least with respect to state-level regulation.

22. Laws and decrees to specific beneficiaries that did not meet their goals could simply be ignored. General-purpose legislation could not be easily ignored, since by leaving it in place kept open the possibility that it could be invoked.

23. The 'negative' incentives constraining regulation targeted to individuals were revocations of concessions (usually for railroad trunk lines or steel plants) or fines.

24. Calógeras, *As minas do Brasil*. Other authors, also with vested interests, relied exclusively on the Calógeras study (Vivacqua, *A nova política do sub-solo*; Junqueira, *Inconstitucionalidade*).

25. N. C. de Senna, *A terra mineira*, 2 vols (Belo Horizonte: Imprensa Oficial do Estado de Minas Gerais, 1926), vol. 2, pp. 33–6.

26. Other factors also affecting the willingness to mine iron ore – such as increasing demand and plentiful resource endowment – cannot offer explanations for either the un-sustained legal trajectory or the difficulties of increasing mineral output.

27. From 1933, the federal government issued 'authorizations' to prospect; these served the same purpose as earlier concessions to prospect. I have combined these two categories, accounting for the sharp upsurge in 1934 and 1937. (The discontinuous pattern resulted from the strengthening of authorization procedures with the amendments to the Mining Code in 1937.) Again, the data are not directly comparable, because they cover different geographic units.

28. Mining and prospecting concessions refer to those issued throughout Minas Gerais. Land transfers refer to those registered in the municipalities of Sabará and Itabira (Minas Gerais): 1934: Number of mining concessions = 19; 1937: Number of prospecting concessions = 124. Source: Appendix Tables A.3 and A.4.

29. Prospecting authorizations (concessions) demonstrate an unusual pattern. The initial use of these instruments was curtailed until definitional problems were resolved in the reforms of 1937.
30. Itabira, 1912 = 42. Source: Appendix Table A.4.
31. For an early announcement of these resources see J. P. Wileman (ed.), *Brazilian Year Book* (Rio de Janeiro, printed in London: 1909), pp. 555–6. Wileman also anticipated the looming infrastructure problems.
32. Other problems, such as beneficial-use requirements and maintaining the seniority of mineral rights for the discoverer, were complicated and expensive, but remediable.
33. In the Itabira project, as it was finally implemented in 1942, the distribution of initial capital improvements was:

	Amount (*Cruzeiros*, mln)	Percentage
Mines	29	8.2
Refining and concentration plant	142	40.3
Railroad development	137	39.0
Ports development	44	12.5
Total	352	100.0

Source Piimenta, 'O minério de ferro, Part 1': 98.

See also *Revista Commercial de Minas Gerais*, 1:1 (October 1937), pp. 43–52.
34. Extensive literatures in economic history and development theory focus on the interrelated centralities of finance and transportation infrastructure in creating the conditions for economic growth. Some of the most prominent examples include A. Gerschenkron, *Economic Backwardness in Historical Perspective, A Book of Essays* (Cambridge, MA: Belknap Press of Harvard University Press, 1962); J. H. Coatsworth, *Growth against Development: The Economic Impact of Railroads in Porfirian Mexico*, The Origins of Modern Mexico Series (DeKalb, IL: Northern Illinois University Press, 1981); A. Fishlow, *American Railroads and the Transformation of the Antebellum Economy*, Harvard Economic Studies Series, 127 (Cambridge, MA: Harvard University Press, 1965); Summerhill, *Order against Progress*.
35. Attempts to produce steel without reliance on coke (the 'Smith process') received little mention, and were not seriously considered. Lobato attributes this lack of attention to the prominence of British methods in the industry (M. Lobato, *Ferro: A solução do problema siderúrgico do Brasil pelo processo Smith* (Rio de Janeiro, 1931), ch. 3). Another proposal also received brief consideration; an A. D. Williams of New Jersey proposed researching the production of low carbon pig iron (MRE, Lata 1260, maço 28384: EC/153/565.12 (Anexo)). Coal became a target of special regulation; three of the thirteen laws that applied to specific metals and/or steel during the period of this study attempted to increase the supply of coal by granting tax reductions and prohibiting exports. As late as 1939, at least one engineering analysis doubted the ability to sustain the steel industry using domestic coal (M. T. C. de Mendonça, 'A Grande Siderúrgia e o carvão nacional' *Mineração e Metalurgia*, 4: 20 (July–August 1939)). As an indication of its importance, the state nationalized the coal industry in 1942, simultaneously with its programmes to construct large ore-export and integrated steel enterprises. Sixteen of the preferential actions applied to steel. On the favourable policy treatment of coal and steel, see Serviço Geológico e Mineralógico do Brasil, Ministerio da Agricultura, Industria e Commercio, *Relatório apresentado ao Ministro da Agricultura, Industria e Commercio* (Rio de Janeiro: Imprensa Nacional, 1922), pp. 145–6. On the long-term struggle to find

sufficient coal for iron ore refining and steelmaking, see Barros, *História da siderurgia no Brasil, século XIX*, pp. 71–117.

36. The wood necessary for making charcoal gained value with its depletion. In the 1930s, the Itabira real-estate registry recorded at least thirty-eight transactions that permitted clearing of ground cover (*matas*), without the transfer of land ownership; these contracts typically were in effect for seven to ten years (as indicated in the Itabira notarial registries). Although not included in this project (because of inadequate data availability) land registries from the municipality of Mariana (adjacent to Sabará) also gives evidence of registering the granting of access to *matas* as transactions of real property. The *matas* of Minas Gerais remain depleted as a result of earlier clearing.

37. United States Department of Commerce and Labor, Bureau of Manufactures, Special Consular Reports, *Coal Trade in Latin America* (Washington DC: Government Printing Office, 1910), pp. 21–5. When labour conditions threatened strikes in Welsh coalfields, imports shifted to the US.

38. M. C. d. S. Minayo, *Os homens de ferro: Estudo sobre os trabalhadores da indústria extrativa de minério de Ferro da Companhia Vale do Rio Doce em Itabira, Minas Gerais* (Rio de Janeiro: Dois Pontos, 1986), pp. 39–47.

39. Four other foreign syndicates also tried to gain access to the ore deposits of the Rio Doce valley (Companhia Vale do Rio Doce, *Companhia Vale do Rio Doce*, pp. 151–61; PF, box 8, folder 104, 'Itabira memoir' by Percival Farquhar (30 July 1942)). This group was a syndicate associated with steel producers who jointly sought to secure iron ore supplies. In 1942, the Itabira mines were estimated to have 700 million tons of iron ore, about 54 per cent of Brazilian reserves (D. J. Pimenta, *Companhia Vale do Rio Doce*, p. 24; C. M. Peláez, 'Itabira Iron e a exportação do minério de ferro do Brasil', *Revista Brasileira de Economia*, 24, 4th edn (1970), pp. 139–74). For a descriptive (non-analytical) narrative of these events, see E. J. Rogers, 'Brazil's Rio Doce Valley Project', *Journal of Interamerican Studies*, 1:2 (1959), pp. 123–40.

40. Derby, 'The Iron Ores of Brazil'; Companhia Vale do Rio Doce, *A mineração no Brasil*, pp. 151–4.

41. PF, box 7, folder 86; cited in 'A Nossa Siderurgia e a Grande Siderurgia' Report attributed to Getúlio Vargas (November 1932); Ministério da Agricultura, Serviço de Fomento da Producção Mineral, memo of 26 May 1936 (the point is also made in Vivacqua, *A nova política do sub-solo*, p. 306). The volume of reserves estimated in Minas Gerais was 13 billion tons (Wirth, 'Brazilian Economic Nationalism', p. 105). The arithmetic discrepancy is not resolved. According to these findings the United States of America possessed 20 per cent of world reserves (though of lower quality), and other countries followed with much smaller shares.

42. The Itabira ore was about 68 per cent iron. Russia and Sweden had ore reserves of comparable quality to Brazil's, but the high-concentration reserves were of smaller quantity (PF, box 5, folder 62, 'Official Note' (1940, re-affirmation of 1936 manifest of mining holdings) box 7, folder 86).

43. In an administrative maneuver with political intent, the *Tribunal de Contas* refused to accept the contract registration and Epitácio Pessoa, President of Brazil, overrode the refusal. For political and procedural reasons the contract remained in dispute (E. Pessôa, *Pela verdade* (Rio de Janeiro: Livraria Francisco Alves, 1925), pp. 375–98). See also PF box 6, folder 77, memo by Epitácio Pessoa (May 1933), on his reasoning with respect to the Itabira project). The issue is also discussed in Pimenta, *Companhia Vale do Rio Doce*.

44. C. A. Gauld, *The Last Titan: Percival Farquhar: American Entrepreneur in Latin America* (Stanford, CA: Institute of Hispanic American and Luso-Brazilian Studies Stanford University Press, 1964); Baer, *The Development of the Brazilian Steel Industry*, pp. 64–8. The Gauld biography is hagiographic; Baer focuses on Farquhar's involvement in iron mining.

45. The Companhia Estrada de Ferro Vitória a Minas obtained its operating concession in 1890, but the company was not capitalized until 1902. Its originally intended purposes were both to service the (anticipated) steel industry and to aid in the generation of large-scale hydropower. Later, scandals concerning the legitimacy of one of its international bond offerings significantly complicated the railroads commercial viability (D. A. Araripe, *História da Estrada de Ferro Vitória e Minas: 1904–1954* (Rio de Janeiro: Ed Cia. Vale do Rio Doce, 1954). See also, CPDOC: EMS, pi 1938.06.10).

46. Farquhar's experience with railways and other infrastructure had been his 'selling point' in acquiring the Itabira Iron Ore options (Gauld, *The Last Titan*; M. M. A. Chiarizia, 'Itabira Iron Ore Company Limited' (Master's dissertation, Universidade Federal Fluminense, 1979), p. 29).

47. Chiarizia, 'Itabira Iron Ore Company Limited', pp. 37–9; Peláez, 'Itabira Iron '; J. D. Wirth, *Economic Nationalism: Trade and Steel Under Vargas* (Stanford, CA: Stanford University Press, 1969); Gauld, *The Last Titan*.

48. A. S. Bernardes, 'Porque não se fez o contrato com a Itabira Iron', in Bernardes, *Discursos e Pronunciamentos de Arthur da Silva Bernardes* (Belo Horizonte: Governo do Estado de Minas Gerais, 1977), p. 181. Committing to build an integrated steel plant within the state of Minas Gerais would reduce the tax by 90 per cent. Bernardes also articulated the widespread complaint that the Itabira Iron Ore Co. acquired its land for a very low price (Bernardes, *Discursos*, p. 162). This complaint did not reflect the economic logic that the land acquired its value only with the large-scale improvements that its previous owners did not make. His arguments often took a tone that would, in later years, be described as protecting infant industry.

49. The plant was to produce 150,000 tons of steel annually; doing so would gain an exemption from the export tax. Although Itabira was the only company with the potential capacity to export ore, this privilege extended to any producer of steel; it was not specifically negotiated with Itabira Iron Ore (Peláez, 'Itabira Iron', p. 163). Even so, many did not accept the premise that foreign-owned steel manufacture would be conducive to a successful steel sector in Brazil (CPDOC: EMS, da Silva, Paul Ribeiro, 'Relatório: Ferro a salvação do Brasil', 1931).

50. PF, box 3, folder 31, letter from Farquhar to Gordon Leith (13 November 1923). The earliest expression of concern about the nationality of mineral access, that I have found, dates to 1901 (*Retrospecto Comercial* (1901)).

51. CPDOC: EMS, pi Silva, R. 1922.08.16.

52. According to Bernardes (*Discursos*, 'Porque não', p. 181) these contracts included sixteen 'favours' from the national government and seven 'favours' from the state government of Minas Gerais. These agreements excluded both the rail transport privilege and the requirement (but not the right) to build an integrated steel plant.

53. The Crash of 1929 forced the cancellation of a planned stock offering. Farquhar and the Vargas government spent the next twelve years arguing on whether the inability of to raise capital was a failure that nullified their contract, or a *force majeur*, which would have kept their original contracts in place (with new deadlines) resulting from the Crash.

54. Pimenta, 'O minério de ferro', part 1; Wirth, 'Brazilian Economic Nationalism'.

55. The 1937 Constitutional reform introduced the prohibition of foreign-owned mines that could be subject to expropriation for reasons of national security. Bernardes led the opposition to (and fueled the controversy about) Itabira's potential monopoly went on for more than three decades (*New York Times*, 20 June 1937, p. 22).
56. C. de Oliveira, *A Concessão Itabira* (Belo Horizonte: n.a., 1934), p. 378. Oliveira offers detailed argument that almost every clause of each version of the Itabira Iron Ore contract disadvantaged Brazilians. Oliveira was a close associate of Artur Bernardes. Also see PF, box 3, folder 33, letter from Sir Alexander Mackenzie to John Tilley (British Ambassador to Brazil, 27 October 1921); box 6, folder 77, 1936, report by Epitácio Pessoa, on the efforts of his government (1919–22) to make iron ore exports viable. Pessoa identified opposition to the arrangement on grounds of mineral depletion). Secondary sources include Wirth, *The Politics of Brazilian* Development, ch. 5; Companhia Vale do Rio Doce, *A mineração no Brasil*, pp. 154–61.
57. CPDOC: EMS, pi 1931.08.14 Soares, E. See also C. de Oliveira, *A Concessão Itabira*, p. 21.
58. All data measured in US$/metric ton.

    Legend of company names:

UQJ:	Usina Queiroz Júnior	CFB:	Cia. Ferro Brasileira
CBUM:	Cia. Bras. de Usinas Metallurgicas	B-Min:	Belgo-Mineira
Mag:	Magnavacca & Filhos		

    Sources: individual company data: Gonsalves, Apheu Dinitz. *O ferro na economia nacional*, 1937; exchange rates: Global Financial Data (based on annual average of monthly close); US iron ore prices: NBER Macrohistory data base, #4010a–c.
59. Lobato, *Ferro*, p. 22.
60. On the Vargas Regime see G. Vargas, 'A industrialização do ferro – base de nova estrutura econômica do Brasil (1931)', in Vargas, *A nova política do Brasil*, pp. 135–6; Wirth, *Economic Nationalism*.
61. In this speech, he explicitly referenced the public-good nature of iron as well as its eventual nationalization (G. Vargas, 'Os saldos ouro e o problema siderúrgica', in Vargas, *A nova política do Brasil*, pp. 93–108). For a highly polemical expression of this view, see Lobato, *Ferro*.
62. Vivacqua, *A nova política do sub-solo*, p. 329. See also Fróes Abreu, *A riqueza mineral do Brasil* (São Paulo: Companhia Editora Nacional, 1937), pp. 27–9.
63. CPDOC: HB, 22.08.16, 19 August, 1938 (1904); J. da Silva Lima, 'O problema siderúrgico brasileiro sob o ponto de vista das indústrias militares', presented at O problema siderúrgico brasileiro conference, Rio de Janeiro, 19 August 1938.
64. Fróes Abreu, *A riqueza mineral do Brasil*, p. 49. Fróes Abreu also immediately recognized the additional requirements of fuel and market demand in order to build the industry.
65. The significant changes to mining regulation were its separation from land and return to the public domain at the national level. Both of these factors contributed to bringing order and security to mining enterprises. Interpretations remained inconsistent about whether ownership of mineral deposits rested with the state or the state's role was to control resources owned by no one (*res nullius*). See, for example United States Tariff Commission, *Mining and Manufacturing Industries in Brazil* (Washington DC: Government Printing Office, 1949), pp. 11–2. For an explicit expression of the industrial ambitions motivating the Mining Code see D. J. Pimenta, 'Exportação de minério de ferro pelo Vale do Rio Doce', *Geologia e metallurgia*, 7 (1949), pp. 62–101, on p. 126.

66. Ribeiro, *A era Vargas*, vol. 1, pp. 123–4.
67. They also fell off rapidly. By 1943, existing companies completed mandatory authorizations for current or anticipated mining. Later practitioners characterized this surge as a 'run' to lay claim to future prospecting, without basis in geological studies (Távora, 'O Código de Minas e desenvolvimento', p. 186).
68. In 1921, the second plan for large-scale industrial iron ore extraction at Itabira projected exports of 3 million metric tons annually. Brazil did not reach this level of output until 1957 (C. de Oliveira, *A Concessão Itabira*; Rache, *A grande siderurgia e a exportação de minério*; United Nations Statistical Office, *Statistical Yearbook* (New York: United Nations, various years)).
69. See, for example, *Revista do Commércio de Minas Gerais*, December 1924, p. 199; July 1925, p. 13; August 1925, p. 33.
70. Duarte Pereira explicitly links (without explanation) the change in property rights and increased ore exports: 'the disappearance of private property of the subsoil produced immediate consequences for iron ore exports' (O. Duarte Pereira, *Ferro e independencia: um desafio à dignidade nacional* (Rio de Janeiro: Ed. Civilização Brasileira, 1967), pp. 44–5).
71. Source: *Mineração e Metalurgia*, 10:57 (July 1945), p. 122; see Appendix Table A.11.
72. Calógeras, *As minas do Brasil*, vol. 1, ch. 9, pp. 227–8. See also DCN, 7 November 1916, pp. 226–7.
73. With the re-introduction of federal mining rights and regulation in 1934, 'authorizations' replaced 'concessions' and took on a new form. As a first attempt to address the complications, the National Department of Mining Production issued authorizations to specific individuals 'by himself or a company that he may form'. This format allowed the initial, risky (but relatively inexpensive) exploration to remain with the individual, but served two purposes by anticipating a successful prospector's conversion to partnership or corporation. It helped to preserve the prospector's preferential right to extraction while also recognizing the need to enlarge the capital base of the enterprise. Without requiring a second form of concession or losing legal right to newly discovered minerals the prospector could change his business structure (Companhia Vale do Rio Doce, *Coletânea da legislação*). Authorizations remained non-transferable. In practice, a corporate organization could allow for continuity of the enterprise without continuity of the original prospector.
74. J. H. Welch, *Capital Markets in Development: The Case of Brazil*, Pitt Latin America Series (Pittsburgh, PA: University of Pittsburgh Press, 1993); N. H. Leff, 'Capital Markets in the Less Developed Countries: The Group Principle', in R. I. McKinnon (ed.), *Money and Finance in Economic Growth and Development* (New York: Dekker, 1976), pp. 97–122; Eakin, *Tropical Capitalism*. Even so, Brazil's was not the most moribund of Latin American capital markets (S. Haber, 'Financial Markets and Industrial Development: A Comparative Study of Governmental Regulation, Financial Innovation and Industrial Structure in Brazil and Mexico, 1840–1930', in S. Haber (ed.), *How Latin America Fell Behind: Essays on the Economic Histories of Brazil and Mexico, 1800–1914* (Stanford, CA: Stanford University Press, 1997), pp. 146–78).
75. Centro Industrial do Brasil, *Brazil: Its Natural Riches and Industries*, 2 vols (Paris: Librairie Aillaud & Co., 1910), vol. 1; Brasil, Directoria Geral de Estatística, *Recenseamento do Brasil de 1920 (4o Censo geral da população e 1o da agricultura e das indústrias)*, Indústria, 5 (1a parte) (Rio de Janeiro: Typ. da Estatística, 1927).

76. Inconsistent evidence from the 1907 industrial census also suggests that metallurgy companies were considerably smaller in 1920 than they had been in 1907 (Industrial Census 1907, as cited in Corrêa do Lago et al., *A indústria brasileira de bens de capital*).

77. Forging and laminating company data are unavailable at this level of detail.

78. Sources: Centro Industrial do Brasil, *Brazil: Its Natural Riches* (1910); Directoria Geral de Estatística. *Recenseamento do Brasil de 1920*; see Appendix Table A.5.

79. Forging and laminating is a subset of total metallurgy. Source: *Recenseamento do Brasil de 1920*, table 16, on p. 186.

80. Serviço Geológico e Mineralógico do Brasil, Ministerio da Agricultura, Industria e Commercio, *Relatório apresentado ao Ministro da Agricultura, Industria e Commercio* (Rio de Janeiro: Imprensa Nacional, 1923), p. 32.

81. Here, I do not distinguish between foreign and domestic investment, since Brazilians and others could invest freely in both markets if they chose to do so.

82. These plans represent those put forward by: the Itabira Iron Ore Company (IIO), The Percival Farquhar Group (PF) and Companhia Vale do Rio Doce (Vale), respectively, in the years indicated. Source: See Appendix Table A.6 for details of construction and data.

83. Haber, 'Financial Markets and Industrial Development'; Musacchio, *Experiments in Financial Democracy*.

84. PF, box 3, folder 30, letters of 1 June 1920 from Henry Leigh Hunt to Farquhar and 15 September 1920 from Sir Alexander Mackenzie, a Farquhar Syndicate investor, to Carlos de Campos. Preferred shares were not allowed until 1943.

85. G. H. B. Franco, *Reforma monetária e instabilidade durante a transição republicana*, 2nd edn (1983; Rio de Janeiro: Banco Nacional de Desenvolvimento Econômico e Social, 1987).

86. Methodology and assumptions see Data Appendix and notes to Appendix Tables. Source: Derived from Appendix Table A.6.

87. For the state, tax revenues were the attraction of private sector precious metals mining. The most important exception to this shift was that the national Treasury blocked gold exports during the Depression. This action fell in the realm of monetary, rather than industrial or production, policy.

88. The methodologies for such a counterfactual analysis would remain highly speculative and fall beyond the scope of this study.

89. Olson, *The Logic of Collective Action*; E. S. Reinert, 'The Role of the State in Economic Growth', in Toninelli (ed.), *The Rise and Fall of State-Owned Enterprise in the Western World*, pp. 73–99; P. A. Toninelli, 'The Rise and Fall of Public Enterprise: The Framework', in Toninelli (ed.), *The Rise and Fall of State-Owned Enterprise in the Western World*, pp. 3–24; A. O. Hirschman, *Shifting Involvements: Private Interest and Public Action* (Princeton, NJ: Princeton University Press, 1982).

90. Transactions costs, in the jargon of institutionalists.

91. Rodrik refers to this problem as one of synchronizing 'coordination externalities' (Rodrik, *One Economics, Many Recipes*, pp. 107–9). Rodrik further identifies the higher probability of coordination failures in 'industries that exhibit scale economies ... or require geographic proximity' (p. 107). These were the defining characteristics that challenged Brazilian mining and metallurgy.

92. Recent considerations of property rights recognize that the path dependence of entrenched rights creates transactions costs in efforts to change rights (Pierson, *Politics in Time*).

93. The Companhia Vale do Rio Doce was chartered, as an SOE, in 1942. Based on its origi-
    nal exploitation of the Itabira iron ore deposits, Vale emerged at the end of the twentieth
    century as one of the largest companies in Brazil and one of the largest mining compa-
    nies in the world.
94. Attempts to develop domestic alternatives to Farquhar's project in Itabira will be dis-
    cussed in Chapter 5.
95. Eakin, *Tropical Capitalism*; Leff, 'Capital Markets in the Less Developed'.

5 Industrializing Iron Ore

1. For a wide variety of views on the level and determinants of growth in the capital goods
   sector, for example, see: B. Gupta, 'The Great Depression and Brazil's Capital Goods
   Sector: A Re-examination', *Revista Brasileira de Economia*, 51:2 (1997), pp. 239–51;
   Baer, *The Development of the Brazilian Steel Industry*; Suzigan, *Indústria brasileira*.
2. O. Dinius, *Brazil's Steel City: Developmentalism, Strategic Position, and Industrial Relations in Volta Redonda (1941–1968)* (Stanford, CA: Stanford University Press, 2010).
   Dinius focuses on the closely related case of the Companhia Siderurgica National (CSN
   or National Steel Company), with particular attention to labour.
3. Levine, *The Vargas Regime*; Dulles, *Vargas of Brazil*; Wirth, *Economic Nationalism*.
4. On the strong and increasing role of the military in domestic politics, see Murilo de
   Carvalho, *Forças armadas e política no Brasil*. Carvalho suggests that the Vargas regime,
   particularly during the Estado Nôvo from 1937 to 1945, came at the initiative of the
   armed forces (pp. 109–10). On the emergence of entrepreneurs and industrialists as
   interest groups, see Diniz and Boschi, *Empresários, interesses e mercado*, pp. 44–54.
5. *Revista Commercial de Minas Gerais*, 30 (March 1940), p. 49.
6. For the theoretical literature on this subject, see Olson, *The Logic of Collective Action*; L.
   Galambos and W. Baumol, 'Conclusion: Schumpeter Revisited', in Toninelli (ed.), *The
   Rise and Fall of State-Owned Enterprise in the Western World*, pp. 303–10.
7. It is not clear whether the argument found an initially sympathetic hearing from Vargas
   (Duarte Pereira, *Ferro e independencia: um desafio à dignidade nacional*, p. 49; Dutra
   Fonseca, *Vargas: O capitalismo em construção*, pp. 263–82).
8. Werneck, *Relatório apresentado*, p. 36. This is the first explicit reference that I have found
   linking national defense and the protection of a domestic iron industry. The politics of
   the Vargas regime also required constant, and increasing, compliance with a growing role
   for the military. Vargas's presidency required the complicity of the Army. As one of the
   strongest national institutions, the Army laid the framework for their future dictatorship
   (1964–85) during the Vargas years.
9. F. R. Versiani, 'Before the Depression: Brazilian Industry in the 1920's', in R. Thorp (ed.),
   Latin America in the 1930's: The Role of the Periphery in World Crisis (Oxford: Macmillan Press, 1984); Suzigan, *Indústria brasileira*; Baer, *The Brazilian Economy*.
10. Instituto Brasileiro de Geografia e Estatística, *Estatísticas históricas do Brasil: Séries
    econômicas, demográficas e sociais 1550 a 1985*, Séries estatísticas históricas do Brasil, 3,
    2nd edn (Rio de Janeiro: IBGE, 1990), table 11.2. Further, annual average export earn-
    ings from 1914–18 fell to 84 per cent of the pre-war quinquenium.
11. The military first articulated its interest in steel development in 1920 (J. da Silva Lima,
    O problema siderúrgico brasileiro sob o ponto de vista das indústrias militares, p. 2). See
    Suzigan, *Indústria brasileira*, on the economic impact for Brazilian industrialization
    efforts of the disruptions to international trade during World War I. The annual average

value of machinery imported into Brazil for the war years of 1914–19 was about one-quarter of the annual average value of machinery imports for the preceding five years. In the five years after World War I, average machinery imports increased 2.5-fold, and they did not reach their pre-war level until 1929. This volume measures machinery imported from the US, Britain and Germany, measured in 1913-pounds-sterling (Suzigan, *Indústria brasiliera*, table 18). See also CPDOC: EMS, pi 'Relatório: Ferro e a Salvação do Brasil' by Raul Ribeiro da Silva (1931).

12. McCann, *Soldiers of the Pátria*, p. 421; Levine, *The Vargas Regime*.

13. CPDOC: EMS, pi Soares 1939.07.26; Draibe, *Rumos e metamorfoses*, p. 106. Draibe offers a cogent explanation that colonial experience had conditioned Brazilians against any activity that may offer an opportunity for foreign (or 'imperial') control. In Chapter 6, I offer an overlapping possibility.

14. E. Ridings, *Business Interest Groups in Nineteenth-Century Brazil*, Cambridge Latin American Studies Series, 78 (Cambridge: Cambridge University Press, 1994).

15. M. A. P. Leopoldi, 'Burocracia, empresariado e arenas decisórias estratégicas: trajetórias do neo-corporativismo no Brasil', presented at XV Encontro ANPOCS conference, Caxambu Minas Gerais, 1991.

16. I. Beloch and A. Alves de Abreu (eds), *Dicionário histórico-biográfico pós 1930*, 2nd edn, 5 vols (Rio de Janeiro: Ed. Fundação Getúlio Vargas, 2001), also available at http:// cpdoc.fgv.br/acervo/dhbb [accessed 3 March 2011].

17. As early as 1933, Siciliano articulated a desire for the public sector to begin national-izing mine exploration and to restrict foreign participation in both mining and steel (CPDOC: HB, 32.02.00; Siciliano's comments at a meeting on the Itabira contract). Guinle was a member of the review commission, Conselho Técnico de Economia e Finanças that reviewed the possibilities for iron ore export and iron and steel enterprises in 1938 (Brasil, Ministério da Fazenda, *A grande siderurgia e a exportação de minério de ferro brasileiro em larga escala; Estudos e conclusões apresentadas ao Presidente da República em 27 de julho de 1938* (Rio de Janeiro: Ministério da Fazenda 1938)).

18. Within the organizing and review efforts, the army was represented by such military-technical personnel as Macedo Soares e Silva (who was instrumental in negotiating the Export–Import Bank loan for Vale), Juarez Távora, Horta Barbosa and Mendonça Lima (Brasil, Ministério da Fazenda, *A grande siderurgia e a exportação de minério de ferro*; E. M. Soares e Silva, *O ferro na história e na economia do Brasil* (Rio de Janeiro, 1972)). I thank my students in the 2007 graduate seminar in Economic Institutions in State-build-ing and Political Development at the Programa de Pós-Graduação em Ciência Política; Universidade Federal Fluminense at Niterói for educating me into the nature of indus-trial–military partnerships of modern Brazil.

19. Draibe, *Rumos e metamorfoses*, pp. 76–85. Some argue that the delay of establishing a steel industry in the 1920s was a result of the political violence of the decade and the 1930 'revolution' that brought Vargas to power (C. de Oliveira, *A Concessão Itabira*, pp. 365–84).

20. Privately owned holdings were grandfathered; manufacturers wanted, and could receive, authorization to mine, whether they had current concessions or not.

21. These reporting requirements remain in effect. The DNPM retains very tight control on them (covering the entire period of the requirement). The reports are exempt from public disclosure laws and the department will not make them available for scholarly research, although they have made the reports available to selected Brazilian entrepre-

neurs (see for example, A. Barrionuevo, 'For Wealthy Brazilian, Money From Ore and Might From the Cosmos', *New York Times*, 2 August 2008).

22. Chiarizia, 'Itabira Iron Ore Company Limited', p. 13; Wirth, *Economic Nationalism*; E. B. Burns, *Nationalism in Brazil: A Historical Survey* (New York: Praeger, 1968).

23. CPDOC: AGM, 1936.07.30, letter from A. Magalhães to Francisco de Chateaubriand 30 July 1936. Even so, pockets of support for foreign investment in mining could still be found (F. E. Miles, 'Se o Brasil quer desenvolver a mineração', *Mineração e Metalurgia*, 8:48 (April 1945), pp. 379–82).

24. Wirth, *Economic Nationalism*.

25. The Brazilian army endorsed the export of iron ore simultaneously with accommodation of its needs to modernize military technology (National Steel Commission Report, 1932).

26. National Steel Commission Report, 1932.

27. PF, box 6, folder 74, Ministério da Guerra, 'Resposta aos quesitos ...' (December 1931).

28. PF, box 3, folder 36, 'Itabira: Preliminary Outline of Organization' (7 February 1928); box 5, folder 75, Percival Farquhar's comments to the National Steel Commission (October 1931). Farquhar's plan kept the financial operations in New York. This action did not convince the Brazilian opponents of the plan. Clodomiro de Oliveira referred to Itabira Iron Ore's 'pretension to ore exports under the mantel of domestic steel' (C. de Oliveira, *A Concessão Itabira*, p. ix).

29. For a strong but succinct discussion of the Vargas regimes objections to the Itabira contract see M. Tavora, 'Analyse do Contracto da "Itabira Iron" e suas relações com a "Vitoria e Minas", a exportação de minérios e a grande siderurgia nacional; Discurso pronunciado na sessão de 28 de julho de 1937', from speech of 28 July 1937 (Rio de Janeiro: Imprensa Nacional, 1938).

30. Brasil, Ministério da Fazenda, *A grande siderurgia e a exportação de minério de ferro*, p. 156; see also Chapter 4.

31. Brasil, Ministério da Fazenda, *A grande siderurgia e a exportação de minério de ferro*, pp. 156–7.

32. Ibid., p. 99.

33. Ibid. The National Security Council ratified the study and accepted that the results were not prejudicial to military security issues in May 1939. The official report of the Council rejected direct federal participation.

34. PF, box 7, folder 87, letter from Percival Farquhar to E. F. Turner [legal secretary of Itabira Iron Ore Co.] (25 October 1938).

35. Brasil, Ministério da Fazenda, *A grande siderurgia e a exportação de minério de ferro*, p. 197. The Commission's review of the contract came in response to a request from the military (Companhia Vale do Rio Doce, *A mineração no Brasil*, p. 181; PF, box 6, folder 74, Ministério da Guerra 'Resposta aos quesitos'; Calógeras, *As minas do Brasil* [1938], vol. 2, pp. 105, 14)).

36. Wirth, *Economic Nationalism*, pp. 101–12; P. P. Z. Bastos, 'Roots of Associated Developmentalism: Comments on the Prussian Style Strategy and Pan-American Cooperation during the Estado Nôvo Regime (1937–1945)', *Revista Economia*, 5:3 (2004), pp. 275–310, on p. 301. Guinle became the first president of the Companhia Siderúrgica Nacional.

37. Brasil, Ministério da Fazenda, *A grande siderurgia e a exportação de minério de ferro*, pp. 36–7.

38. For a strong and succinct discussion of the Vargas regime's objections to the Itabira contract, see Tavora, 'Analyse do Contracto da 'Itabira Iron'; *Revista Commercial de Minas Gerais*, 24 (September 1939), p. 143; CPDOC: EMS, pi, Soares, E. 1939.07.26, 'Observações a respeito do parecer da Comissão Especial do Conselho Federal do Comercio Exterior'. In fact, this separation of the two projects had first been studied as early as the 1932 review of the Itabira Contract (CPDOC: HB, Rio de Janeiro, CPDOC).

39. CPDOC: EMS, pi; Soares E., 1939.07.26.

40. MRE, Lata 1259, maço 28361:Emb. Washington 177/563.51/1938/Anexo, Emb. Washington/559/811.(42)(22)/1940 and MRE, MDB 48/5/2: 844.(00)(42). In an attempt to prevent his options for shares of Itabira Iron Ore from losing their total value, Farquhar organized, and remained a shareholder of, the Companhia Brasileira de Mineração e Siderurgia (CBMS) as a Brazilian-chartered company and began promoting this project for the Export-Import Bank to participate in iron ore mining in the Rio Doce Valley. Farquhar hoped to sell his Itabira Iron Ore Co. options to CBMS, who would, in this plan, be the corporate venue for Export–Import Bank-financed ore mining (PF, box 7, folder 95, letters by Farquhar to Minister of Communication and Public Works (19 June 1940), Leith (13 March 1939) and Vice President (of Brazil) Eurico Dutra (undated)). For material on CBMS, see PF, box 7, folder 87, letter to Malezomoff (5 April 1939) and folder 88; MRE, *Lata* 1454, *maço* 33153; letter from Malezomoff to Carlos Martins, Brazilian Ambassador to W. S., 14 January 1941. See also 'Financing Sought Here for Brazil', *New York Times*, 23 April 1939.

41. CPDOC: OA, 1936.07.17/02, 1938.01.22, 1940.07.24.

42. *Monitor Mercantil*, 13 January 1940, p. 30. An earlier joint project proposal with the General Reduction Corporation of Detroit also did not come to fruition (MRE, Lata 1260, maço 28384: Emb. Washington 118/1935/Anexo letter, 12 March 1936 from William Smith, President of General Reduction Corp. to Osvaldo Aranha, Minister of Foreign Relations).

43. MRE: Lata 1454, Caixa 37119: EC/Sn/565.1/1941/Annexo, Letter to W. Clayton, President of Reconstruction Finance Corporation from I. F. L. Elliot, 25 November 1940; Emb. London 812/60/(42) 26 September 1940; *Revista Commercial de Minas Gerais*, 46 (December 1941), p. 33.

44. Beyond a substantial presence of ideologically sympathetic Brazilians, Farquhar had worked with Fritz Thyssen of Vereinigte Stahlwerke AG to develop German participation in Itabira, both as an equity holder (for as much as 30 per cent of total equity) and as a consumer of Itabira iron. In April 1936, they worked on an agreement in which Vereinigte Stahlwerke would commit to purchase 1.5–2 million tons of ore per year, with payments partially in coal (coke to fuel the IIO steel factory. PF, box 6, folder 80, various letters from Farquhar to Thyssen (1930–6) and folder 83, letter from Farquhar to Fred Brandi, Dillon Reed (21 January 1935)).

45. For a parallel history with respect to manganese, see Priest, *Global Gambits*.

46. Wirth, *The Politics of Brazilian Development*. Discussion with the Export–Import Bank for foreign, state-guaranteed, credit first occurred during 1937, and the following year, a proposal was seriously considered for a state-owned monopoly-protected steel plant, which included provisions to expropriate the iron mines. The reliance on imported coke was recognized as a vulnerability, which could be partially offset by domestic charcoal in an emergency. The initial capacity of the Volta Redonda plant was planned to be 335,000 tons per year of steel in various forms and strengths; this plan was expanded as early as 1942 (Vivacqua, *A nova política do sub-solo*, p. 334.

47. MRE, MDB 48/5/2: Emb. Washington /11C/812.(42)/1942/Anexo 1; PF, box 5, folder 69. The enabling legislation within Brazil for the Accords is *Leis, Decreto-lei* #4352, 1 June 1942. Discussions between the US Export–Import Bank and Brazilian industrialists, military and financial official and Percival Farquhar about the possibility of aid to Brazilian steel development had, in fact, begun in 1939 (Companhia Vale do Rio Doce, *A mineração no Brasil*, pp. 186–8; M. Zorzal e Silva, 'A Companhia Vale do Rio Doce no contexto do estado desenvolvimentista', ch. 3).

48. MRE, MDB 48/5/2; Emb. Washington/11C/812.(42)/1942 Anexo 2. Options for the shares of the Estrado de Ferra Vitória a Minas were also transferred to the Brazilian government with the Itabira Iron Ore Co. shares (free of dubious obligations on bonds issued in France), with the concession to improve and operate the railroad issued to the Cia. Brasileira de Mineração e Siderurgia – the Brazilian chartered firm that Farquhar organized in 1940 to accommodate the national-origin requirements of mining rights. See also Pimenta, 'Exportação de minério de ferro pelo Vale do Rio Doce'.

49. MRE, Lata 2058 Caixa 37119; 565.1 T275359, 'Indústria Siderúrgica no Brasil; Relatório Conjunto das Comissões Brasileira e Americana' (1940) discusses the primacy that the US officials attached to the transportation problems. See also *New York Times*, 4 March 1942, p. 9.

50. PF, box 7, folder 89; Pimenta, *Companhia Vale do Rio Doce*, p. 47. This level of production compares with the 4 million tons per year that Farquhar projected in 1919.

51. The value of Itabira Iron Ore and the railroad increased infinitely, from being worthless (without Brazilian agreement for all components of the project) to an initial market value of Cr$310 million (or about US$10.9 million at the prevailing exchange rate). When first quoted on the Rio de Janeiro stock exchange (based on the initial quotations for Vale shares when first quoted on the Rio de Janeiro stock exchange in January 1945).

52. Farquhar went on to become one of the organizing partners and major shareholders of Acesita (Companhia Aços Especiaes de Itabira), an important specialty steel manufacturer in the Brazilian market (PF, box 6, folder 73). Acesita remains in operation.

53. A. Ribeiro Soares, *Formação histórica e papel do setor estatal da economia brasileira 1930–1989* (São Paulo: Lume, 1991), p. 21. Soares estimates that two-thirds of SOEs were in railroads; in the banking sector, state capital was found in the Banco do Brasil, savings banks (Caixas Econômicas) and banks owned by individual states (most notably, in São Paulo).

54. United States Department of Commerce and Labor, Bureau of Manufactures, Special Consular Reports, *Coal Trade in Latin America*, pp. 5–6.

55. Implications of the original SOE to produce iron ore will be the subject of Chapter 7.

56. The magnitude of the differential between iron ore and pig iron/crude steel does not alter significantly if the growth comparisons are constrained to the years for which all data are available.

57. Initially, Vale developed the Carajás deposits in partnership with US Steel. US Steel sold their share of the partnership to Vale. An interview with Roberto Castelo Branco, managing director for Investor Relations of Vale, characterized the sale of the Carajás deposits as having occurred at a very favourable price for Vale; but he was unwilling to discuss the reasons for US Steel's willingness to sell at a low price. Others have indicated that federal government unwillingness to allow foreign control of the mine, demonstrated through slowed approval processes, etc, was the motivating factor (S. Raw, *The Making of a State-Owned Conglomerate: A Brazilian Case Study*, Working Paper: Helen Kellogg Institute for International Studies, 97 (South Bend, IN:

Kellogg Institute, University of Notre Dame, 1987), p. 24). Currently, Carajás is the largest iron ore mine in the world. See http://www.mining-technology.com/projects/carajas/ [accessed 13 June 2010].

58. Index based on volume (metric tons) of production. Data for iron ore not available beyond 1990. Source: United Nations *Statistical Yearbook*, various years.
59. Source: United Nations, *Statistical Yearbook*, various years.
60. Exports could, and often did, exceed production because of the non-perishable nature of ore.
61. The correlation coefficient of export growth of pig iron as a function of iron ore export is .003, and is not statistically significant. Brazil was the largest exporter of pig iron in 1984, and intermittently retained that position until 1997. United Nations Statistical Office, *International Trade Statistics Yearbook*.
62. Source: United Nations, *International Trade Statistics*, various years.
63. Based on volume (metric tons) of production. Sources: United Nations, *Statistical Yearbook*; and United Nations, *International Trade Statistics* various years.
64. Wirth, 'Brazilian Economic Nationalism', pp. 116–21.
65. G. Dutra de Morais, *Jazidos de ferro do Brasil* (Biblioteca de Estudos Mineralógicas, 1944), pp. 30–75.
66. A number of firms manufactured steel, and at least ten new producers had opened during the 1930s, while Brazilian manufacturers continued to import 75 per cent of the laminated steel that it used (PF, box 7, folder 86, citing a survey from 1935; de Senna, *A terra mineira*, vol. 1, p. 239; M. A. M. Dantes and J. Souza Santos, 'Siderurgia e tecnologia (1918–1964)', in S. Motoyama (ed.), *Tecnologia e industrialização no Brasil: Uma perspectiva histórica* (São Paulo: Editora da Universidade Estadual, 1994), pp. 213–32).
67. Based on volume (metric tons) of production. Sources: Vale Annual Report (various years) and Brasil, *Anuário Estatístico* (various years).
68. Based on volume (metric tons) of production and exports. Sources: Vale Annual Report (various years; consistent data are not available after 1978).
69. Vale, *Annual Reports*, various years. 1955–63 are the only years in which the railroads are identified as a separate asset category in the financial statements. By comparison, mines accounted for 10 per cent of total assets in 1955, and 5 per cent in 1963. (Both categories are measured before depreciation.)
70. Arguably, this decision had been taken, but not effected, in 1939 with the cancellation of the Itabira Iron Ore contract.
71. This conversion is based on the fixed annual exchange rate of Cr$19.6 = US$1, for the period 1942–4 (M. P. Abreu (ed.), *A ordem do progresso: Cem anos de política econômica republicana* (Rio de Janeiro: Editora Campus, 1990), statistical appendix, col. 32).
72. Vale, Annual Report (1954), pp. 24–5.
73. The most important condition imposed on US Export–Import Bank loans was that their proceeds were used to procure US-produced goods and services.
74. Reinert, 'The Role of the State in Economic Growth'.
75. V. F. Bouças, *História da dívida externa* (Rio de Janeiro: Edições Financeiras, 1950).
76. These notional calculations assume that Vale (with government guarantees) would have access in international financial markets to the sovereign interest rate without a risk premium, and it uses the black market exchange rate (see discussion below and Data Appendix). Thus, they represent the lower-bound estimate of the value of the subsidy. The calculation on gross revenues also requires the currency translation from Brazilian cruzeiros to US dollars for revenues, with the complication of incorporating a spread between the black market and official exchange rate. I back into the estimate of the effect on net funding requirements, by deducting from total assets (including depreciation) all

statutory capital, reserves, provisions and retained earnings. See Appendix Tables A.7A and A.7B for Vale financial data.

77. Sources: Vale Annual Report (various years); *Commercial and Financial Chronicle*, various issues.

78. Privately owned steel companies and large investors with iron ore interests held the privately owned shares available to the public.

79. In 1944, the state took 83.7 per cent of the Cr$100 million capital increase, raising state ownership to 65 per cent (Pimenta, *Companhia Vale do Rio Doce*, pp. 9–12).

80. Excludes five capital increases and revaluations, 1956–64, which do not significantly change the distribution of ownership. Sources: Vale Annual Report, various years; Pimenta, *Companhia Vale do Rio Doce*.

81. The original shares were divided between stocks with 'ordinary' and 'preferred' provisions. Amending the Commercial Code to permit preferred equity had been a provision that Farquhar lobbied hard to achieve. This form of equity was permitted from 1943, with Vale and CSN among the earliest corporations to raise capital in this manner. The preferred shares gave their owners guaranteed minimum dividends of 6 per cent (after achieving profitability, on a gross profits basis), the ability to acquire shares at their initial offering on the market on an installment plan (initial investment of 20 per cent of book value, and 18 month pay-in period), and a place in the creditors' line, in the event of liquidation, in front of ordinary shareholders. This division of the stock served to protect investors in the private sector by keeping the ordinary shares in the Treasury. Financial theory generates expectations of a lower price for preferred shares in order to compensate for the reduced risk (and the spread between the prices on preferred and ordinary shares could be interpreted as a measure of the market's expectation of the risk of bankruptcy). Quotes for Vale shares did not display this behaviour.

82. The standard shares on the exchanges at the time had book values denominated at Cr$200, an amount that would not impede purchases by individual investors; CSN shares (also traded on the stock exchange) had a book value of Cr$200. Participation of a wide swath of Brazilian citizens was a stated goal in the financial organization of CSN ('O Lançamento na Bolsa das Ações da Grande Siderúrgia (entrevista com o Sr. Juvenal de Queiroz Vieira)'; *O Economista*, Rio de Janeiro (March 1941), p. 395.

83. The stock exchanges have been regulated by varying bodies under the jurisdiction of Treasury Ministry. The Câmaras Sindicais dos Corretores of each exchange emerged in 1894 followed by a selection of bodies. The current Comissão de Valores Mobiliários was organized in 1976. No comprehensive analytic history of financial market regulation has been written.

84. These standards are not unusual in Brazil; they allow public traded corporations to attract investors from large and anonymous pools of participants. These concepts, of course, do not address the efficacy or the enforcement of the requirements.

85. The Companhia Vale do Rio Doce annual report of 1970 anticipated privatization by 1980.

86. MRE, MDR – Washington; Oficios, Mar-Abr/ 1942; 48/5/2, letter from Brazilian Ambassador to US Artur de Souza Costa, to US Secretary of State Sumner Wells, 3 March 1942.

87. Vale's higher market-to-book value relative to other mining companies (though in parallel with them) is difficult to interpret, given the heightened vulnerabilities of mining companies in financial parameters and the small number of mining companies whose shares traded on the Rio de Janeiro exchange (Appendix Tables A.8B and A.8C).

88. Movimento da Bolsa, various years, Arquivo Nacional, Rio de Janeiro. These quotations referred to prices at which a transaction would take place, though actual sales were rare (see n. 89 below).

89. Source: CS *Relatório*, various years (Appendix Table A8.A).

90. Vale, 1960: quotes are for bearer bonds (or unspecified, prior to March when distinction began). Belgo-Mineira, 1950: used initial Cr$200 through the year; the new issue (cr$1000) picked up in subsequent years (to allow consistent series). Source: AN: *Movimento da Bolsa*.

91. Derived from Câmara Syndical dos Corretores de Fundos Públicos da Capital Federal, *Relatórios da Câmara Syndical dos Corretores de Fundos Públicos da Capital Federal* (Rio de Janeiro: Imprensa Nacional, 1942–4).

92. I compare them to industrial concerns, excluding such sectors as railroads, banks and insurance both because of the early appearance of these sectors on the bolsa (in keeping with financial history practices generally) and because of the government guarantees and special provisions that frequently accompanied these firms.

93. Belgo-Mineira was organized in 1927, and it was the first firm in Brazil to engage in all three stages of steel production: producing pig iron, refining it for use in steel and producing laminated steel. As one of the early beneficiaries of state and national benefits, this firm and its rival Usinas Queiroz Júnior, may have been the intended beneficiaries of Bernardes's obstructive policies against the Itabira Iron Ore Co. The firm had been listed on the Rio de Janeiro exchange since 1938; it was the most successful privately owned steel firm, and mined its own iron ore (J. B. de Araujo, 'Informações sobre a Companhia Belgo-Mineira', *Mineração e Metalurgia*, 1:6 (1937), pp. 251–8.; C. de Oliveira, *A Concessão Itabira*, pp. 372–8).

94. Source: CS *Relatório*, various years (See Appendix Tables A.8B and C).

95. Source: AN *Movimento da Bolsa*.

96. W. Suzigan, 'As empresas do governo e o papel do governo na economia brasileira', in F. Rezende, J. Monteiro, Vianna, W. Suzigan, D. Carneiro and F. P. Castelo Branco (eds), *Aspectos da participação do governo na economia* (Rio de Janeiro: IEA/INPES, 1976), pp. 77–131, on p. 88.

97. Exchange regulations from 1946 required that hard currency be exchanged for local currency.

98. For a descriptive summary of the exchange rate regimes during this period, see Baer, *The Brazilian Economy*, pp. 47–58.

99. Further, capital goods industries, including Vale, received beneficial exchange rates and tariff exemptions for imported capital equipment.

100. Dutra Fonseca, *Vargas: O capitalismo em construção*, pp. 267–9.

101. Raw, *The Making of a State-Owned Conglomerate*, p. 14; O. Brito, 'Privatação não afeta planos de crescimento', *Brasil Mineral*, 14:151 (1997), pp. 22–8, on p. 24.

102. These estimates are based on the Vale financial statements (see Appendix Tables A.7B), exchange rates (black market rates, as reported in Global Financial Data (www.globalfinancialdata.com) and the money supply time series in IBGE, *Estatísticas Históricas*, table 10.2).

103. For a useful overview see J. L. Love, 'The Rise and Decline of Economic Structuralism in Latin America: New Dimensions', *Latin American Research Review*, 40:3 (2005), pp. 100–25. Love also identifies that structuralist policies were widely in effect in the 1930s and 1940s (p. 107).

104. Chiarizia, 'Itabira Iron Ore Company Limited'; P. R. A. Rodrigues, 'A cultura empresarial brasileira e a Cia. Vale do Rio Doce', *Revista da Administração Pública*, 35:6 (2001), pp. 23–32.

6 Minerals and the Formation of Economic Ideology

1. Gerschenkron, *Economic Backwardness*; S. Haber (ed.), *How Latin America Fell Behind: Essays in the Economic Histories of Brazil and Mexico, 1800–1914* (Stanford, CA: Stanford Unviversity Press, 1997).
2. O. Munteal Filho, 'O liberalismo num outro Ocidente', in L. M. P. Guimarães and M. E. Prado (eds), *O liberalismo no Brasil imperial* (Rio de Janeiro: Editora Revan, 2001).
3. Questions raised by the philosophy of science, with respect to interpretation, conclusiveness and mutability of evidence are not under discussion here.
4. R. Lemos, *Benjamin Constant: Vida e história* (Rio de Janeiro: Topbooks, 1999). Positivism's strongest impact on Brazil was to perpetuate entrenched social hierarchies, relying upon new ideas, in the wake of abolition. The ideology was prevalent throughout Latin America at the turn of the twentieth century.
5. The simultaneous selective applications of these ideologies to different fields of economic activity deserve further study. I know of no research that has been done in this area.
6. Calmon, *Direito de propriedade*, pp. 153–98.
7. Werneck 'O Brasil: Seu presente e seu futuro', as cited in E. Carone, *O pensamento industrial no Brasil, 1880–1945*, Corpo e alma do Brasil, 54 (Rio de Janeiro: Difel, 1977), pp. 31–2. Werneck's comments of 1892 came in the midst of the worst economic crisis that Brazil had experienced until then, the *encilhamento*.
8. I. C. Serzedello, ' O problema econômico do Brasil, 1903', in (compilation of articles from) *A Tribuna* (Rio de Janeiro: Imprensa Nacional, 1903), pp. 153–9. The concept of comparative advantage will be discussed in more detail below.
9. Brazilian positivism relied on seemingly contradictory positions that its practices would lead society to 'universal peace', obviating the need for armies, in juxtaposition with the belief that 'soldier-citizens' would merit leading roles in civil society (J. Murilo de Carvalho, 'As forças armadas na Primeira República: O poder desestabilizador', in B. Fausto (ed.), *História geral: o Brasil republicano; v. 2* (Rio de Janeiro: ed. Bertrand Brasil, 1989), pp. 38–9).
10. J. Murilo de Carvalho, 'Armed Forces and Politics in Brazil: 1930–1945', *Hispanic American Historical Review*, 62:2 (1982), pp. 194–200; McCann, *Soldiers of the Pátria*, ch. 4.
11. P. C. Dutra Fonseca, 'Vargas no contexto da Primeira República', in T. Szmrescsányi and R. G. Granziera (eds), *Getúlio Vargas e a economia contemporânea* (Campinas SP: Editora de Unicamp, 2004), pp. 171–92. In this sense, as Eli Diniz points out, Vargas's policies from 1930 to 1934 were at least as important for their ideological engineering of political institutions as they were for their proto-Keynesian counter-cyclicality (Diniz, 'A progressiva subordinação das oligarquias regionais ao governo central', pp. 41–2).
12. Some of the military officers directly involved in iron and steel development included João Mendonça Lima (who served as Minister of Public Works, under Vargas), Eduardo Macedo Soares (also spent time as Minister of Public Works), and Raul Tavares (served a period as Vargas's Chief of Staff); Pedro Aurélio de Góis Monteiro (periods as Chief of Staff and Minister of War) (Brasil, Ministério da Fazenda, *A grande siderurgia e a exportação de minério de ferro*; Beloch and Abreu (eds), *Dicionário histórico-biográfico pós 1930*).
13. In contrast, positivism was a social theory with strong economic implications, and 'dependency', arising out of structuralism, advanced a politicized view of the world that ultimately extended far beyond economics.

14. Theories about comparative advantage usually attribute their origins to David Ricardo's *On the Principles of Political Economy and Taxation* (1817) and were most notably formalized by the Heckscher-Ohlin general equilibrium model of international trade. Its application in this instance will be discussed below.

15. See J. L. Love, *Crafting the Third World: Theorizing Underdevelopment in Rumania and Brazil* (Stanford, CA: Stanford University Press, 1996). The two best known, and very different primary-source discussions of these theories are F. H. Cardoso and E. Faletto, *Dependency and development in Latin America* (Berkeley, CA: University of California Press, 1979); J. D. Cockcroft, D. L. Johnson and A. Gunder Frank, *Dependence and Underdevelopment: Latin America's Political Economy*, 1st edn (Garden City, NY: Anchor Books, 1972). Dependency theory, a more aggressive offshoot of structuralism, quickly expanded to cover themes far afield from the economic theory of structuralism. The purpose, here, is not to argue the empirical 'correctness' of structuralist ideas but only to delineate briefly their arguments in order to demonstrate their impact on mineral policy. Debate over the theory was widespread and loud; and it motivated much empirical research in economic history during the 1960s to 1980s.

16. L. C. Bresser-Pereira, 'From the National Bourgeois to the Associated Dependency Interpretation of Latin America', *Fundação Getúlio Vargas Escola de Economia, Working Paper 185* (São Paulo: Fundação Getúlio Vargas, Escola de Economia, 2009).

17. Love, *Crafting the Third World*, p. 153.

18. Structuralism and its variants accepted the tenet that industrialization was necessary for development (Bresser-Pereira, 'From the National Bourgeois', p. 8).

19. Love, *Crafting the Third World*. Love particularly cites M. Manoilescu and A. Amaral's *O século do corporativismo; doutrina do corporativismo integral e puro* (Rio de Janeiro: J. Olympio, 1938); M. Manoilescu, *The Theory of Protection and International Trade* (London: P. S. King & Son, Ltd, 1931); see also Love, 'The Rise and Decline of Economic Structuralism in Latin America'.

20. N. V. Luz, *A luta pela industrialização do Brasil 1808–1930* (São Paulo: Ed. Alfa Omega, 1978).

21. Dantes and Souza Santos, 'Siderurgia e tecnologia (1918–1964)', pp. 59–78; A. C. Pinheiro and F. Giambiagi, 'The Macroeconomic Background and Institutional Framework of Brazilian Privatization', presented at the Privatization in Brazil: The Case of Public Utilities conference, Rio de Janeiro, 1999, p. 114.

22. Love, *Crafting the Third World*, p. 120; H. F. Bain and T. T. Read, *Ores and Industry in South America* (New York: Harper & Brothers for the Council on Foreign Relations, 1938), p. 41. The Bain and Read report may have been among the earliest to articulate the point that developmentalism was an ideology closely related to economic nationalism.

23. The major works by these authors include: R. Prebisch, *The Economic Development of Latin America and its Principal Problems* (New York: United Nations, 1950), reprinted in *Economic Bulletin for Latin America*, 7:1 (1962), pp. 1–22; A. Gunder Frank, *Capitalism and Underdevelopment in Latin America: Historical Studies of Chile and Brazil* (New York: Monthly Review Press, 1967).

24. On ISI, see, among others: A. Fishlow, 'Origins and Consequences of Import Substitution in Brazil', in M. Luís Eugenio di and P. Raúl (eds), *International Economics and Development: Essays in Honor of Raúl Prebisch* (New York: Academic Press, 1972), pp. 311–65.

25. C. Furtado, *Accumulation and Development: The Logic of Industrial Civilization* (New York: St Martin's Press, 1983).
26. CPDOC: GC, pi Sampaio, A. 1961.03.02, '"O nacionalismo econômico" Aula inaugural dos cursos da Faculdade de Ciências Econômicas da Universidade do Brasil'. This lecture emphasizes both the importance of natural resources and the pernicious effects of foreign capital as core to the ideology of economic nationalism.
27. Dutra Fonseca, *Vargas: O capitalismo em construção*. Dutra Fonseca unequivocally states: 'A reading of Vargas's speeches from the period of the Estado Novo leaves no doubt: the principal purpose of the government was to consolidate the domestic market, whose expansion he judged to be associated directly to the 'national economic resistance', meaning to its "independence". Vargas advocated, completely consciously, a transformation of the level of Brazilian development. The situation of countries immediately dependent on the export of primary goods and whose commercial balance is subject, immediately, to the world market live at the mercy of frequent collapses of their economic forces. World prices are constantly becoming less remunerative for the countries that supple primary goods and food products.' (pp. 264–5).
28. Dutra Fonseca also focuses on this strategy and identifies it as a predecessor to ECLA's articulation of import substituting industrialization policies (*O capitalismo em construção*, pp. 274–6).
29. Burns, *Nationalism in Brazil*, pp. 81–2; Wirth, *Economic Nationalism*. Burns also contextualized the monopolization of petroleum as a subsequent articulation of the importance of natural resources for economic nationalism.
30. Bedran, *A mineração à luz do direito brasileiro*, pp. 20–2. Bedran also cites Alcides Pinheiro in putting forward this idea.
31. CPDOC: GC, pi Sampaio, A. 1961.03.02; Távora, 'O Código de Minas e desenvolvimento', pp. 152–9.
32. E. Carone, *Estado Nôvo (1937–1945)*, Corpo e Alma do Brasil, 47 (Rio de Janeiro: Difel, 1976), p. 77.
33. Petroleum exploration, drilling, refining, and transport was nationalized in 1953, through the vehicle of Petróleo Brasileiro, S. A. Petrobras (*Lei* 2004, 3 October 1953). See Chapter 7.
34. Other forms of deepening state intervention in the Brazilian economy during the Vargas regime included price controls on coffee and the provision of infrastructure, exchange controls and opening the first ethanol institute (Ribeiro Soares, *Formação histórica e papel*, pp. 22–3).
35. Galambos and Baumol, 'Conclusion: Schumpeter Revisited', pp. 303–10.
36. Toninelli, 'The Rise and Fall of Public Enterprise: The Framework', pp. 7–8; Reinert, 'The Role of the State in Economic Growth', p. 75. The determination of economic justification is an empirical question that requires examination on a case-by-case basis.
37. M. M. Shirley, 'Bureaucrats in Business: The Roles of Privatization versus Corporatization in State-Owned Enterprise Reform', *World Development*, 27:1 (1999), pp. 115–36, on p. 116.
38. These are the preferences that many believe to allow SOEs to overcome the market failures that motivate their formation.
39. For a wide display of this thinking, see Bedran, *A mineração a luz do direito brasileiro*, 11–9.
40. Pinheiro, *Direito das minas*, p. 78. Pinheiro's explanation for state intervention in the case of iron rested predominantly with the concerns of national security.

41. See Trebat, *Brazil's State-Owned Enterprises*, p. 42.

42. Although Vargas had no expectation of SOEs having profit maximizing goals, they also were not to have a claim on Treasury funding.

43. During the 1938 review of the Itabira contract by the Technical Economic and Finance Council, the Ministry of the Treasury rejected one proposed alternative plan (the 'Denizot Plan') because it rested on sovereign guarantee of privately issued debt (Rache, *A grande siderúrgia e a exportação de minério*).

44. Hirschman, *Shifting Involvements: Private Interest and Public Action*.

45. Toninelli, 'The Rise and Fall of Public Enterprise: The Framework', pp. 5–6.

46. Xisto, *Limitação do direito de propriedade*; Calmon, *Direito de propriedade*; de Lima Pereira, *Da propriedade no Brasil*.

47. Calógeras and Alcides Pinheiro were among the prominent legislators who continued to support foreign investment in the mining sector (Bedran, *A mineração a luz do direito brasileiro*, pp. 20–8; Pinheiro, *Direito das minas*, p. 125).

48. Includes all SOEs, industrial and non-industrial firms. Source: Trebat, 1983, tables 3.1 and 3.6.

49. The constraints on foreign participation in the sector strengthened with the Constitution of 1988 (see Chapter 2) even as many focused on the extensive control by multinationals of existing mineral enterprises that arose from 'phantom' investments and companies in which nominal Brazilian ownership served to hide foreign-sourced capital (CPDOC: HS, pi 1990.02.01; F. R. C. Fernandes, 'Quem controla o subsolo brasileiro?', *Revista Brasiliera de Tenologia*, 19:3 (1988), pp. 5–12). Fernandes also implies that the 'anti-trust' provision imposing a limit of fifty concessions was mainly, but ineffectively, aimed at foreigners.

50. Musacchio, *Experiments in Financial Democracy*. Musacchio has shown that some firms did undertake these measures. However, they did not achieve the scale necessary to reassure investors for a firm the size of Vale.

51. Villela Souto, 'O programa brasileiro de privatização de empresas estatais', p. 57.

52. J. A. de Souza, L. Burlamaqui and N. H. Barbosa-Filho, 'Institutional Change and Economic Transformation in Brazil, 1945–2004: From Industrial Catching-Up to Financial Fragility', presented at the XXXIII Encontro Nacional de Economia 2005, Natal, Rio Grande do Norte, Brazil.

53. Trebat, *Brazil's State-Owned Enterprises*, ch. 3. SOEs were only one component of the expanded developmental policy; other actions included exchange controls, credit allocation, wage and price controls.

54. J. R. Mendonça de Barros and D. H. Graham, 'The Brazilian Miracle Revisited: Private and Public Sector Initiative in a Market Economy', *Latin American Research Review*, 13:2 (1978), pp. 5–38.

55. Trebat, *Brazil's State-Owned Enterprises*, ch. 8. Trebat attributes the slow development of Brazilian capital markets at least partially to the dominance of the SOEs. This parallels the conclusion that I extended back to the 1930s and 1940s in Chapter 5.

56. Other minerals in Vale's product mix during the twentieth century included bauxite, aluminum, manganese and titanium (Brito, 'Privatação não afeta planos de crescimento', p. 24).

57. Suzigan, 'As empresas do governo'.

58. Source: Suzigan 'As empresas do governo' (1976), table III.3.

59. Burns also found distant origins of economic nationalism in the eighteenth century, but identified the Vargas regime as a transformative period for these ideas. In a differing

assessment from mine, he asserts that economic nationalism in Brazil was one form of expressing national exceptionalism and he suggests that the SOE was a preference of the state, rather than an expedient tool, that resulted from economic nationalism (Burns, *Nationalism in Brazil*). On this point, see also Pinheiro, *Direito das minas*, p. 124.

60. R. P. Colistete, 'Revisiting Import-Substituting Industrialization in Post-War Brazil', in *Munich Personal RePEc Archive* (MPRA paper, 2010) offers a useful and recent summary of the prior generation of assessments on import-substituting industrialization.

61. A. Gómez-Galvarriato and C. L. Guerrero-Luchtenberg, 'Timing of Protectionism', in *Serie-AD* (Alicante: Universidad de Alicante, Instituto Valenciano de Investigaciones Económicas, 2010), pp. 1–71. The model that these authors present is not directly applicable to the case of Brazilian iron ore, since the model assumes indifference to the nationality of ownership and a preference for more, rather than less, competition. The first assumption clearly did not hold for Brazilian iron ore; and I have not examined the second assumption in detail. Nevertheless, extensions to the basic model to account for these exceptions may complicate the model, but should not negate the idea behind it.

62. Colistete, 'Revisiting'.

63. C. F. Díaz-Alejandro, 'Latin America in the 1930s' (unpublished paper, Yale University, 1982). Many saw the beginning of the process with World War I (Versiani, 'Before the Depression'; Suzigan, *Indústria brasileira*).

64. The authors in the above note 63 also recognized that large economies had more latitude in instituting counter-cyclical policy than did small ones.

65. Gerschenkron, *Economic Backwardness*; H.-J. Chang, *Kicking Away the Ladder: Development Strategy in Historical Perspective* (London: Anthem, 2002).

66. Shirley, 'Bureaucrats in Business'. Without an official census of federally-owned companies prior to 1980 in Brazil or consistent treatment globally of SOEs in national accounting procedures, meaningful international comparisons are untenable (Trebat, *Brazil's State-owned Enterprises*, p. 35).

67. MRE: Emb. Washington/585/565.(22)/1942. This file reports on a US mission to Brazil for the purpose of surveying manufacturing development possibilities. The report specifically refers to mining and metals, and the language of early policies in support of infant industry was prominent. See also United States Deparment of Commerce; Bureau of Foreign and Domestic Commerce; International Reference Service, *Brazil in 1944* (Washington DC: Government Printing Office, 1944).

7 Iron Ore as Precedent and Example

1. A. L. Villas-Bôas, *Mineração e desenvolvimento econômico: A questão nacional nas estratégias de desenvolvimento do setor mineral (1930–1946)* (Rio de Janeiro: Ministério da Ciência e Tecnologia/CNPq/CETEM (Centro de Tecnologia Mineral), 1995), p. 23.

2. Mizael de Souza, 'Será que o Brasil acordará para a importância da mineração?'; C. Mamen, 'Minério de ferro no Brasil – reserva para o mundo', *Engenharia Mineração e Metalurgia*, 52:808 (1970), pp. 53–9.

3. P. de Sá and I. Marques, 'O impasse da política mineral brasileira', *Revista Brasileira de Tecnologia*, 19:3 (1988), pp. 12–7. These authors find that oscillating mining regulation with respect to foreign investment from 1964 for the following two decades also impeded consistent expectations.

4. I do not offer a comprehensive history of Brazilian state intervention in petroleum. For a more detailed account and bibliography of the sector, see P. R. de Almeida, 'Monteiro

Lobato e a emergência da política do petróleo no Brasil', in O. L. de Barros Filho and S. Bojunga (eds), *Potência Brasil: Gás natural, energia limpa para um futuro sustentável* (Porto Alegre: Laser Press, 2008), pp. 12–33.

5. See for example G. Vargas, *A política nacionalista do petróleo no Brasil* (Rio de Janeiro: Tempo Brasileiro, 1964), 'Discurso em Salvador', pp. 60–1.

6. The separation of petroleum from minerals for regulatory purposes was codified in Constitution of 1946 (Távora, 'O Código de Minas e desenvolvimento', pp. 164–5).

7. CPDOC: AN, c. 1928.0202, letter to Goís Monteiro from Monteiro Lobato, 3 May 1940. An amendment to the Mining Code solidified this separation in 1940 (Leis, *Decreto-Lei* 1985, 29 January 1940, and *Decreto-Lei* 3236, 7 May 1941) regulated petroleum and natural gas.

8. M. A. T. Miranda, *O petróleo é nosso: A luta contra o 'entreguismo', pelo monopólio estatal–1947–1953, 1953–1981* (Petrópolis: Vozes, 1983), p. 28.

9. The first attempt to establish a national petroleum company, the Companhia Nacional de Petróleo, occurred in 1939 (Vivacqua, *A nova política do sub-solo*, pp. 353–6, 488). Petrobras remains state-owned; it is a monopoly provider of petroleum, ethanol and other fuels in Brazil.

10. Freire, Comentários, p. 168.

11. M. Vaitsman, *O petróleo no império e na república* (1948; Rio de Janeiro: Editora Interciência, 2001); Dulles, *Vargas of Brazil*, p. 237.

12. Vargas, *A política nacionalista do petróleo no Brasil*, Discourso em Leopoldina, Minas, 24 October 1939, pp. 54–5.

13. Fróes Abreu, *A riqueza mineral do Brasil*, p. 201.

14. The incipient campaign that came to advocate a nationalized monopoly interpreted this action as pandering to foreign interests (Miranda, *O petróleo é nosso*, p. 259; de Almeida, 'Monteiro Lobato').

15. L. J. de Morais, 'Minerais estratégicos', *Mining and Metallurgy*, 5:25 (1940), pp. 10–16.

16. Vaitsman, *O petróleo*, p. 183.

17. Leis, *Decreto* 395, 29 April 1938; M. Victor, *A batalha do petróleo brasileiro* (Rio de Janeiro: Ed. Civilização Brasileira, 1970).

18. J. Soares Pereira, 'Depoimento', in A. Marques Vianna (ed.), *A política nacionalista do petróleo no Brasil* (Rio de Janeiro: Tempo Brasileiro, 1964), pp. 29–53, on p. 42.

19. Victor, *A batalha do petróleo*, pp. 63–98.

20. Ibid., p. 93.

21. de Almeida, 'Monteiro Lobato', p. 14.

22. The phrase originated with the title of an article by Francisco Duarte Burity in *O Correio da Manhã*, 18 September 1948; see also Miranda, *O petróleo é nosso*; O. D. C. Gondin da Fonseca, *Qué sabe você sobre petróleo?* (Rio de Janeiro: Livraria São José, 1957); Vaitsman, *O petróleo*; Victor, *A batalha do petróleo*.

23. Miranda, *O petróleo é nosso*, pp. 236–40. This highly opinionated source is the memoir of the campaign by one of its leaders.

24. Victor, *A batalha do petróleo*, pp. 147–54.

25. Cited in ibid., p. 109.

26. Leis, *Lei* 2004 of 3 October 1953. A campaign to establish a monopoly SOE in petroleum began in 1949 (Victor, *A batalha do petróleo*, p. 226).

27. Trebat, *Brazil's State-Owned Enterprises*, pp. 105–6.

28. Gondin da Fonseca, *Qué sabe você sobre petróleo?*

29. Prior to 2000, exports of petroleum were insignificant and inconsistent (United Nations Statistical Abstract, available at http://data.un.org/Data.aspx [accessed 13 August 2010]).
30. Data do no include production of natural gas or petroleum derivatives. Sources: 1935–87: IBGE *Estatísticas Históricas*, table 9.5; 1990–2007: United Nations, *Statistical Abstract*; http://data.un.org/Data.aspx?q=petroleum&d=EDATA&f=cmID%3aCR [accessed 23 June 2010].
31. Apparent Consumption = Extraction + Imports – Exports. Date do not include production of natural gas or petroleum derivatives. Sources: 1935–1987: IBGE *Estatísticas Históricas*, table 9.5; 1990–2007: United Nations, *Statistical Abstract*; http://data.un.org/Data.aspx?q=petroleum&d=EDATA&f=cmID%3aCR [accessed 23 June 2010].
32. Instituto Brasileiro de Geografia e Estatística, Conselho Nacional de Estatística, *Anuário estatístico do Brasil* (Rio de Janeiro: Impresa Nacional, various years); United Nations Statistical Office, *Statistical Yearbook*.
33. Petrobras, available at http://www.petrobras.com.br/en/about%2Dus/our%2Dhistory/ [accessed 27 July 2010]. As of the date this section is written, any repercussions to the technologies and activities of deep-sea drilling that may arise from the British Petroleum Deepwater Horizon spill remain unknown.
34. As of the year-end 2009, sharholders' equity in Petrobas was R$164.2 billion (US$94.3 billion, of which paid-in capital represented R$79.0 billion (US$45.4 billion) (Petrobras Annual Report, http://petrobrasri.infoinvest.com.br/ [accessed 17 August 2010]). Prior to the confirmation of the deep-sea deposits in the Santos Basin, Petrobras in 2005 was the world's seventh largest energy company, and in 2006 it ranked twentieth globally in size of reserves. See http://www.petrobras.com.br and http://www.bloomberg.com/news/2010-08-19/petrobras-loses-spot-as-latin-america-s-top-company-as-sale-fuels-25-drop.html [accessed 3 March 2011]. Prior to the confirmation of the deep-sea deposits in the Santos Basin, Petrobras in 2005 was the world's seventh largest energy company, and in 2006 it ranked twentieth globally in size of reserves (see http://www.petrobras.com.br and *Petroleum Intelligence Weekly*, 9 May 2006 (http://www.energyintel.com/publicationhomepage.asp?publication_id=4&issueID=853 [accessed 12 May 2006]).
35. Constitutional Amendment, number 9, 9 November 1997.
36. M. A. P. Leopoldi, 'O difícil caminho do meio: Estado, burguesia e industrialização no segundo governo Vargas (1951–1954)', in de Castro Gomes (ed.), *Vargas e a crise dos anos 50*, pp. 161–203, on p. 178.
37. Soares d'Araújo, 'A volta de Vargas ao poder e a polarização das forças políticas e sociais', p. 120.
38. M. A. P. Leopoldi, 'Crescendo em meio à incerteza: A política econômica do govern JK (1956–60)', in de Castro Gomes (ed.), *O Brasil de JK*, pp. 113–7.
39. Some of the sectors in which state enterprises dominated included steel, paper, concrete, aircraft, chemicals, telecommunications, and pharmaceuticals.
40. The first major break in the trajectory of increasing state economic intervention since the formation of Vale and CSN occurred during the interregnum of the Dutra presidency (1946–January 1951) between Vargas's two periods in office. Dutra's classically liberal orientation sought to avoid such intervention (R. Almeida, 'Política econômica do segundo Governo Vargas', in T. Szmrescsányi and R. G. Granziera (eds), *Getúlio Vargas e a economia contemporânea* (Campinas SP: Editora da Unicamp, 2004), pp. 125–40, on p. 127).
41. Pinheiro and Giambiagi, 'The Macroeconomic Background'. These concerns became central political and economic issues throughout Latin America, as pre-reform practices became untenable (F. G. Carneiro and C. H. Rocha, 'Reforming the Public Sector in

Latin America: A Cross-Country Comparison', presented at the Conference on Privatization in Brazil: The Case of Public Utilities, Rio de Janeiro, 1999).

42. In 1982, Brazil's total debt service burden as a share of total exports of goods and services (one common measure of debt capacity) was the highest in the world; in 1973, at the beginning of the oil crises, Brazil had ranked ninth. During the period of the maximum effects of the oil shocks Brazilian debt service burden was:

	Total debt service, % total exports of goods and services		Total debt service, % total exports of goods and services
1973	28.8	1979	70.6
1974	40.2	1980	69.4
1975	46.3	1981	72.0
1976	39.8	1982	89.6
1977	44.9	1983	57.3
1978	62.7	1984	48.4

Source: World Bank Database, available at http://databank.worldbank.org/.
Note: Total debt service includes public, public-guaranteed and private debt; these data are not available prior to 1970.

43. Diniz and Boschi, *Empresários, interesses e mercado*, pp. 33. Tagging the 1980s as a 'lost decade' has become the umbrella term in Brazil (and throughout Latin America) to designate this period of hyperinflation, stagnating growth, rampant political instability and social inequality.

44. Arguments against privatization also continued to be voiced quite loudly, and they tended to focus on the concern about national sovereignty that had consolidated in the economic nationalism debates (J. Seroa de Santa Maria, *Sociedades de economia mista e empresas públicas* (Rio de Janeiro: Ed. Liber Juris, 1979); Fernandes, 'Quem controla o subsolo brasileiro?').

45. These industries typically required, at least initially, the import of their plant and equipment, technology and often management.

46. B. J. Clements, 'State Enterprise and Employment Generation', *Economic Development and Cultural Change*, 41:1 (1992), pp. 51–62, on p. 51. Clements specifically notes the role of metallurgy in this argument. However, he finds mixed support for it with respect in Brazil.

47. L. de Mello Jr, 'Privatization and Corporate Governance', presented at the Conference on Privatization in Brazil: The Case of Public Utilities, Rio de Janeiro, 1999; P. A. P. de Britto, 'Estrutura de propriedade e eficiência: Uma análise com teoria dos incentivos', *Revista de Economia Política*, 19:3 (1999), pp. 57–66; Pinheiro and Giambiagi, 'Macroeconomic Background'.

48. de Mello Jr, 'Privatization and Corporate Governance'.

49. For a survey of this literature, see Raw, *The Making of a State-Owned Conglomerate*.

50. A. D. Novaes, 'Rentabilidade e risco: empresas estatais *versus* empresas privadas', *Revista Brasileira de Economia*, 44:1 (1990), pp. 53–84. The steel companies contributed negatively to the average risk-adjusted return on equity of SOEs in this study.

51. Villela Souto, 'O programa brasileiro de privatização de empresas estatais'.

52. As President, Cardoso had suggested that these policies were logical extensions of structuralism that would remediate the negative outcomes that his earlier academic work uncovered.

53. Ribeiro Soares, *Formação histórica e papel*; Pinheiro and Giambiagi, 'Macroeconomic Background'.

54. Pinheiro and Giambiagi, 'Macroeconomic Background'. Eighty-four of the firms had been owned by the federal government, and twenty-eight were owned by states and municipalities. See also Diniz and Boschi, *Empresários, interesses e mercado*, ch. 2.

55. M. L. Amarante de Andrade, L. M. da Silva Cunha, G. Tavares Gandra and C. C. Ribeiro, 'Impactos da privatização no setor siderúrgico', BNDES Working Paper Área de Operações Industriais 2 – AO2 (2001), pp. 1–14. Vale acquired one of the steel firms. Siderbrás was formed in 1974.

56. The belief was widespread that foreigners were able to enter the Brazilian mining sector by forming 'phantom companies' in collaboration with Brazilian front-people. Fernandes asserts that almost 25 per cent of mines were held by phantom companies, covering an area approximately the combined size of Germany France, Britain, Spain and Portugal (Fernandes, 'Quem controla o subsolo', p. 5; L. B. de Freitas, 'As perspectivas para o setor mineral', *Brasil Mineral*, 11:121 (1994), pp. 24–6).

57. J. C. F. Pinheiro, *Companhia Vale do Rio Doce: O engasgo dos neoliberais* (Belo Horizonte: Centro de Documentação e Informação, Ltda, 1996), pp. 13–14, 90.

58. The vast increase in scale did in fact occur (R. Castello Branco, interview, 5 June 2008 managing director for Investor Relations, Companhia Vale do Rio Doce).

59. BNDES financing of the federal employees' pension fund in order to acquire the majority of Vale added controversy (and sense of impropriety) to the privatization.

60. See http://www45.bb.com.br/docs/ri/ra2009/index.html [accessed 12 June 2010]. Although as recently as June 2010, the investment community referred to Petrobras as 'state owned' (*New York Times*, 'Dealbook Blog', 6 June 2010). This source does not reveal the distribution of the current shareholder base, between corporate, public sector, investment fund entities and individual investors

61. In 2003, 40 per cent of Petrobras equity shares were held by the federal government (32 per cent) and its major financing agent, BNDES (8 per cent); 7 per cent was in the hands of 'foreigners' (although 32 per cent in the form of ADRs may also have been held by foreign owners) (S. W. Lewis, *Critical Issues in Brazil's Energy Sector: Deregulating and Privatizing Brazil's Oil and Gas Sector* (Houston TX: The James A. Baker III Institute for Public Policy of Rice University, 2004), p. 19).

62. CPDOC: HS, 1992.03.31, 'Uma proposta para Volta Redonda'.

63. Diniz and Boschi, *Empresários, interesses e mercado*.

64. E. R. Gomes and F. C. Guimarães, 'Como as instituições contam: O apoio à pequenas e médias empresas no Brasil e na Argentina', *33 Encontro Annual da ANPOCS* (Caxambu MG, October 2009), pp 1–35. These authors cite R. Boschi and F. Gaitán, 'Intervencionismo estatal e políticas de desenvolvimento na América Latina', *Caderno CRH*, 21:53 (2008), pp. 305–22. The data about the increase in SOEs since 2003 come from O. Ribas, 'A volta das estatais: após ciclo de privatização, surgem novas empresas públicas', *Problemas Brasileiras*, 43:373 (2006), pp. 10–13.

65. R. Ramamurti, 'Why Haven't Developing Countries Privatized Deeper and Faster?', *World Development*, 27:1 (1999), pp. 137–55; G. Yarrow, 'A Theory of Privatization, or Why Bureaucrats are Still in Business', *World Development*, 27:1 (1999), pp. 157–68. These studies counter-pose the touchstone World Bank study of privatized enterprise (Shirley, 'Bureaucrats in Business).

66. Ramamurti, 'Why Haven't Developing Countries Privatized Deeper and Faster?', p. 147.

67. Yarrow, 'A Theory of Privatization', pp. 159–62.

68. See also P. Mandetta, V. P. Pereira, M. T. V. Mello, C. Chiodi Filho and A. Conrado, 'Empresa Estadual de Mineração', *Brasil Mineral*, 117:107 (1988), pp. 18–20, 33–4.
69. A. Barrionuevo, 'In Latin America a Mine of Riches and an Economic Sinkhole', *New York Times*, 12 September 2010, available at http://www.nytimes.com/2010/09/12/weekinreview/12barrionuevo.html?ref=weekinreview [accessed 12 September 2010].
70. MV, Board Letters; *passim*. This was an almost-continuous topic of communication between the local supervisor and the Board of Directors through the 1860s and 1870s.
71. I thank Douglas Cole Libby for help in clarifying this point.
72. Venâncio Filho, *Intervenção do Estado no domínio* econômico, pp. 168–75. Water is the subject of very little historical scholarship in Brazil.
73. See for example, A. Barrionuevo's article in the *New York Times* on expropriation of land and homes (A. Barrionuevo, 'Bypassing Resistance, Brazil Prepares to Build a Dam', *New York Times*, 16 August 2010, available at http://www.nytimes.com/2010/08/16/world/americas/16brazil.html?ref=world, [accessed 16 August 2010]).
74. Associated Press, 22 June 2010 [accessed 22 June 2010]. This article asserts that President Lula da Silva supports the move as a means of guaranteeing Brazilian food independence. The effects on the substantial installations of international agro-industrial firms are unknown.
75. Victor, *A batalha do petróleo*, pp. 117–19.
76. Lewis, *Critical Issues in Brazil's Energy Sector*, p. 7.
77. Petrobras Annual Report 2009, available at http://www2.petrobras.com.br/ri/ing/DestaquesOperacionais/Internacional/pdf/ProducaoInternacional_2009_Ing.pdf [accessed 23 August 2010]; Petrobras, available at http://www.petrobras.com.br/en/about%2Dus/our%2Dhistory/ [accessed 22 June 2010]

Conclusion

1. Wright, 'The Origins of American Industrial Success', pp. 660–1. While the same may hold for other economies, I am not aware of scholarship that addresses the point.
2. Bresser-Pereira, 'From the National Bourgeois'.
3. C. A. Britto, 'Direito de propriedade (O novo e sempre velho perfil constitucional da propriedade)', *Revista do Direito Público*, 22:9 (1989), pp. 44–51, on p. 46.
4. Currently, mining companies and Petrobras manage and finance extensive environmental reclamation and repair programs, which they feature prominently on their web sites.
5. Freire, *Comentários*, pp. 196–202.

Data Appendix

1. Companhia Vale do Rio Doce, *Coletânea da legislação*. Although the corporate history (*A mineração no Brasil e a Companhia Vale do Rio Doce*) is not analytic in nature, it offers a useful summary of events. The value of the historical narrative is limited by its uncritical acceptance of Vale's positive role in Brazilian society and economy and the absence of an analytic framework. Nevertheless, the accompanying volumes are extremely helpful compendia of national level mining legislation, parliamentary debates and archival and bibliographic guides; all of which cover the period 1889–1946. CVRD does not open its archives to outside researchers. The company was privatized in 1997; as such, it is not covered by federal disclosure laws, even for the period during which it was an SOE. The company's library in Rio de Janeiro seems to be the only location with a complete set of

the company's annual reports; with a great deal of effort, researchers can get access to this material. (As of May 2007, CVRD claimed to be digitizing the entire set of annual reports, although they have not indicated if they will be made publicly accessible.)

2. See http://www2.camara.gov.br/publicacoes [accessed 6 june 2010].
3. J. A. Mendoza de Azevedo, *Índice systemático da legislação brasileira* (Belo Horizonte: Silveiro Costa, Cia., 1939), Parte I – Império.
4. Since cataloguing and incorporating the attempts to regulate mining in each of the states would be an unwieldy task, this paper keeps its focus on the location that was the focus of Brazilian development.
5. Based in Roman (or Napoleonic) concepts, codified laws and decrees rather than case precedent established the boundaries of permissible activity.
6. As one caveat to this classification, the laws and decrees affecting railroad concessions are included only when initially granted or when changed to significantly affect mining capabilities. The multitude of intermediary decrees that approved specific feasibility studies, expenditures and minor routing changes (of lines that had previous approval) are not included.
7. From 1934, the Mining Code replaced 'concessions' to prospect with 'authorizations' to prospect. They served essentially the same purpose. I have included them as concessions to prospect in order to avoid the unnecessary complication of introducing another term/ variable.
8. Concessions to prospect usually had a time period of three years, but could be renewed. Typical concessions to mine were granted for thirty years.
9. In fact, the state of Minas Gerais did not enact laws to enable concessionary powers until 1911.
10. Brazilian municipalities are the rough equivalent of counties in the US.
11. Eakin, *British Enterprise in Brazil*; Carsalade Villela, *Nova Lima: Formação histórica*. Gold mining continued through the twentieth century in Sabará.
12. I rely on the notaries to have accurately identified mining lands, and I have no consistent way to test whether they did so. The magnitude of the task of going through individual land transfer records for sixty years (and of obtaining judicial permission in each jurisdiction to do so) recommended the limited, but judicious, selection that I have employed.
13. At this time, foreign capital markets would not invest in Brazilian private sector enterprise (usually railroads) without federal government guarantees. From an analytic perspective, benchmark measures of necessary interest rates, the cost of investment at the time and in the place planned, are equally infeasible.
14. While the attraction of large-scale iron mining lay in the externalities that Brazilians believed it could create, investors in a specific enterprise would evaluate its prospects relative to its direct returns. Therefore, that is the appropriate basis for this consideration.
15. In 1942, when actually initiated, the opportunity cost of the project was 38 per cent of public debt service. This amount reflects that low debt servicing during the rescheduling of sovereign debt. I judge the anticipated proportion of debt service to be quite high.
16. For the years when private capital inflow data are available (1914 and 1930,) the project would have accounted for 97 per cent and 10 per cent of private inflows, respectively.
17. The small size of Brazilian capital markets inhibited the ability to finance it because of both the volume of capital and the mechanisms available within Brazilian financial structures. When Percival Farquhar first structured a plan to mine and export Itabira ore, one of his important stumbling blocks was the inability to issue preferred shares on the Rio exchange. The Brazilian financial regulatory officials remained unwilling to introduce

this innovation (PF, box 3, folder 30, letter from Henry Leigh Hunt to Farquhar, 1 June 1920; letter from Alexander Mackenzie to Carlos de Campos, 15 September 1920).

18. Câmara Syndical dos Corretores de Fundos Públicos da Capital Federal, *Relatórios da Câmara syndical dos corretores de fundos públicos da capital federal*, various years.

19. The 'Movimento da Bolsa' was uncatalogued at the time that I accumulated the data (May–June 2007); therefore additional citation material is not available.

20. A promise of assistance in this matter was never forthcoming, in keeping with the company's overall policy of not responding to requests of academic researchers.

21. Personal email communication of 26 August 2006.

WORKS CITED

Manuscript Sources

Arquivo Nacional, Rio de Janeiro.

    Movimento da Bolsa (uncatalogued collection of Bolsa de Valores price quotations).

Arquivo Público Mineiro, Belo Horizonte, Minas Gerais.

    Artur Bernardes collection.

    Percival Farquhar collection.

Centro de Pesquisa e Documentação de História Contempôraneo do Brasil, Fundação Getúlio Vargas, Rio de Janeiro, papers of:

    Agamenom Magalhães.

    Clemente Mariani.

    Eduardo Macedo Soares.

    Gustavo Capenema.

    Herbert de Souza.

    Júlio Caetano Horta Barbosa.

    Juarez Távora.

    Oswaldo Aranha.

Percival Farquhar Papers, Yale University, Beinecke Rare Books and Manuscripts Library, Manuscript Group 205.

St John d'el Rey Company Ltd Archives at Centro de Memória, Morro Velho, Nova Lima, Brazil.

    Anon. [J. H. Wharrier?], 'Historical Notes', MV Imobiliário 13/10/66, [1960?].

    Official letters from St John d'el Rey Board of Directors to Superintendent, Casa de Memória.

    Morro Velho Imobiliário (Real Estate Department files).

    Registro de Documentos, Morro Velho Imobiliário.

St John d'el Rey Company Ltd Archives held at Nettie Lee Benson Library, University of Texas, Austin Texas.

    Annual Report to Shareholders, London, 1830–1960.

    Morro Velho Survey Map, May 1954.

Serials and Statistical Data

Câmara Syndical dos Corretores de Fundos Públicos da Capital Federal, *Relatórios da Câmara syndical dos corretores de fundos públicos da capital federal* (Rio de Janeiro: Imprensa Nacional, various years).

Chronicle of Finance and Commerce (New York: William B. Dana Co.).

Companhia Vale do Rio Doce, *Relatório da Diretoria ... apresentado α Assembléia Geral Ordinária* (Rio de Janeiro: Companhia Vale do Rio Doce), various years (from 1999, online at http://www.vale.com/en-us/investidores/Pages/default.aspx [accessed 3 January 2011].

O Correio de Manhã, Rio de Janeiro.

Economist, London.

Global Financial Data, online at http://www-globalfinancialdata.com [restricted; accessed 22 October 2010].

Itabira (Minas Gerais), public registries, land transfer registration, 1872–1940.

Jornal do Commércio.

Minas Gerais, Assembléa do Estado, Biblioteca, catalogue of laws & decrees passed, 1890–1930; Excel spreadsheet.

Mineração e Metalurgia, Rio de Janeiro.

Monitor Mercantile, Rio de Janeiro.

National Bureau of Economic Research; Macrohistory database: NBER04010a–c.

New York Times, New York.

O Economista, Rio de Janeiro.

Retrospecto Comercial de Jornal do Commércio (Rio de Janeiro: Jornal de Commércio de Rodrigues e Cia, Annual Series).

Revista Commercial de Minas Gerais.

Revista Industrial de Minas Gerais, Juiz de Fora, Minas Gerais (1893–7).

Sabará (Minas Gerais), public registries, land transfer registration, 1872–1940.

Sweden, Statistiska centralbyrån, *Sveriges oficialla statistic*, Handel, Berättelse för ar ... av Kommerskol.

United Nations Statistical Office, *Statistical Yearbook* (New York: United Nations, various years).

United Nations Statistical Office, *International Trade Statistics Yearbook* (New York: United Nations, various years).

Brazilian Government Serials and Archives

Assembléia Nacional Constituinte, *Anais da Assembléa Nacional Constituinte (1933–34)* (Rio de Janeiro: Imprensa Nacional), online at http://imagem.camara.gov.br/diarios. asp [accessed 22 October 2010].

Câmara dos Deputados, *Anais da Câmara dos Deputados* (Rio de Janeiro: Imprensa Nacional), online at http://imagem.camara.gov.br/diarios.asp [accessed 22 October 2010].

'Coleção das Leis e Decretos' (Imprensa Nacional), online at http://www2.camara.gov.br/ atividade-legislativa/legislacao [accessed 22 October 2010].

Congresso Nacional, *Anais do Congresso Constituinte de 1890/91* (Rio de Janeiro: Imprensa Nacional), online at http://imagem.camara.gov.br/diarios.asp [accessed 22 October 2010].

Congresso Nacional, *Diários da Assembléia Nacional Constituinte de 1933/34* (Rio de Janeiro: Imprensa Nacional), online at http://imagem.camara.gov.br/diarios.asp [accessed 22 October 2010].

Congresso Nacional, *Diário do Congresso Nacional* (Rio de Janeiro: Imprensa Nacional), online at http://imagem.camara.gov.br/diarios.asp [accessed 22 October 2010].

Constituição dos Estados Unidos do Brasil (Rio de Janeiro: Impresa nacional), online at http://www2.camara.gov.br/atividade-legislativa/legislacao [accessed 22 October 2010]. Constitutions of 1891, 1934, 1937, 1946, 1967 and 1988.

Departamento de Justiça e Negocios Interiores, *Anteprojecto de constituição para o Brasil* (Rio de Janeiro: Imprensa Nacional, 1946).

Directoria Geral de Estatísticl, *Recenseamento do Brasil de 1920 (4o Censo geral da população e 1o da agricultura e das indústrias)*, Indústria, 5 (1a parte) (Indústria. Rio de Janeiro: Typ. da Estatística, 1927).

Instituto Brasileiro de Geografia e Estatística, Conselho Nacional de Estatística, *Anuário estatístico do Brasil* (Rio de Janeiro: Impresa Nacional).

Instituto Brasileiro de Geografia e Estatística, *Estatísticas históricas do Brasil: Séries econômicas, demográficas e sociais 1550 a 1985*, Séries estatísticas históricas do Brasil, 3, 2nd edn (Rio de Janeiro: IBGE, 1990).

Ministério da Agricultura (Departamento Nacional de Producção Mineral, Serviço de Fomento e Producção Mineral) *Relatório da Directoria* (Rio de Janeiro: Impresa Natcional, 1934–5).

Ministério da Agricultura, I.e.C, *Relatório apresentado ao Ministro da Agricultura, Indústria e Commércio* (Rio de Janeiro: Imprensa Nacional, various years).

Ministério da Fazenda, *Relatório apresentado ao Presidente da República dos Estados Unidos do Brasil pelo Ministro de Estado dos negócios da fazenda* (Rio de Janeiro: Imprensa Nacional, various years).

Ministério das Relações Exteriores, Rio de Janeiro.

Minas Gerais, *Annaes do Congresso Constituinte de Estado de Minas Gerais, 1891* (Ouro Preto MG: Imprensa Oficial de Minas Gerais, 1896).

Minas Gerais, Presidente do Estado, *Mensagem dirigida pelo Presidente do Estado ao Congresso Mineiro em sua xx sessão ordinária da xx legislatura, no anno* (Imprensa Nacional, various years), online at http://www.crl.edu/content/brazil/mina.htm [accessed 3 March 2011].

Serviço Geológico e Mineralógico do Brasil, Ministerio da Agricultura, Industria e Commercio, *Relatório apresentado ao Ministro da Agricultura, Industria e Commercio* (Rio de Janeiro: Imprensa Nacional, various years).

Published Sources

Abreu, M. P. (ed.), *A ordem do progresso: Cem anos de política econômica republicana* (Rio de Janeiro: Editora Campus, 1990).

Acemoglu, D., S. Johnson and J. Robinson., 'The Colonial Origins of Comparative Development: An Empirical Investigation', *American Economic Review*, 91:5 (2002), pp. 1369–401; also available in *Revista de Economia Institucional*, 7 (2005).

Alchian, A. A., and H. Demsetz. 'The Property Rights Paradigm', *Journal of Economic History*, 33:1 (1973), pp. 16–27.

Almeida, R., 'Política econômica do segundo Governo Vargas', in T. Szmrescsányi and R. G. Granziera (eds), *Getúlio Vargas e a economia contemporânea* (Campinas SP: Editora da Unicamp, 2004), pp. 125–40.

Alston, L. J., G. D. Libecap and B. Mueller, *Titles, Conflict, and Land Use: The Development of Property Rights and Land Reform on the Brazilian Amazon Frontier* (Ann Arbor, MI: University of Michigan Press, 1999).

Alvarenga, O. M., *Teoria e prática do direito agrário* (Rio de Janeiro: CONSAGR-Comunicações Sociais Agrárias, 1983).

Amarante de Andrade, M. L., L. M. da Silva Cunha and M. do Carmo Silva., 'Balança comercial do setor mínero-metalúrgico: Desafios para o crescimento', *Mineração e Metalurgia*, 16 (2002), pp. 105–22.

Amarante de Andrade, M. L., L. M. da Silva Cunha, G. Tavares Gandra and C. C. Ribeiro, 'Impactos da privatização no setor siderúrgico', 'Impactos da privatização no setor siderúrgico', BNDES Working Paper Área de Operações Industriais 2 – AO2 (2001), pp. 1–14.

Antunes, A., *Do diamante ao aço: A trajectória do Intendente Câmara* (Belo Horizonte: UNA, 1999).

Araripe, D. A., *História da Estrada de Ferro Vitória e Minas: 1904–1954* (Rio de Janeiro: Ed Cia. Vale do Rio Doce, 1954).

Baer, W., *The Development of the Brazilian Steel Industry* (Nashville, TN: Vanderbilt University Press, 1969).

—, *The Brazilian Economy: Growth and Development*, 4th edn (Westport, CT: Praeger, 1995).

Bain, H. F. and T. T. Read., *Ores and Industry in South America* (New York: Harper & Brothers for the Council on Foreign Relations, 1938).

Barbosa, A. R., 'Breve panorama da legislação minerária', *Revista de Direito* Administrativo, 197 (1994), pp. 64–73.

Barman, R. J., *Brazil: The Forging of a Nation, 1798–1852* (Stanford, CA: Stanford University Press, 1988).

Barrionuevo, A., 'For Wealthy Brazilian, Money From Ore and Might From the Cosmos', *New York Times*, 2 August 2008

—, 'Bypassing Resistance, Brazil Prepares to Build a Dam', *New York Times*, 16 August 2010, online at http://www.nytimes.com/2010/08/16/world/americas/16brazil.html?ref=world, [accessed 16 August 2010].

—, 'In Latin America a Mine of Riches and an Economic Sinkhole', *New York Times*, 12 September 2010, online at http://www.nytimes.com/2010/09/12/weekinreview/12barrionuevo.html?ref=weekinreview [accessed 12 September 2010].

Barros, G. M., *História da siderurgia no Brasil, século XIX* (Belo Horizonte: Imprensa Oficial de Minas Gerais, 1989).

Barzel, Y., *A Theory of the State: Economic Rights, Legal Rights, and the Scope of the State*, Political Economy of Institutions and Decisions Series (Cambridge and New York: Cambridge University Press, 2002).

Bastos, P. P. Z., 'Roots of Associated Developmentalism: Comments on the Prussian Style Strategy and Pan-American Cooperation during the Estado Nôvo Regime (1937–1945)', *Revista Economia*, 5:3 (2004), pp. 275–310.

Bedran, E., *A mineração à luz do direito brasileiro: Comentário, doutrina e jurisprudência* (Rio de Janeiro: Editora Alba, Limitada, 1957).

Beloch, I., and A. Alves de Abreu (eds), *Dicionário histórico-biográfico brasileiro, pós-1930*, 2nd edn, 5 vols (Rio de Janeiro: Ed. Fundação Getúlio Vargas, 2001); online at http://cpdoc.fgv.br/acervo/dhbb [accessed 3 March 2011].

Bernardes, A. S., *Discursos e pronunciamentos de Arthur da Silva Bernardes* (Belo Horizonte: Governo do Estado de Minas Gerais, 1977).

Bethell, L. (ed.), *The Cambridge History of Latin America*, 11 vols (New York: Cambridge University Press, 1984).

Boschi, R., and F. Gaitán, 'Intervencionismo estatal e políticas de desenvolvimento na América Latina', *Caderno CRH*, 21:53 (2008), pp. 305–22.

Bouças, V. F., *História da dívida externa* (Rio de Janeiro: Edições Financeiras, 1950).

Brasil, Ministério da Fazenda, *A grande siderurgia e a exportação de minério de ferro brasileiro em larga escala; Estudos e conclusões apresentadas ao Presidente da República em 27 de julho de 1938* (Rio de Janeiro: Ministério da Fazenda, 1938).

Brasil, Ministério da Fazenda, Museu da Fazenda, *Ciclo da mineração* (Rio de Janeiro: Ministério da Fazenda, 1984).

Brasil, Instituto Brasileiro de Mineração, *Mineração e constituinte: histórico e sugestões a nova constituição brasileira* (Belo Horizonte: Instituto Brasileiro de Mineração, 1986).

Bresser-Pereira, L. C., 'From the National Bourgeois to the Associated Dependency Interpretation of Latin America', *Fundação Getúlio Vargas Escola de Economia, Working Paper 185* (São Paulo: Fundação Getúlio Vargas, Escola de Economia, 2009).

Brito, O., 'Privatização não afeta planos de crescimento', *Brasil Mineral*, 14:151 (1997), pp. 22–8.

Britto, C. A., 'Direito de propriedade (O novo e sempre velho perfil constitucional da propriedade)', *Revista do Direito Público*, 22:9 (1989), pp. 44–51.

Burns, E. B., *Nationalism in Brazil: A Historical Survey* (New York: Praeger, 1968).

Caldeira, J., *A nação mercantilista: Ensaio sobre o Brasil*, 1st edn (São Paulo: Editora 34, 1999).

Calmon, P., *Direito de propriedade: A margem dos seus problemas juridicos, sociologicos, historicos e politicos* (Rio de Janeiro: Imprensa Nacional, 1925).

Calógeras, J. P., *As minas do Brasil e sua legislação geológica econômica do Brasil*, expanded by Djalma Guimarães, 2nd edn, 3 vols (1904/05; Biblioteca pedagógica brasileira. São Paulo: Companhia Editora Nacional, 1938).

Canabrava, A. P., 'A repartição da terra na capitania de São Paulo, 1818', *Estudos Econômicos*, 2:6 (1972), pp. 77–129.

Cardoso, F. H. and E. Faletto, *Dependency and Development in Latin America* (Berkeley, CA: University of California Press, 1979).

Cardozo, M. S., 'The Collection of the Fifths in Brazil, 1695–1708', *Hispanic American Historical Review*, 20:3 (1940), pp. 359–79.

Carneiro de Mendonça, M., *O Intendente Câmara: Manuel Ferreira da Câmara Bethencourt e Sá, Intendente Geral das Minas e Diamantes: 1764–1835* (São Paulo: Companhia Editora Nacional, 1958), vol. 301.

Carneiro, F. G. and C. H. Rocha, 'Reforming the Public Sector in Latin America: A Cross-Country Comparison', presented at the Conference on Privatization in Brazil: The Case of Public Utilities, Rio de Janeiro, 1999.

Carone, E., *Estado Nôvo (1937–1945)*, Corpo e Alma do Brasil, 47 (Rio de Janeiro: Difel, 1976).

—, *O pensamento industrial no Brasil, 1880–1945*, Corpo e Alma do Brasil, 54 (Rio de Janeiro: Difel, 1977).

Carsalade Villela, B., *Nova Lima: Formação histórica* (Belo Horizonte: Editora Cultura, 1998).

Carvalho, J. L., 'Private Sector Development and Property Rights in Latin America', *Revista Brasileira de Economia*, 50:3 (1996), pp. 351–77.

Castello Branco, R., managing director for Investor Relations, Companhia Vale do Rio Doce, interview with author, 5 June 2008.

Centro Industrial do Brasil, *Brazil: Its Natural Riches and Industries*, 2 vols (Paris: Librairie Aillaud & Co., 1910), vol. 1.

Chang, H.-J., *Kicking Away the Ladder: Development Strategy in Historical Perspective* (London: Anthem, 2002).

Chiarizia, M. M. A., 'Itabira Iron Ore Company Limited' (MA dissertation, Universidade Federal Fluminense, 1979).

Clay, K. and G. Wright., 'Order Without Law? Property Rights During the California Gold Rush', *Explorations in Economic History*, 42:2 (2005), pp. 155–83.

Clements, B. J., 'State Enterprise and Employment Generation', *Economic Development and Cultural Change*, 41:1 (1992), pp. 51–62.

Coatsworth, J. H., *Growth against Development: The Economic Impact of Railroads in Porfirian Mexico*. The Origins of Modern Mexico Series (DeKalb, IL: Northern Illinois University Press, 1981).

—, 'Structures, Endowments, and Institutions in the Economic History of Latin America', *Latin American Research Review*, 40:3 (2005), pp. 14–53.

—, 'Inequality, Institutions and Economic Growth in Latin America', *Journal of Latin American Studies*, 40 (2008), pp. 145–69.

Cockcroft, J. D., D. L. Johnson and A. Gunder Frank, *Dependence and Underdevelopment: Latin America's Political Economy*, 1st edn (Garden City, NY: Anchor Books, 1972).

Colistete, R. P., 'Revisiting Import-Substituting Industrialisation in Post-War Brazil', in *Munich Personal RePEc Archive* (MPRA paper; 2010).

Companhia Vale do Rio Doce *A mineração no Brasil e a Companhia Vale do Rio Doce* (Rio de Janeiro: CVRD, 1992).

—, *Coletânea da legislação sobre mineração no Brasil* (Rio de Janeiro: Companhia Vale do Rio Doce, 1993).

Corrêa do Lago, L. A., F. Lopes de Almeida and B. M. F. de Lima, *A indústria brasileira de bens de capital: Origens, situação recente, perspectivas* (Rio de Janeiro: Fundação Getúlio Vargas, 1979).

Coutinho, D. R. S., in A. M. D. Silva (ed.), *Colecção de Obras Clássicas do Pensamento Económico Português* (Lisboa: Banco do Portugal, 1993).

da Costa Sena, J. C., 'Viagem e estudos metallurgicos no centro da provincia de Minas Gerais', *Annaes da Escola de Minas de Ouro Preto*, 1 (1881), pp. 106–43.

da Matta, C., *O direito de propriedade e a utilidade publica: Das expropriações* (Coimbra: Imprensa da Universidade, 1906).

da Silva, A. R. C., *Construção da nação e escravidão no pensamento de José Bonifácio, 1783–1823* (São Paulo: Editora da Unicamp, 1999).

da Silva Lima, J., 'O problema siderúrgico brasileiro sob o ponto de vista das indústrias militares', presented at O problema siderúrgico brasileiro conference, Rio de Janeiro, 19 August 1938.

Dantas, M. D., *Fronteiras movediças: Relações sociais na Bahia do século XI (a comarca Itapicaru e a formação do arraial de Canudos)* (São Paulo: Aderaldo & Rothschild Editores: FAPESP, 2007).

Dantes, M. A. M. and J. Souza Santos, 'Siderurgia e tecnologia (1918–1964)', in S. Motoyama (ed.), *Tecnologia e industrialização no Brasil: Uma perspectiva histórica* (São Paulo: Editora da Universidade Estadual, 1994), pp. 213–32.

Davidson, D. M., 'How the Brazilian West was Won: Freelance and State on the Mato Grosso Frontier, 1737–1752', in D. Alden (ed.), *Colonial Roots of Modern Brazil* (Berkeley and Los Angeles, CA: University of California Press, 1973), pp. 61–106.

de Almeida, P. R., 'A formação econômica brasileira a caminho do autonomia política: Uma análise estrutural e conjuntural do período pré-Independência', in L. V. de Oliveira, R. Ricupero and A. Domingues (eds), _A abertura dos portos_ (São Paulo, SP: Editora Senac São Paulo, 2007), pp. 256–83.

—, 'Monteiro Lobato e a emergência da política do petróleo no Brasil', in O. L. de Barros Filho and S. Bojunga (eds), _Potência Brasil: Gás natural, energia limpa para um futuro sustentável_ (Porto Alegre: Laser Press, 2008), pp. 12–33.

de Andrade Arruda, J. J., _Uma colônia entre dois impérios: A abertura dos portos brasileiros, 1800–1808_ (Rio de Janeiro: Edusc, 2006).

de Araujo, J. B., 'Informações sobre a Companhia Belgo–Mineira', _Mineração e Metalurgia_, 1:6 (1937), pp. 251–7.

de Assis Barbosa, F., _Dom João VI e a siderúrgia no Brasil_ (Rio de Janeiro: Biblioteca do Exército; Coleção Tauney, 1958).

de Barros Penteado, A. A., _A legislação mineira do Brasil_ (Rio de Janeiro: Cruzeiro do Sul, 1941).

de Britto, P. A. P., 'Estrutura de propriedade e eficiência: Uma análise com teoria dos incentivos', _Revista de Economia Política_, 19:3 (1999), pp. 57–66.

de Castro Gomes, A. (ed.), _O Brasil de JK_ (Rio de Janeiro: Fundação Getúlio Vargas, 2002).

de Freitas e Souza, R., 'Trabalho e cotidiano na mineração inglesa em Minas Gerais: A mina da Passagem de Mariana (1863–1927)' (MA dissertation, Universidade de São Paulo, 2009).

de Freitas, L. B., 'As perspectivas para o setor mineral', _Brasil Mineral_, 11:121 (1994), pp. 24–6.

de Góis Monteiro, N. (ed.), _Dicionário Biográfico de Minas Gerais: Período Republicano, 1889–1930_, 2 vols (Belo Horizonte: Assembléia Legislativa do Estado de Minas Gerais, 1994).

de Lima Pereira, J. O., _Da propriedade no Brasil_ (São Paulo: Casa Duprat, 1932).

de Mello Jr, L., 'Privatization and Corporate Governance', presented at the Conference on Privatization in Brazil: The Case of Public Utilities, Rio de Janeiro, 1999.

de Menezes, J. R., 'Exposição sobre o estado da decadência da Capitania de Minas Geraes e meios de remedial-a', _Revista do Arquivo Público Mineiro_, 2:18 (1780;1897), p. 320.

de Morais, L. J., 'Minerais estratégicos', _Mining and Metallurgy_, 5:25 (1940), pp. 10–16.

de Oliveira, C., _A Concessão Itabira_ (Belo Horizonte: n.a., 1934).

de Oliveira, E. P., 'A política do ouro (October 1934)', _Mineração e Metalurgia Avulso_, 29 (1937), pp. 25–6.

de Oliveira Lima, M., _Dom João VI no Brasil_ (1908; Rio de Janeiro: Topbooks, 2006).

de Queiros Mattoso, K. M., _To Be a Slave in Brazil, 1550–1888_ (New Brunswick, NJ: Rutgers University Press, 1986).

de Roure, A., _A constituinte republicana_ (Rio de Janeiro: Imprensa Nacional, 1918).

de Sá, P. and I. Marques, 'O impasse da política mineral brasileira', _Revista Brasileira de Tecnologia_, 19:3 (1988), pp. 12–7.

de Seabra, A. L., *A propriedade: Philosophia do direito*. Coimbra: Imprensa da Universidade, 1850.

de Senna, N. C., 'A função social do Estado e a desapropriação de minas para fins públicos', *Anais da Câmara dos Deputados do Congresso Mineiro* (Rio de Janeiro: Belo Horizonte, Imprensa Ofical, 1907), pp. 247–60.

—, *A terra mineira*, 2 vols (Belo Horizonte: Imprensa Oficial do Estado de Minas Gerais, 1926).

de Souza Bandeira, A. H., *A propriedade das minas: estudo de direito administrativo* (Rio de Janeiro: Imprensa Nacional, 1885).

de Souza, J. A., L. Burlamaqui and N. H. Barbosa Filho, 'Institutional Change and Economic Transformation in Brazil, 1945–2004: From Industrial Catching-Up to Financial Fragility', presented at the XXXIII Encontro Nacional de Economia, 2005, Natal, Rio Grande do Norte, Brazil.

Dean, W., *The Industrialization of São Paulo* (Austin, TX: Institute of Latin American Studies by the University of Texas Press, 1969).

—, 'Latifundia and Land Policy in Nineteenth-Century Brazil', *Hispanic American Historical Review*, 51:44 (1971), pp. 606–25.

—, *Rio Claro: a Brazilian Plantation System, 1820–1920* (Stanford, CA: Stanford University Press, 1976).

—, *With Broadax and Firebrand: The Destruction of the Brazilian Atlantic Forest* (Berkeley, CA: University of California Press, 1995).

Demsetz, H., 'Toward a Theory of Property Rights', *American Economic Review*, 56:2 (1967), pp. 347–59.

Derby, O., 'The Iron Ores of Brazil', in *The Iron Ore Resources of the World: An Inquiry Made upon the Initiative of the Executive Committee of the XI International Geological Congress*, 2 (Stockholm, 1910), pp. 813–22.

Díaz-Alejandro, C. F., 'Latin America in the 1930s' (unpublished paper, Yale University, 1982).

Dinius, O., *Brazil's Steel City: Developmentalism, Strategic Position, and Industrial Relations in Volta Redonda (1941–1968)* (Stanford, CA: Stanford University Press, 2010).

Diniz, E., *Estado e capitalismo no Brasil: 1930–1945* (Rio de Janeiro: Editora Paz e Terra, 1978).

—, 'A progressiva subordinação das oligarquias regionais ao governo central', in T. Szmrescsányi and R. G. Granziera (eds), *Getúlio Vargas e a economia contemporânea* (Campinas SP: Editora da Unicamp, 2004), pp. 38–46.

Diniz, E. and R. R. Boschi., *Empresários, interesses e mercado: Dilemas do desenvolvimento no Brasil* (Belo Horizonte and Rio de Janeiro: Editora UFMG; IUPERJ, 2004).

Draibe, S., *Rumos e metamorfoses: um estudo sobre a constituição do Estado e as alternativas da industrialização no Brasil, 1930–1960* (Rio de Janeiro, RJ: Paz e Terra, 1985).

Duarte Pereira, O., *Ferro e independencia: um desafio à dignidade nacional* (Rio de Janeiro: Ed. Civilização Brasileira, 1967).

Dulles, J. W. F., *Vargas of Brazil: A Political Biography* (Austin, TX: University of Texas Press, 1967).

Dutra de Morais, G., *Jazidos de ferro do Brasil* (Biblioteca de Estudos Mineralógicas, 1944).

Dutra Fonseca, P. C., *Vargas: O capitalismo em construção* (São Paulo: Brasiliense, 1987).

—, 'Vargas no contexto da Primeira República', in T. Szmrescsányi and R. G. Granziera (eds), *Getúlio Vargas e a economia contemporânea* (Campinas SP: Editora de Unicamp, 2004), pp. 171–92.

Eakin, M. C., *British Enterprise in Brazil: The St. John d'el Rey Mining Company and the Morro Velho Gold Mine, 1830–1960* (Durham, NC: Duke University Press, 1989).

—, *Tropical Capitalism: The Industrialization of Belo Horizonte, Brazil* (New York Houndmills: Palgrave, 2001).

Earp, F. S. S., *A questão mineral na Constituição de 1988* (Rio de Janeiro: CETEM/CNPq, 1988).

Eisenberg, P. L., *The Sugar Industry in Pernambuco: Modernization without Change, 1840–1910* (Berkeley, CA: University of California Press, 1974).

Engerman, S. L. and K. L. Sokoloff., 'Factor Endowments, Inequality, and Paths of Development Among New World Economies', *Economia*, 3:1 (2002), pp. 41–109, including comments.

Fausto, B., *História geral da civilização brasileira (III) O Brasil republicano (1) Estrutura de poder e economia (1889–1930)* (Rio de Janeiro: Ed. Bertrand Brasil, 1989).

Fernandes, F. R. C., 'Quem controla o subsolo brasileiro?', *Revista Brasiliera de Tecnologia*, 19:3 (1988), pp. 5–12.

Ferreira, F. I., *Legislação das minas, repertório jurídico do mineiro, consolidação alphabética e chronológica* (Rio de Janeiro: Typographia Nacional, 1884).

Field, A. J., 'The Problem with Neoclassical Institutional Economics: A Critique with Special Reference to the North/Thomas Model of Pre-1500 Europe', *Explorations in Economic History*, 18:3 (1981), pp. 174–98.

Figueirôa, S. F., *As ciências geológicas no Brasil: Uma história social e institucional, 1875–1934* (São Paulo: Editora Hucitec, 1997).

Fishlow, A., *American Railroads and the Transformation of the Antebellum Economy*, Harvard Economic Studies Series, 127 (Cambridge, MA: Harvard University Press, 1965).

—, 'Origins and Consequences of Import Substitution in Brazil', in M. Luís Eugenio di and P. Raúl (eds), *International Economics and Development: Essays in Honor of Raúl Prebisch* (New York: Academic Press, 1972), pp. 311–65.

Franco, G. H. B., *Reforma monetária e instabilidade durante a transição republicana*, 2nd edn (1983; Rio de Janeiro: Banco Nacional de Desenvolvimento Econômico e Social, 1987).

Frank, Z. L., *Dutra's World: Wealth and Family in Nineteenth-Century Rio de Janeiro* (Albuquerque, NM: University of New Mexico Press, 2004).

Freire, W., *Comentários ao Código de Mineração* (Rio de Janeiro: Aide Editora e Comércio de Livros, 1995).

Fritsch, W., *External Constraints on Economic Policy in Brazil, 1889–1930* (Pittsburgh, PA: University of Pittsburgh Press, 1988).

Fróes Abreu, S., *A riqueza mineral do Brasil* (São Paulo: Companhia Editora Nacional, 1937).

Furtado, C., *Formação econômica do Brasil*, 40th edn (1959; São Paulo: Ed. Brasiliense, 1993).

—, *Accumulation and Development: The Logic of Industrial Civilization* (New York: St Martin's Press, 1983).

Galambos, L. and W. Baumol, 'Conclusion: Schumpeter Revisited', in Toninelli (ed.), *The Rise and Fall of State-Owned Enterprise in the Western World*, pp. 303–10.

Gauld, C. A., *The Last Titan: Percival Farquhar: American Entrepreneur in Latin America* (Stanford, CA: Institute of Hispanic American and Luso-Brazilian Studies, Stanford University, 1964).

Gerschenkron, A., *Economic Backwardness in Historical Perspective, A Book of Essays* (Cambridge, MA: Belknap Press of Harvard University Press, 1962).

Gomes, E. R. and F. C. Guimarães, 'Como as instituições contam: O apoio à pequenas e médias empresas no Brasil e na Argentina' *33 Encontro Annual da ANPOCS* (Caxambu MG, October 2009), pp 1–35.

Gómez-Galvarriato, A. and C. L. Guerrero-Luchtenberg, 'Timing of Protectionism', in *Serie-AD* (Alicante: Universidad de Alicante, Instituto Valenciano de Investigaciones Económicas, 2010), pp. 1–71.

Gondin da Fonseca, O. D. C., *Qué sabe você sobre petróleo?* (Rio de Janeiro: Livraria São José, 1957).

Gonsalves, A. D., *O ferro na economia nacional* (Rio de Janeiro: Ministério da Agricultura, Directoria de Estatística da Producão, Secão de Estatística da Producção Extrativa, 1937).

Graham, R., 'Government Expenditures and Political Change in Brazil, 1880–1899: Who Got What', *Journal of Interamerican Studies and World Affairs*, 19:3 (1977), pp. 339–68.

Gunder Frank, A., *Capitalism and Underdevelopment in Latin America: Historical Studies of Chile and Brazil* (New York: Monthly Review Press, 1967).

Gupta, B., 'The Great Depression and Brazil's Capital Goods Sector: A Re-examination', *Revista Brasileira de Economia*, 51:2 (1997), pp. 239–51.

Haber, S., 'Financial Markets and Industrial Development: A Comparative Study of Governmental Regulation, Financial Innovation and Industrial Structure in Brazil and Mexico, 1840–1930', in S. Haber (ed.), *How Latin America Fell Behind: Essays on the Economic Histories of Brazil and Mexico, 1800–1914* (Stanford CA: Stanford University Press, 1997), pp. 146–78.

— (ed.), *How Latin America Fell Behind: Essays in the Economic Histories of Brazil and Mexico, 1800–1914* (Stanford, CA: Stanford Unviversity Press, 1997).

Haber, S., N. Maurer and A. Razo., 'When the Law Does Not Matter: The Rise and Decline of the Mexican Oil Industry', *Journal of Economic History*, 63:1 (2003), pp. 1–32.

Hall, L. B., *Oil, Banks, and Politics: The United States and Postrevolutionary Mexico, 1917–1924* (Austin, TX: University of Texas Press, 1995).

Hanley, A. G., *Native Capital: Financial Institutions and Economic Development in São Paulo, Brazil, 1850–1920* (Stanford, CA: Stanford University Press, 2005).

Hira, A. and R. Hira., 'The New Institutionalism: Contradictory Notions of Change', *American Journal of Economics and Sociology*, 59:2 (2000), pp. 268–82.

Hirschman, A. O., *Shifting Involvements: Private Interest and Public Action* (Princeton, NJ: Princeton University Press, 1982).

Jacob, R., *Minas Geraes no século XX* (Rio de Janeiro: Gomes Irmão & Cia., 1911).

Junqueira, M., *Inconstitucionalidade do Código de Minas: Impugnação da Fazenda do Estado de São Paulo á applicabilidade do Decreto Federal No. 24642* (São Paulo: Procuradoria de Terras do Estado de São Paulo, 1936).

Krautkraemer, J. A., 'Nonrenewable Resource Scarcity', *Journal of Economic Literature*, 36:4 (1998), pp. 2065–107.

Lacerda Rocha, L., *Das minas e jazidas no direito brasileiro (Comentários ao Código de Minas atualizado e legislação subseqüente)* (Rio de Janeiro: Ed. Livraria Agir, 1947).

Lamoreaux, N. R. and J.-L. Rosenthal, 'Legal Regime and Business's Organizational Choice: A Comparison of France and the United States during the Nineteenth Century', in *NBER Working Paper No. 10288* (Cambridge, MA: National Bureau of Economic Research, 2004).

LaPorta, R., F. Lopez-de-Salinas, A. Shleifer and R. Vishny, 'Law and Finance', *Journal of Political Economy*, 106:6 (1998), pp. 1113–55.

Lauderdale Graham, S., *Caetana Says No: Women's Stories from a Brazilian Slave Society* (Cambridge and New York: Cambridge University Press, 2002).

Leff, N. H., 'Capital Markets in the Less Developed Countries: The Group Principle', in R. I. McKinnon (ed.), *Money and Finance in Economic Growth and Development* (New York: Dekker, 1976), pp. 97–122.

Lemos, R., *Benjamin Constant: Vida e história* (Rio de Janeiro: Topbooks, 1999).

Leopoldi, M. A. P., 'Burocracia, empresariado e arenas decisórias estratégicas: trajetórias do neo-corporativismo no Brasil', presented at XV Encontro ANPOCS conference, Caxambu Minas Gerais, 1991.

—, 'O difícil caminho do meio: Estado, burguesia e industrialização no segundo governo Vargas (1951–1954)', in de Castro Gomes (ed.), *Vargas e a crise dos anos 50*, pp. 161–203.

—, 'Crescendo em meio à incerteza: A política econômica do govern JK (1956–60)', in de Castro Gomes (ed.), *O Brasil de JK*, pp. 107–42.

Levine, R. M., *The Vargas Regime; The Critical Years, 1934–1938* (New York: Columbia University Press, 1970).

Levy, M. B., *História da bolsa de valores do Rio de Janeiro* (Rio de Janeiro: IBMEC, 1977).

Lewin, L., *Surprise Heirs*, 2 vols (Stanford, CA: Stanford University Press, 2003).

Lewis, S. W., *Critical Issues in Brazil's Energy Sector: Deregulating and Privatizing Brazil's Oil and Gas Sector* (Houston, TX: The James A. Baker III Institute for Public Policy of Rice University, 2004).

Libby, D. C., *Trabalho escravo e capital estrangeiro no Brasil: o caso de Morro Velho* Biblioteca de estudos brasileiros, 1 (Belo Horizonte: Editora Itatiaia, 1984).

—, *Transformação e trabalho em uma economia escravista: Minas Gerais no século XIX* (São Paulo: Editora Brasiliense, 1988).

Libecap, G. D., *The Evolution of Private Mineral Rights: Nevada's Comstock Lode* (New York: Arno Press, 1978).

—, 'Property Rights in Economic History: Implications for Research', *Explorations in Economic History*, 23:3 (1986), pp. 227–52.

Lobato, M., *Ferro: A solução do problema siderúrgico do Brasil pelo processo Smith* (Rio de Janeiro, 1931).

Love, J. L., *Crafting the Third World: Theorizing Underdevelopment in Rumania and Brazil* (Stanford, CA: Stanford University Press, 1996).

—, 'The Rise and Decline of Economic Structuralism in Latin America: New Dimensions', *Latin American Research Review*, 40:3 (2005), pp. 100–25.

Luz, N. V., *A luta pela industrialização do Brasil 1808–1930* (Corpo e Alma, 5. São Paulo: Ed. Alfa Omega, 1978).

Maia, A. M. C., *O instituto das terras devoltas e a legislação fundiária do Estado de Minas Gerais* (Belo Horizonte: Fundação Rural Mineira de Colonização e Desenvolvimento Agrária, 1994).

Maloney, W. F., 'Missed Opportunities: Innovation and Resource-Based Growth in Latin America', *Economia*, 3:1 (2002), pp. 111–67.

Mamen, C., 'Minério de ferro no Brasil – reserva para o mundo', *Engenharia Mineração e Metalurgia*, 52:808 (1970), pp. 53–9.

Manchester, A. K., *British Preeminence in Brazil, Its Rise and Decline: A Study in European Expansion* (Chapel Hill: University of North Carolina Press, 1933).

Mandetta, P., V. P. Pereira, M. T. V. Mello, C. Chiodi Filho and A. Conrado, 'Empresa Estadual de Mineração', *Brasil Mineral*, 117:107 (1988), pp. 18–20, 33–4.

Manoilescu, M., *The Theory of Protection and International Trade* (London: P. S. King & Son, Ltd, 1931).

Manoilescu, M. and A. Amaral, *O século do corporativismo; doutrina do corporativismo integral e puro* (Rio de Janeiro: J. Olympio, 1938).

Martins, R. and O. E. A. Brito, *História da mineração no Brasil* (São Paulo: Empresas das Artes, 1989).

Maxwell, K., *Pombal, Paradox of the Enlightenment* (Cambridge and New York, NY: Cambridge University Press, 1995).

McCann, F. D., *Soldiers of the Pátria: A History of the Brazilian Army, 1889–1937* (Stanford, CA: Stanford University Press, 2004).

McDowell, A. G., 'From Commons to Claims: Property in the California Gold Rush', *Yale Journal of Law and the Humanities*, 14:1 (2002), pp. 1–72.

Ménard, C., *Institutions, Contracts and Organizations: Perspectives from New Institutional Economics* (Cheltenham and Northampton, MA: Edward Elgar Publishing, 2000).

Mendonça de Azevedo, J. A., *Elaborando a constituição nacional: Atas da subcomissão elaboradora do anteprojeto 1932/33*, Edição Fac-Similar (Brasília: Imprensa Nacional, 1993).

Mendonça de Barros, J. R. and D. H. Graham. 'The Brazilian Miracle Revisited: Private and Public Sector Initiative in a Market Economy', *Latin American Research Review*, 13:2 (1978), pp. 5–38.

Mendoza de Azevedo, J. A., *Índice sistemático da legislação brasileira* (Belo Horizonte: Silveiro Costa, Cia., 1939), Parte I – Império.

Metcalf, A. C., *Family and Frontier in Colonial Brazil: Santana de Parnaíba, 1580–1822* (Berkeley, CA: University of California Press, 1992).

Miles, F. E., 'Se o Brasil quer desenvolver a mineração', *Mineração e Metalurgia*, 8:48 (April 1945), pp. 379–82

Miller, S. W., *Fruitless Trees: Portuguese Conservation and Brazil's Colonial Timber* (Stanford, CA: Stanford University Press, 2000).

Milton, A., *A constituição do Brasil: Notícia, histórica, texto e commentário* (Rio de Janeiro: Imprensa Nacional, 1898).

Minayo, M. C. d. S., *Os homens de ferro: Estudo sobre os trabalhadores da indústria extrativa de minério de Ferro da Companhia Vale do Rio Doce em Itabira, Minas Gerais* (Rio de Janeiro: Dois Pontos, 1986).

Miranda, M. A. T., *O petróleo é nosso: A luta contra o 'entreguismo', pelo monopólio estatal–1947–1953, 1953–1981* (Petrópolis: Vozes, 1983).

Mizael de Souza, J. M., 'Será que o Brasil acordará para a importância da mineração?', in A. D. Leite and J. P. d. Reis (eds), *O novo Governo e os desafios do desenvolvimento* (Rio de Janeiro: Ed José Olympio, 2002), pp. 528–48.

Moog, C. V., *Bandeirantes e pioneiros; paralelo entre duas culturas* (Rio de Janeiro,: Editôra Globo, 1954).

Mota, C. G., 'Da ordem imperial pombalina à fundação do Império brasileiro (1750–1831) o significado da Abertura dos Portos (1808)', in L. V. d. Oliveira, R. Ricupero and A. Domingues (eds), *A abertura dos portos* (São Paulo, SP: Editora Senac São Paulo, 2007), pp. 60–99.

Mueller, B., 'A evolução histórica dos direitos de propriedade sobre as terras no Brasil e nos EUA', *História Econômica & História de Empresas*, 9:2 (2006), pp. 23–54.

Munteal Filho, O., 'O liberalismo num outro Ocidente', in L. M. P. Guimarães and M. E. Prado (eds), *O liberalismo no Brasil imperial* (Rio de Janeiro: Editora Revan, 2001), pp. 31–72.

Murilo de Carvalho, J., 'Armed Forces and Politics in Brazil: 1930–1945', *Hispanic American Historical Review*, 62:2 (1982), pp. 193–223.

—, *Teatro de sombras: A política imperial*, Formação do Brasil, 4 (Rio de Janeiro: IUPERJ; Vertice, 1988).

—, 'As forças armadas na Primeira República: O poder desestabilizador', in B. Fausto (ed.), *História geral: o Brasil republicano; v. 2* (Rio de Janeiro: ed. Bertrand Brasil, 1989).

—, *A Escola de Minas de Ouro Preto: O peso da glória* (Belo Horizonte: Editora UFMG, 2002).

—, *Forças armadas e política no Brasil* (Rio de Janeiro RJ: Jorge Zahar Editor, 2005).

Musacchio, A., 'Laws versus Contracts: Legal Origins, Shareholder Protections and Ownership Concentration in Brazil, 1890–1950', *Business History Review*, 82:3 (2008), pp. 445–73.

—, *Experiments in Financial Democracy: Corporate Governance and Financial Development in Brazil, 1882–1950* (New York: Cambridge University Press, 2009).

Nabuco, J., *Abolitionism: The Brazilian Antislavery Struggle (O abolicionismo)* (1880; Urbana, IL: University of Illinois Press, 1977).

Nazzari, M., 'Widows as Obstacles to Business: British Objections to Brazilian Marriage and Inheritance Laws', *Comparative Studies in Society and History*, 37:4 (1995), pp. 781–802.

Needell, J. D., *The Party of Order: The Conservatives, the State, and Slavery in the Brazilian Monarchy, 1831–1871* (Stanford, CA: Stanford University Press, 2006).

North, D. C., *Structure and Change in Economic History* (New York: Norton, 1981).

—, *Institutions, Institutional Change, and Economic Performance* (Cambridge: Cambridge University Press, 1990).

North, D. C., and R. P. Thomas., *The Rise of the Western World: A New Economic History* (Cambridge: University Press, 1973).

Novaes, A. D., 'Rentabilidade e risco: empresas estatais *versus* empresas privadas', *Revista Brasileira de Economia*, 44:1 (1990), pp. 53–84.

Novais, F. A., *Portugal e Brasil na crise do antigo sistema colonial (1777–1808)* (Coleção Estudos historicos. São Paulo: Editora HUCITEC, 1979).

Nugent, J. B. and V. Saddi., 'Abolition and the Evolution of Property Rights in Land: The Role of Immigrant Labor and its Recruitment in Brazil' (unpublished paper, University of Southern California, 2007).

Octavio, R., *Do domínio da União e dos Estados, segunda a Constituição Federal* (São Paulo: Saraiva & Co., 1924).

Olson, M., *The Logic of Collective Action: Public Goods and the Theory of Groups* (Cambridge, MA: Harvard University Press, 1971).

Olson, M., and R. Zeckhauser, 'The Efficient Production of External Economies', *American Economic Review*, 60:3 (1970), pp. 512–7.

Paiva, G., 'O código de minas e o incremento da mineração no Brasil em 1940', in *Ministério da Agricultura, DNPM, Serviço de Fomento da Producção Mineral, Avulso 47* (Rio de Janeiro: Imprensa Nacional, 1942).

'Pandiá Calógeras na opinião de seus contemporâneos' (Belo Horizonte, 1934).

Peláez, C. M., 'Itabira Iron e a exportação do minério de ferro do Brasil', *Revista Brasileira de Economia*, 24, 4th edn (1970), pp. 139–74.

Pessôa, E., *Pela verdade* (Rio de Janeiro: Livraria Francisco Alves, 1925).

Pierson, P., *Politics in Time: History, Institutions, and Social Analysis* (Princeton, NJ: Princeton University Press, 2004).

Pimenta, D. J., '*Companhia Vale do Rio Doce' Relatório Apresentado ao Ministro da Fazenda; Programa de Obras* (Rio de Janeiro: Imprensa Oficial, 1947).

—, 'Exportação de minério de ferro pelo Vale do Rio Doce', *Geologia e metallurgia*, 7 (1949), pp. 62–101.

—, 'O minério de ferro na economia nacional: Evolução do minério de ferro; Part 1', *Revista do Serviço Público*, 4:1 (1949), pp. 101–12.

—, 'O minério de ferro na economia nacional: Evolução do minério de ferro; Part 2', *Revista do Serviço Público*, 4:3 (1949), pp. 107–17.

Pinheiro, A., *Direito das minas: Comentários e legislação* (Rio de Janeiro: Imprensa do 'Jornal do Commercio', 1939).

Pinheiro, A. C. and F. Giambiagi, 'The Macroeconomic Background and Institutional Framework of Brazilian Privatization', presented at the Privatization in Brazil: The Case of Public Utilities conference, Rio de Janeiro, 1999.

Pinheiro, J. C. F., *Companhia Vale do Rio Doce: O engasgo dos neoliberais* (Belo Horizonte: Centro de Documentação e Informação, Ltda, 1996).

Prado Jr, C., *História econômica do Brasil* (1942; São Paulo: Editora Brasilense, 1993).

Prebisch, R., *The Economic Development of Latin America and its Principal Problems* (New York: United Nations, 1950), reprinted in *Economic Bulletin for Latin America*, 7:1 (1962), pp. 1–22.

Priest, T., *Global Gambits: Big Steel and the U.S. Quest for Manganese*, International History Series (Westport, CT: Praeger, 2003).

Rache, P., *A grande siderurgia e a exportação de minério de ferro brasileiro em larga escala* (Rio de Janeiro: Imprensa Oficial, 1939).

Rady, D. E., *Volta Redonda: A Steel Mill comes to a Brazilian Coffee Plantation; Industrial Entrepreneurship in a Developing Economy* (Albuquerque, NM: Rio Grande Publishing Co., 1973).

Ramamurti, R., 'Why Haven't Developing Countries Privatized Deeper and Faster?', *World Development*, 27:1 (1999), pp. 137–55.

Raw, S., *The Making of a State-Owned Conglomerate: A Brazilian Case Study*, Working Paper: Helen Kellogg Institute for International Studies, 97 (South Bend, IN: Kellogg Institute, University of Notre Dame, 1987).

Reinert, E. S., 'The Role of the State in Economic Growth', in Toninelli (ed.), *The Rise and Fall of State-Owned Enterprise in the Western World*, pp. 73–99.

Ribas, O., 'A volta das estatais: após ciclo de privatização, surgem novas empresas públicas', *Problemas Brasileiras*, 43:373 (2006), pp. 10–13.

Ribeiro, J. A., *A era Vargas*, 3 vols (Rio de Janeiro, RJ: Casa Jorge, 2001).

Ribeiro Soares, A., *Formação histórica e papel do setor estatal da economia brasileira 1930–1989* (São Paulo: Lume, 1991).

Ricupero, R., 'O problema da abertura dos portos', in L. V. Oliveira, R. Ricupero and A. Domingues (eds), *A abertura dos portos* (São Paulo SP: Editora Senac São Paulo, 2007), pp. 16–59.

Ridings, E., *Business Interest Groups in Nineteenth-Century Brazil*, Cambridge Latin American Studies Series, 78 (Cambridge: Cambridge University Press, 1994).

Rodrigues, P. R. A., 'A cultura empresarial brasileira e a Cia. Vale do Rio Doce', *Revista da Administração Pública*, 35:6 (2001), pp. 23–32.

Rodrik, D., *One Economics, Many Recipes: Globalization, Institutions, and Economic Growth* (Princeton, NJ: Princeton University Press, 2007).

Rogers, E. J., 'Brazil's Rio Doce Valley Project', *Journal of Interamerican Studies*, 1:2 (1959), pp. 123–40.

—, 'The Iron and Steel Industry in Colonial and Imperial Brazil', *Americas*, 19:2 (1962), pp. 172–85.

Russell-Wood, A. J. R., 'Technology and Society: The Impact of Gold Mining on the Institution of Slavery in Portuguese America', *Journal of Economic History*, 37:1 (1977), pp. 59–83.

Ryan, J. J., 'Credit Where Credit is Due: The Evolution of the Rio de Janeiro Credit Market, 1820–1900' (PhD dissertation, University of California, 2007).

Sarmento, A., 'A exploração de minas: defesa da lei de 6 de Janeiro de 1915', Discurso pronunciado na Camara dos Deputados na sessão de 7 de nov de 1916 (Rio de Janeiro: Imprensa Nacional, 1916).

Schultz, K., *Tropical Versailles: Empire, Monarchy, and the Portuguese Royal Court in Rio de Janeiro, 1808–1821* (New York: Routledge, 2001).

Schwartz, S. B., *Sugar Plantations in the Formation of Brazilian Society: Bahia 1550–1835*, Cambridge Latin American Studies Series, 52 (Cambridge: Cambridge University Press, 1985).

Seroa de Santa Maria, J., *Sociedades de economia mista e empresas públicas* (Rio de Janeiro: Ed. Liber Juris, 1979).

Serra, S. H., *Direitos minerários: Formação, condicionamentos e extinção* (São Paulo: Ed. Signus, 2000).

Serzedello, I. C., 'O problema econômico do Brasil, 1903', in (a compilation of articles from) *A Tribuna* (Rio de Janeiro: Imprensa Nacional, 1903).

Shirley, M. M., 'Bureaucrats in Business: The Roles of Privatization versus Corporatization in State-Owned Enterprise Reform', *World Development*, 27:1 (1999), pp. 115–36.

Silva, L. M. O., *Terras devolutas e latifúndio: Efeitos da lei de 1850* (Campinas, SP, Brasil: Editora da Unicamp, 1996).

Simonsen, R. C., *História econômica do Brasil, 1500–1820* (São Paulo: Editora Nacional, 1962).

Soares d'Araújo, M. C., 'A volta de Vargas ao poder e a polarização das forças políticas e sociais', in T. Szmrescsányi and R. G. Granziera (eds), *Getúlio Vargas e a economia contemporânea* (Campinas SP: Editora da Unicamp, 2004), pp. 112–24.

Soares e Silva, E. M. *O ferro na história e na economia do Brasil*. Rio de Janeiro1972.

Soares Pereira, J., 'Depoimento', in A. Marques Vianna (ed.), *A política nacionalista do petróleo no Brasil* (Rio de Janeiro: Tempo Brasileiro, 1964), pp. 29–53.

Stein, S. J., *Vassouras, a Brazilian Coffee County, 1850–1900*, Harvard Historical Studies Series, 69(Cambridge MA: Harvard University Press, 1957).

Summerhill III, W. R., *Order against Progress: Government, Foreign Investment, and Railroads in Brazil, 1854–1913* (Stanford, CA: Stanford University Press, 2003).

—, *Inglorious Revolution: Political Institutions, Public Debt and Financial Development in Imperial Brazil* (New Haven, CT: Yale University Press, forthcoming).

Suzigan, W., 'As empresas do governo e o papel do governo na economia brasileira', in F. Rezende, J. Monteiro, Vianna, W. Suzigan, D. Carneiro and F. P. Castelo Branco (eds), *Aspectos da participação do governo na economia* (Rio de Janeiro: IEA/INPES, 1976), pp. 77–131.

—, *Indústria brasileira: origem e desenvolvimento* (São Paulo: Brasiliense, 1986).

Távora, J., 'O Código de Minas e desenvolvimento', *Geologia e metallurgia*, 14 (1956), pp. 152–94.

Tavora, M., 'Analise do Contracto da "Itabira Iron" e suas relações com a "Vitoria e Minas", a exportação de minérios e a grande siderurgia nacional; Discurso pronunciado na sessão de 28 de julho de 1937', from speech of 28 July 1937 (Rio de Janeiro: Imprensa Nacional, 1938).

Toninelli, P. A (ed.), *The Rise and Fall of State-Owned Enterprise in the Western World* (Cambridge and New York: Cambridge University Press, 2000).

—, 'The Rise and Fall of Public Enterprise: The Framework', in Toninelli (ed.), *The Rise and Fall of State-Owned Enterprise in the Western World*, pp. 3–24.

Topik, S., *The Political Economy of the Brazilian State, 1889–1930* (Austin, TX: University of Texas Press, 1987).

Trebat, T. J., *Brazil's State-Owned Enterprises: A Case Study of the State as Entrepreneur* (Cambridge and New York: Cambridge University Press, 1983).

Triner, G. D., *Banking and Economic Development: Brazil, 1889–1930* (New York: Palgrave Press, 2000).

—, 'Property Rights, Family and Business Partnerships in Nineteenth- and Twentieth-Century Brazil', *Enterprise and Society*, 8:1 (2007), pp. 35–67.

Umbeck, J. 'The California Gold Rush: A Study of Emerging Property Rights', *Explorations in Economic History*, 14 (1977), pp. 197–226.

United States Deparment of Commerce; Bureau of Foreign and Domestic Commerce; International Reference Service, *Brazil in 1944* (Washington DC: Government Printing Office, 1944).

United States Department of Commerce and Labor, Bureau of Manufactures, Special Consular Reports, *Coal Trade in Latin America* (Washington DC: Government Printing Office, 1910).

United States Tariff Commission, *Mining and Manufacturing Industries in Brazil* (Washington, DC: Government Printing Office, 1949).

Vaitsman, M., *O petróleo no império e na república* (1948; Rio de Janeiro: Editora Interciência, 2001).

Vargas, G., 'A industrialização do ferro – base de nova estrutura econômica do Brasil (1931)', in G. Vargo, *A nova política do Brasil*, pp. 135–6.

—, 'Os saldos ouro e o problema siderúrgica', in Vargas, *A nova política do Brasil*, pp. 93–108.

—, *A nova política do Brasil* (Rio de Janeiro: J. Olympio Editora, 1938).

—, *A política nacionalista do petróleo no Brasil* (1951; Rio de Janeiro: Tempo Brasileiro, 1964).

Vasconcellos, F. M. d., 'O novo Código de Mineração: Palestra Instituto Brasileiro de Geografia e Estatística, Conselho Nacional de Estatística, *Anuário estatístico do Brasil* (Rio de Janeiro: Impresa Nacional).

proferida no Centro Moraes Rêgo' (São Paulo, 1967).

Venâncio Filho, A., *Intervenção do Estado no domínio econômico: o direito público econômico no Brasil* (Rio de Janeiro: Fundação Getúlio Vargas, 1968).

Versiani, F. R., 'Industrialização e economia de exportação antes de 1914', *Revista Brasileira de Economia*, 34:1 (1980), pp. 3–40.

—, 'Before the Depression: Brazilian Industry in the 1920's', in R. Thorp (ed.) *Latin America in the 1930's: The Role of the Periphery in World Crisis* (Oxford: Macmillan Press, 1984), pp. 163–87.

Victor, M., *A batalha do petróleo brasileiro* (Rio de Janeiro: Ed. Civilização Brasileira, 1970).

Vieira Couto, J., *Memória sobre a Capitania das Minas Gerais; seu território, clima e produções metálicas: sobre a necessidade de restabelecer e animar a mineração decadente do Brasil; sobre o commércio e exportação dos metaes e interesses regiões* (Belo Horizonte: Sistema Estadual de Planejamento, Fundação João Pinheiro, Centro de Estudos Históricos e Culturais, 1994).

Villas-Bôas, A. L., *Mineração e desenvolvimento econômico: A questão nacional nas estratégias de desenvolvimento do setor mineral (1930–1946)* (Rio de Janeiro: Ministério da Ciência e Tecnologia/CNPq/CETEM (Centro de Tecnologia Mineral), 1995).

Villela Souto, M. J., 'O programa brasileiro de privatização de empresas estatais', *Revista de Direito Mercantil*, 29:80 (1990), pp. 54–65.

Vinhosa, F. L. T., *Brasil sede da monarquia: Brasil reino (2a parte)*, História Administrativa do Brasil, 8 (Brasília, DF: Editora Universidade de Brasília: Fundação Centro de Formação do Servidor Público, 1984).

Viotti da Costa, E., *The Brazilian Empire: Myths and Histories* (Chicago, IL: University of Chicago Press, 1985).

Vivacqua, A., *A nova política do sub-solo e o regime legal das minas* (Rio de Janeiro: Editora Panamericana, 1942).

Weinstein, B., *For Social Peace in Brazil: Industrialists and the Remaking of the Working Class in São Paulo, 1920–1964* (Chapel Hill, NC: University of North Carolina Press, 1996).

Welch, J. H., *Capital Markets in Development: The Case of Brazil*, Pitt Latin America Series (Pittsburgh, PA: University of Pittsburgh Press, 1993).

Werneck, A., *Relatório apresentado ao Dr. Presidente do estado de Minas pelo Secretário de Estado dos Negócios da Agricultura, Commércio e Obras Públicas* (Cidade de Minas: Imprensa Official de Minas Gerais, 1899).

Wilcken, P., *Empire Adrift: The Portuguese Court in Rio de Janeiro, 1808–1821* (London: Bloomsbury, 2004).

Wileman, J. P. (ed.), *Brazilian Year Book* (Rio de Janeiro, printed in London, 1909).

Williamson, O. E., *The Economic Institutions of Capitalism: Firms, Markets, Relational Contracting* (New York and London: Free Press Collier Macmillan, 1985).

Wirth, J. D., 'Brazilian Economic Nationalism: Trade and Steel under Vargas', DAI-A 27/04 (PhD dissertation, Stanford University, 1966).

—, *Economic Nationalism: Trade and Steel Under Vargas* (Stanford, CA: Stanford University Press, 1969).

—, *The Politics of Brazilian Development 1930–1954* (Stanford, CA: Stanford University Press, 1970).

—, *Minas Gerais in the Brazilian Federation, 1889–1937* (Stanford, CA: Stanford University Press, 1977).

Wright, G., 'The Origins of American Industrial Success', *American Economic Review*, 80: 4 (1990), pp. 651–68.

Xisto, P., 'Limitação do direito de propriedade' (PhD dissertation, Recife: Escolas Profissionaes do Colegio Salesiano, 1923).

Yarrow, G., 'A Theory of Privatization, or Why Bureaucrats are Still in Business', *World Development*, 27:1 (1999), pp. 157–68.

Yeager, T. J., *Institutions, Transition Economies, and Economic Development* (Boulder, CO: Westview Press, 1999).

Zorzal e Silva, M., 'A Companhia Vale do Rio Doce no contexto do estado desenvolvimentista' (PhD disseration, Universidade de São Paulo, 2001).

INDEX

Italics have been used to identify figures and tables.

For Product Safety Concerns and Information please contact our EU
representative GPSR@taylorandfrancis.com
Taylor & Francis Verlag GmbH, Kaufingerstraße 24, 80331 München, Germany